EXPOSITORY SCIENCE: FORMS AND FUNCTIONS OF POPULARISATION

Edited by

TERRY SHINN

Centre National de la Recherche Scientifique, Paris, France

and

RICHARD WHITLEY

Manchester Business School, Manchester, U.K.

D. REIDEL PUBLISHING COMPANY

A MEMBER OF THE KLUWER ACADEMIC PUBLISHERS GROUP

DORDRECHT / BOSTON / LANCASTER

Library of Congress Cataloging in Publication Data
Main entry under title:
Expository science.
    (Sociology of the sciences ; no. 9)
    Includes index.
    1.   Science news—Addresses, essays, lectures.   2.   Communica-
tion in science—Addresses, essays, lectures.   3.   Science—Social aspects—
Addresses, essays, lectures.   4.   Knowledge, Theory of—Addresses,
essays, lectures.   I.   Shinn, Terry.   II.   Whitley, Richard.   III.   Series.
W225.E95   1985   306'.45   85–10921
ISBN 90–277–1831–8
ISBN 90–277–1832–6 (pbk.)

Published by D. Reidel Publishing Company,
P.O. Box 17, 3300 AA Dordrecht, Holland

Sold and distributed in the U.S.A. and Canada
by Kluwer Academic Publishers,
190 Old Derby Street, Hingham, MA 02043, U.S.A.

In all other countries, sold and distributed
by Kluwer Academic Publishers Group,
P.O. Box 322, 3300 AH Dordrecht, Holland

Printed in The Netherlands

TABLE OF CONTENTS

PART III

The Social Appropriation of Science

PART IV

A Practitioner's View of Popularisation

EDITORIAL PREFACE

The prevailing view of scientific popularization, both within academic circles and beyond, affirms that its objectives and procedures are unrelated to tasks of cognitive development and that its pertinence is by and large restricted to the lay public. Consistent with this view, popularization is frequently portrayed as a logical and hence inescapable consequence of a culture dominated by science-based products and procedures and by a scientistic ideology. On another level, it is depicted as a quasi-political device for chan-nelling the energies of the general public along predetermined paths; examples of this are the nineteenth-century Industrial Revolution and the U.S.–Soviet space race.

Alternatively, scientific popularization is described as a carefully contrived plan which enables scientists or their spokesmen to allege that scientific learn-ing is equitably shared by scientists and non-scientists alike. This manoeuvre is intended to weaken the claims of anti-scientific protesters that scientists monopolize knowledge as a means of sustaining their social privileges. Pop-ularization is also sometimes presented as a psychological crutch. This, in an era of increasing scientific specialisation, permits the researchers involved to believe that by transcending the boundaries of their narrow fields, their endeavours assume a degree of general cognitive importance and even extra-scientific relevance. Regardless of the particular thrust of these different analyses it is important to point out that all are predicated on the tacit presupposition that scientific popularization belongs essentially to the realm of non-science, or only concerns the periphery of scientific activity. Accord-ing to conventional wisdom, then, scientific popularization is irrevocably separated from the central core of scientific research and thus from the process of knowledge production.

This volume questions the reality of a radical demarcation between the goals and instruments of scientific popularization and the ways in which scientists articulate research results, ideas and objectives within purely pro-fessional texts. In the essays published here the traditional notion of scientific

Terry Shinn and Richard Whitley (eds.), Expository Science: Forms and Functions of Popularisation. Sociology of the Science, Volume IX, 1985, vii–xi.
© 1985 *by D. Reidel Publishing Company.*

popularization has, to varying degrees, given way to an alternative concept, scientific exposition. Exposition refers to the entire gamut of techniques and strategies that mark the formal exchanges that occur within the sphere of science where the latter is very broadly defined. Exposition, thus, embraces all the instruments for communicating results and ideas, among an extended range of initiators and audiences. This includes specialists conducting research in the same field, specialists communicating across disciplinary boundaries, professors instructing students, scientists and journalists addressing the lay public and civil servants and industrialists treating matters associated with science and technology. Put differently, exposition is defined here as a sort of continuum of methods and practices utilized both within research and far beyond, for purposes of conveying science-based information, whether as pure cognition, pedagogy, or in terms of social and economic problems.

Research built around the concept of exposition enjoys several advantages over the classical notion of popularization. First it opens the way for a systematic comparison between structural components of various categories of science-related texts. More precisely it raises the questions: to what extent and in what respect does each genre evince distinct attributes which effectively isolate it from other types of publications? Conversely, to what degree and in what ways do sets of basic underlying structures traverse and thereby transcend a host of genres? Thus the principal task is to isolate the similarities and the particularities of intra- and inter-specialist texts, pedagogical writings, and articles in periodicals and the daily press which are intended for a broad, rather heterogeneous, audience.

Analysis may be conducted along several lines. It can, for example, focus on the presence and the proportional importance of varying types of discourse, symbolic formalisms, instruments of persuasion and strategies for attracting audiences. Alternatively, study may bear on the arguments, imagery and range of subject matter contained in different genres. Such analysis is particularly significant because it is capable of explaining why different categories of texts are compartmentalized and exclusive of one another and how they are also highly integrated and interactive segments of a general network.

Expository practices transcend, however, the domains of intra- and inter-scientific communication. On another level the concept of exposition assists in understanding certain details of the process of cognitive development. In the same way that categories of scientific texts are not professionally and socially neutral, neither are they epistemologically and intellectually neutral. Projects, ideas and results regarding given phenomena that are fully admissible in one genre are frequently unacceptable in another. Statements presented in pedagogical texts cannot necessarily withstand criticism coming from the specialist perspective. Notions and conclusions articulated in inter-specialist articles obey different epistemological rules and tests of validation from those pronounced in newspapers and in journals designed for a broad public, even when this public consists mainly of scientists. Whatever the combination, the same holds true across all the spectrum. This is a consequence of the fact that every textual category possesses definite cognitive norms in terms of language, logics, representations, subject matter, etc. Each category thus corresponds to a cognitive niche, and thoughts which can be legitimately expressed in one defy the standards of certain others. The transfer of knowledge from one niche to another is not merely an exercise in occupying the widest possible intellectual area. It is also the process which both guides and accompanies the elaboration and maturation of ideas, and a structure which often stringently delimits the direction and even the content of propositions.

Finally, the expository framework provides a promising vantage point for explaining the relationships between segments of the research community and for examining the concatenation of influences between scientific professionals and publics either indirectly involved in science or only peripherally interested in it. Expository techniques and strategies are, for example, sometimes wielded as a weapon in moments of conflict between hostile factions within the scientific community. Scientists who dominate a given expository category, or further still several genres, are able to impose favoured results and concepts on neighbouring disciplines. This may also serve to enhance their social recognition. In the same vein scientists rely, among other things, on expository procedures to convince politicians, civil servants and relevant interest groups of the need to sustain and even to increase the sum of resources allocated to them. For this purpose they conceive special reports or books which uniquely marry some of the attributes of pedagogical, inter-specialist and popular texts. Conversely non-scientists, amateurs and ex-scientists often publish in the popular scientific press, pedagogical journals or newspapers in order to affect the outcome of scientific controversies, to influence the orientation of future research or to modify the relations and the balance of power between the scientific community and groups marginal to science. Professional scientists read such publications more frequently and more attentively than has often been appreciated. Such purely socially motivated articles appearing in the very centre of the expository constellation tend to weigh heavily on the course of events.

In the light of what is admittedly only a preliminary understanding of the concept of exposition, this volume has been arranged around three distinct yet complementary themes. Part I 'Expository Contexts and Knowledge Types', contains five papers which together set out to identify the principal expository genres employed by scientists in their efforts to communicate various types of information to other scientists and to non-scientists. The authors examine the particularities of different expository categories as well as the components that they have in common. Equally important in this series of articles, an attempt is made to measure both the cognitive and social potential of each of the genres under study.

Part II, 'The Scientific Appropriation of Major Publics', demonstrates the numerical magnitude and the heterogeneity of the audiences addressed by the scientific community and by other communities allied to it. These six papers suggest that scientists deploy a panoply of expository techniques and strategies to obtain symbolic and material concessions from society at large. Exposition is similarly called upon to recast power relations within the research community proper. Scientists depend on exposition as a vehicle for influencing science and society directly. But they also seek to influence science indirectly through the manipulation of society by dint of expository procedures.

The third part of the volume, 'The Social Appropriation of Science', includes two papers. These provide readers with case studies that reveal how, in particular circumstances, the image of science and its ideological trappings are seized by those relatively removed from active scientific practices, in order to garner social advantages either in the name of individual ambition or for the realizations of political and economic projects. The book begins with an introductory chapter which juxtaposes the expository concept with that of popularization and which analyses the strengths and inadequacies of this concept in terms of contemporary sociological and historical issues.

In common with many collective ventures this one frequently proved perilous both intellectually and administratively. The reader is best placed to judge the former. As for the latter, the editors and authors are indebted to two *Centre National de la Recherche Scientifique* programmes, namely the *Direction de l'Information Scientifique et Technique* and *Science, Technologie et Société*, which fully financed the December 1983 Conference, some of the papers of which serve as the basis for this volume. We are equally grateful to the *Maison des Sciences de l'Homme* which subsidised two preliminary meetings between the editors in 1981 and 1982.

March 1984   TERRY SHINN
                                                      RICHARD WHITLEY

CONTRIBUTORS TO THIS VOLUME

Kurt Bayertz, *University of Bielefeld*

Michel Biezunski, 1 *Boulevard du Temple, Paris*

Christine Blondel, *Musée National des Sciences, des Techniques et des Industries, Paris*

Joske Bunders, *The Free University, Amsterdam*

Gregory Claeys, *University of Hannover*

Michel Cloître, *Laboratoire d'Hydrodynamique et Mécanique Physique ERA CNRS 1000, ESPCI, Paris*

Jacqueline Eidelman, *Sociologie de l'Éducation, CNRS, Paris*

Max Goldstrom, *The Queen's University of Belfast*

Jeremy Green, *University of Lancaster*

Hans Harbers, *The State University of Groningen*

Victor K. McElheny, *MIT, Cambridge, Mass.*

Nathan Reingold, *Smithsonian Institution*

Terry Shinn, *Gemas – ERA CNRS, Paris*

Gerard de Vries, *The State University of Groningen*

Richard Whitley, *Manchester Business School*

Steven Yearley, *The Queen's University of Belfast*

Edward Yoxen, *University of Manchester*

INTRODUCTORY ESSAY

KNOWLEDGE PRODUCERS AND KNOWLEDGE ACQUIRERS

Popularisation as a Relation Between Scientific Fields and Their Publics

RICHARD WHITLEY

Manchester Business School

The Popularisation of Scientific Knowledge: The Traditional View

Popularisation has traditionally been considered as the transmission of scientific knowledge from scientists to the lay public for purposes of edification, legitimation and training. Typically, it is seen as a low status activity, unrelated to research work, which scientists are often unwilling to do and for which they are ill-equipped, as the two Dutch symposia mentioned by Bunders and Whitley (1) exemplify. Essentially, popularisation is not viewed as part of the knowledge production and validation process but as something external to research which can be left to non-scientists, failed scientists or ex-scientists as part of the general public relations effort of the research enterprise. The critical activity of the modern scientists in this view, commonly held by many researchers in the natural sciences, is to produce true knowledge about the world and communicate findings to fellow initiates. Dissemination to other groups is at best a subsidiary activity which does not enhance, and may actually decrease, a researcher's scientific reputation and prestige.

In this introductory essay I shall consider this view as one which reflects a particular conception of scientific knowledge, of how and by whom it is produced, and of its connections to lay knowledge and audiences. This conception has come under considerable attack in recent years in the history and sociology of science and seems increasingly inapplicable to the contemporary sciences. Alternative approaches to the study of the sciences, such as those presented in the papers published in this book, imply a richer and more sophisticated view of the popularisation process and its consequences for intellectual developments in different scientific fields. In this latter view, the

Terry Shinn and Richard Whitley (eds.), Expository Science: Forms and Functions of Popularisation. Sociology of the Sciences, Volume IX, 1985, 3–28
© *1985 by D. Reidel Publishing Company.*

dissemination of particular results and ideas to non-scientific publics is a more complex phenomenon, involving a variety of actors and audiences, that impinges upon the research process and cannot be totally isolated from it. Furthermore, the expansion and specialisation of scientific research in the past 200 or so years has resulted in many scientists popularising their work to other groups of scientists as well as to non-scientists — for a variety of purposes — so that the term has to be broadened beyond the simple traditional usage.

Initially, I shall draw out the common presumptions of the traditional view of the popularisation of scientific research to highlight its reliance upon an inappropriate conception of the modern sciences. Next I shall suggest a broader view of the phenomenon based on different conceptions of the sciences and outline some differences between various forms of popularisation. Finally, I shall consider some of the major contextual circumstances in which these different forms are likely to develop and the sorts of functions that can be fulfilled by the popularisation of scientific knowledge.

Popularisation in general can be analysed on a number of dimensions such as its assumptions about: (1) the audiences for scientific knowledge, (2) the producers of knowledge, (3) the knowledge itself and its transformation and (4) the effects of popularisation upon the production and validation of new knowledge. To facilitate the comparison of the traditional view with the broader conception and the exposition of the latter I shall consider each of these dimensions separately, although, of course, they are interconnected.

In the common conception of scientific popularisation the audience is typically viewed as large, diffuse, undifferentiated and passive. Whether it is the fashionable audiences attending Davy's lectures at the Royal Institution in the 1800s or the "modernisers" addressed by Häckel and others in 19th-century Germany (Bayertz), or the television audiences subjected to the claims of molecular biology in the 1960s (2) their sole distinguishing characteristic is their exclusion from the process of knowledge production and validation and hence their incompetence to judge the status of what they are acquiring. In a similar manner to many studies of mass communication in the 1940s and 1950s (3) the traditional view of popularisation of scientific ideas assumes audiences to be atomistic receivers of information, with little or no collective internal structure, who passively internalise knowledge in isolation from other social activities and structures. They are unorganised, vaguely or very weakly bounded and their acquisition of knowledge has few social consequences.

Leaving aside the important set of audiences constituted by other scientists, this view is clearly misleading for lay recipients of scientific knowledge just as it was for television and radio audiences. First of all, they were usually restricted to the educated public, particularly those with some scientific training since the 19th century. Secondly, a major non-scientific public for scientific ideas and results has been, and remains, the varied set of professional occupations which claim some legitimacy from their use of scientific knowledge and which constitute an important market for scientific ideas, both through providing trainees and students to be educated and through demonstrating the relevance and importance of scientific knowledge in their work. This set of audiences is scarcely unorganised, nor do they absorb knowledge passively or lack influence upon research strategies and resource allocation decisions. Thirdly, a major audience is constituted by secondary school children and university students which collectively served to justify the employment of researchers and enabled them to exert considerable control over their conditions of employment, and over the performance and significance standards applied to their work (4). While this audience is relatively dependent upon scientists, it is scarcely unstructured and has great importance for scientific research, both as a source of recruits and as an increasing proportion of the general public which could support the claims of scientists to produce true, stable and coherent knowledge. Finally, of course, there is the increasingly important audience of military and business groups who seek knowledge for their own uses and exert influence upon the overall purposes and direction of much research. The growth of "big science" has accelerated the increasing dependence of many researchers upon these groups and successful popularisation of ideas, strategies and results to them has become critical for many scientific fields. Thus we can see that there are a number of readily identifiable audiences for scientific knowledge which pursue a variety of goals and which are important for scientific research in a number of ways. Furthermore these audiences are clearly historically specific and so too are the forms and functions of popularisation.

In contrast to the perception of lay audiences being unorganised, the conventional view of the second aspect of popularisation, the producers or discoverers of knowledge, conceives them as a highly organised community with clear boundaries who use their esoteric and elaborate skills to generate "true" knowledge in isolation from non-scientists. Whether they are organised as paradigm bound specialist communities (5) or as a more diffuse, normatively constituted scientific community (6), researchers are implicitly portrayed as an elite group with highly specialised and extensive training who produce "truth" in esoteric ways which can then be translated into ordinary language for public dissemination. This "truth" production process is commonly seen as being very different from profane, everyday activities and one which requires, or is guaranteed by, a strong community structure that is largely self governing through distinctive norms and traditions. In some approaches to the study of knowledge production it is this highly cohesive and integrated social structure that is a prerequisite for "mature" science (7). Thus a structured intellectual elite of knowledge producers is contrasted to the diffuse mass of ignorant knowledge consumers in the traditional approach to popularisation.

This portrait of knowledge producers has been extensively criticised, both on theoretical and empirical grounds (8), and the presumption of scientific knowledge necessary being generated by cohesive autonomous communities is not as widely held as it was. "Truth" is increasingly viewed as a sociologically contingent construction which varies between sciences and historical periods (9). However, the considerable differences between scientific fields, and the increasingly differentiated and specialised organisation of scientific research, have not led to many systematic analyses of how researchers in many fields have to communicate their work to other scientific groups if they are to gain wide reputations and cooperation. In general, popularisation is still viewed as communication to the general public rather than as communication to a variety of distinct audiences, including researchers from other fields and disciplines. Yet the expansion of scientific research and diversity of specialised interests of researchers have meant that scientists seeking reputations from a broader audience than their immediate specialist colleagues have to transform their ideas and results into a form that other groups can understand. This aspect of popularisation has become critical to much contemporary research and will be discussed further in the next section.

The third aspect of popularisation concerns the nature of scientific knowledge and its change in the transformation process. Since knowledge is, in the traditional view, produced in esoteric ways by autonomous, exclusive communities, it is clearly not directly accessible to non-scientists. Thus it has to be transformed into everyday terms if it is to be popularised successfully. This transformation cannot affect the truth status of scientific knowledge, since that is guaranteed by the procedures and norms of the scientific community, but it obviously changes the form in which this knowledge is expressed. The conventional view of the transformation process is to treat it as a technical problem which can be surmounted by increasing the general level of scientific training in the population and to develop new, better ways of communicating complex ideas. The knowledge itself is assumed to remain unchanged throughout the transformation process. According to de Vries and Harbers, this view was taken by van Heek in his popularisation efforts in the 1960s.

If, in fact, knowledge was produced by cohesive, autonomous communities governed by their own paradigms then it is difficult to see how its communication to other audiences could fail to alter its nature since the meaning of research results would be determined by the paradigm that generated them. If Wittgensteinian "forms of life" govern the use of concepts and rules determining correct descriptions of social actions (10) in particular scientific communities then the transformation of knowledge produced by one community into the language and concepts of another is very difficult, if not impossible, without seriously changing the nature of that knowledge (11). Thus popularisation, in the sense of communicating the meaning of scientific knowledge to a large, lay public, is infeasible once strong barriers are perceived between the producers of scientific knowledge and the general laity.

If we take cognisance of the differentiated nature of the sciences, and of various non-scientific groups who constitute audiences for scientific knowledge, the translation or transformation "problem" becomes more tractable, but it is still difficult to see how knowledge can be translated without changing it. Indeed as Fleck (12) and Latour (13) argued, any communication of knowledge claims involves some redescription which subtly alters them so that the popularisation of true knowledge to a wide audience always results in alterations to it. This is not simply a matter of "distortion" of the true message, but is rather an inevitable concomitant of translation from one system of discourse to another. The greater the linguistic and cognitive distance between such systems, the more alteration occurs and it is worthwhile bearing in mind that knowledge producers and non-specialist audiences vary in their conceptual overlap and proximity, both across fields and across historical periods, as the papers in the volume demonstrate.

These differences also affect the fourth aspect of popularisation to be considered here: the extent and nature of feedback from popularisation to knowledge production and validation. In the conventional view, scientific knowledge is disseminated to a lay audience after it has been discovered and this process is separate from research. Since the scientific community is autonomous and distinct from the general public, the latter's acquisition of translated knowledge cannot affect the production and validation of new knowledge. Thus feedback from popularisation to scientific research is non-existent.

This simple view of the relationship between knowledge production and its communication to the lay public is obviously incorrect for the many intellectual fields whose vocabulary and concepts are quite close to those of ordinary language and whose results are of clear public interest, such as most of the social sciences and humanities in many historical periods. In these fields, lay standards and terms are often involved in intellectual debates and controversies so that what counts as knowledge is often affected by successful mobilisation of lay elites and/or diffusion of doctrines to a wide audience, such as the notion of productive/unproductive labour in political economy discussed by Claeys. The closer scientific fields are to everyday discourse and concerns, then, the stronger the feedback from popularisation to knowledge production is likely to be.

Even in fields which seem more autonomous from lay standards and symbol structures popularisation can readily be seen to affect research strategies once the differentiated nature of sceintific and non-scientific audiences is recognised. First of all, much research in the natural sciences nowadays requires resources from external agencies who have to be convinced that the work is worth undertaking. Even where this is decided by strict peer review methods, the applicants still have to translate their ideas and goals into a form that specialists from other, related, fields can understand and appreciate. Additionally, of course, lay officials within funding agencies also need to understand proposals if they are to handle them competently. Thus popularisation in a broad sense is necessary to obtain funds and so affects what work is done. Furthermore, many scientific fields — most notably cancer research — rely on general public support for funds and legitimacy so that popularisation of their results to other professions, semi-professions and the laity is a necessary activity for research being continued. Whether the critical audience is a professional group, industry leaders, administrative officials or the general public, successful communication of results and goals is a major factor in the support of research into particular problems and of particular approaches to them, as the case of molecular biology indicates (14).

This need to obtain resources from outsiders is not simply a matter of general support for broad goals which researchers can then allocate on purely "internal" standards. As several authors have recently emphasised (15), in many scientific fields non-specialists are directly involved in the determination of research strategies, of topics to be pursued and of approaches to be followed. This is especially the case in areas where organisational objectives are broader than any single specialism and cooperation between researchers with different skills is a prerequisite of successful research, such as many bio-medical areas and state directed research institutions or programmes. Here, the process of communicating ideas and results to non-specialists and non-scientists can affect the direction of research as these different audiences respond in different ways and actively become involved in the research process. Non-specialist audiences thus are not always passive recipients of scientific knowledge in the contemporary, differentiated sciences but can be significant actors in intellectual development so that popularisation often has a direct impact upon what research is done, how it is done and how it is interpreted.

Furthermore, of course, much popularisation of contemporary scientific knowledge is intended to gain wider social support for a particular position or approach within a scientific controversy. While this is perhaps mostly obvious in the social sciences and humanities, as in current disputes over the proper status and nature of knowledge in English Literature, it also occurs in the natural sciences where particular views of the hierarchy of the sciences, or of *the* scientific method, or of *the* appropriate way research should be conducted and organised are presented as fixed, eternal and universal truths (16). The strong sanctions imposed on Velikovsky for his popularisation efforts (17) should not obscure the everyday and continuous popularisation of contingent and changing scientific ideas, results and procedures as true knowledge through textbooks, public lectures, the mass media and other means by current scientific elites who are concerned to present a coherent picture of progress and accumulation of knowledge by qualified experts (Eidelman). Because the conventional view of popularisation conceives scientific knowledge to be unitary and epistemologically privileged, it is incapable of appreciating the partial nature of popularising currently accepted knowledge as truth.

The expansion and differentiation of the sciences during the present century has, of course, broadened the scope of motives for non-specialist communication. While in the 17th, 18th and 19th centuries in many fields it was possible to seek support from the educated laity for particular positions and approaches, as in for example geology and natural history (18), the professionalisation and specialisation of research over the past 150 or so years has increasingly necessitated intrascientific popularisation as well. As scientists gained more control over resource allocation criteria and became able to determine significance standards, so researchers had to convince scientific establishments of the scientific respectability of their procedures. Thus they had to popularise their research within the sciences and allied organisations to gain control over resources and over the direction of research programmes. Popularisation in these instances is more a matter of collective assertion and claim to authority than sharing one's knowledge with an interested public. Similar motives, of course, can be imputed to scientists seeking to communicate their results to professional audiences who, indirectly, provide the basis of social legitimacy and resources for research, as was discussed above (Green).

This brief consideration of the main tenets or presumptions underlying the traditional view of popularisation has indicated its many difficulties and limitations. While it may be something of an artificial construction, I suggest that many of these tenets are implicit in much current discussion of the phenomenon and it is useful to clarify their inadequacies as a preliminary to developing a broader and less limited approach. At the very least this discussion has demonstrated the strong connection between one's view of popularisation and more general presuppositions about the nature of scientific knowledge and its production. Different assumptions imply a different approach to the popularisation of scientific knowledge as will be clear in the next section which sketches a broader view.

The Communication of Scientific Knowledge to Non-Specialists: A Broader View of Popularisation

The above discussion has emphasised the close connections between general conceptions of scientific knowledge, its generation and validation, and particular conceptions of popularisation processes. The study of communication of scientific knowledge to lay publics involves assumptions about the nature of scientific knowledge, how its production is organised and controlled, how audiences are constituted, differentiated and change, and how the organisation of knowledge production is connected to its dissemination to non-specialist audiences. Variations in these assumptions imply variations in how popularisation is conceptualised and analysed.

In criticising the traditional view of popularisation, I suggested that it rested upon an inadequate and ahistorical view of the sciences. Recent work has shown that scientific fields vary considerably in their degree of internal cohesion, of intellectual pluralism, of standardisation of research procedures, of control over performance and significance standards and of formalisation of symbols (19). These differences apply not only to the contemporary sciences but also to fields in different historical periods, as Jungnickel's discussion of the standardisation of error limits in "physics" illustrates (20). Thus the "scientific community" is not a monolithic, stable and wholly autonomous entity but rather comprises a number of variously organised social structures, whose internal relationships change and whose connections with non-scientific groups are also varied and changeable. Furthermore, what constitutes scientific knowledge has changed and depends upon particular social relationships and collective judgements. "Facts" are socially constructed cognitive objects, liable to reinterpretation and change, which become established through negotiations and extensive communication among scientists (21). The exposition of research results to scientific audiences is a crucial component of these processes which affects what comes to constitute knowledge in that field at that time. Expository practices are not epistemologically neutral.

What are the implications of these points for the analysis of popularisation? The variability of the organisation and control of research suggests that relationships between scientists and lay publics are also variable and changeable so that no single type of connection can be assumed to be general. The variability and constructed nature of scientific knowledge suggest that popularisation cannot be separated from knowledge generation and development but needs to be considered as part of the overall process of intellectual change. Its forms and functions, then, need to be broadened beyond those implied in the traditional view sketched above.

The communication of knowledge from the group which produced and validated it to a wider audience can take a number of forms, from textbooks to television programmes, and can lead to a number of consequences, from ostracism, as in the case of Velikovsky, to enhanced prestige, as in the case of Nobel prize lectures, but always involves the communication of ideas, results and "facts" from the context of their production, however organised, to some less specialised and usually larger group. Popularisation thus implies the separation, however minimal, of knowledge constitution from other social processes and activities. It presupposes that the social organisation of intellectual work is differentiated from general cultural activities and is governed by esoteric standards. For knowledge to be popularised it has to be generated and validated in relatively distinct and esoteric ways which are not directly accessible to the general public. The transmission of intellectual products from the context of their production to other contexts, then, seems to me to be the key feature of popularisation.

A number of points follow from this general characterisation. First, popularisation clearly is part of the overall set of relations between specialist groups of researchers and their various audiences, reference groups, sponsors and legitimators. Thus, the form it takes, and the functions it performs, are dependent on general connections between scientists and non-scientists and between the particular scientific field and other sciences. As scientific knowledge became more distinct from other forms of understanding, and scientists gained more autonomy over performance and significance standards, popularisation to the lay public involved greater simplification and more extensive transformation. Its growing prestige in the 19th century led to social movements utilising particular "laws" and results for advancing their goals in a way which would have been ineffective in earlier centuries (Bayertz and Goldstrom). The expansion of secondary education and its control by intellectuals not only provided jobs for researchers and entrenched their standards in major social institutions, but also expanded the range and scope of textbook popularisations and distinguished levels of public sophistication about scientific terminology and ideas.

Second, the particular form that popularisation takes, and possible functions it fulfils, depend upon the way research is organised and controlled in the scientific field which produced the ideas and results, and on its relationship to the audiences being addressed. Communicating knowledge to neighbouring scientists who may share some educational experiences but are using different technical procedures or forms of representation to explore different problems involves less translation and simplification than it would if school children were being addressed (Cloître and Shinn). Similarly, it is easier to convince lay publics of the validity of one's results if they follow general notions of how scientific knowledge should be expressed and are not the subject of intense disputes (Biezunski). The more removed the context of research is from the context of reception in terms of language, intellectual prestige and skill levels, the easier it is for scientists to present their work as certain, decontextualised from the conditions of its production, and authoritative. The more they rely on everyday discursive language, lack full control over performance standards and significance standards and are prone to conflict over priorities and procedures, the closer popularisation becomes to collegiate communication, as we see in the human sciences where books often constitute contributions to collective intellectual goals as well as texts for students, and research results have direct political implications as in the case discussed by de Vries and Harbers.

Thirdly, popularisation includes intra-scientific communication across organisational boundaries. In addition to addressing the general public, students, professionals and administrators, scientists frequently popularise their ideas and results to colleagues in other fields for a variety of reasons. The high degree of specialisation in many contemporary sciences has resulted in researchers having to transform their results into more general terms and frameworks to gain reputations from disciplinary colleagues and to obtain the assistance of specialists from other areas, as Bunders and Whitley suggest. Where employers and/or state agencies organise programmes around general social goals which necessitate researchers collaborating across skill and intellectual boundaries, popularisation skills are required to ensure adequate coordination of research topics and approaches. Scientists also communicate their work to other scientists outside their immediate area of concern when they compete with other specialists for access to scarce facilities or materials and when they seek to increase their scientific status by demonstrating the correctness of their work and its general scientific significance (Green).

Claims to have solved major intellectual problems which cross fields, such as those made by the molecular biologists and sociobiologists, frequently involved popularisation since they translate specific contributions into general scientific issues and seek to re-order general intellectual standards (Yoxen).

This broadening of the concept of popularisation highlights its contingent and varied nature, as well as drawing attention to the variety of audiences and relations between them and researchers in the contemporary sciences. As an important part of relationships between reputational organisations producing and validating scientific knowledge (22) and their environments, popularisation clearly takes many forms and has many consequences for researchers. The studies gathered together in this volume illustrate the variety of popularisation processes in the sciences, and their different roles. In order to begin to make some sense of this variety, I shall now suggest a simple means of classifying forms of popularisation, and then briefly discuss some reasons for their occurrence and their consequences in the next section.

In considering how the popularisation of scientific knowledge varies between, say, textbooks, articles in *Scientific American*, Davy's lectures at the Royal Institution, summaries of biological research for medical doctors and *The Double Helix*, an immediate difference is the degree to which ordinary, everyday language is used as opposed to an esoteric and technical symbol system. While the mass media obviously use discursive language and try to avoid technical details, and university student textbooks are highly technical, there is a wide range in between these two extremes. Communication to scientific colleagues in a cognate area is likely to be highly technical but general reports for a scientifically literate audience such as those published in *Scientific American*, or *New Scientist*, are written in ordinary language yet use technical terms quite freely and rely upon a common background in school and early university science. Similarly, scientists writing for medical practitioners and other professional groups are able to use quite technical terms and rely upon a considerable degree of understanding of the intellectual background to their work, even if the audiences' interests and goals are different as reported by the neurophysiologists in the case reported by Bunders and Whitley. In general, then, we can distinguish forms of popularisation in terms of the degree of formalisation and technical precision used to communicate results. The more they rely on diffuse, discursive means of communication, the lower the degree of formalisation.

The second dimension for differentiating forms of popularisation stems from its tendency to present current, changeable conclusions as universal, stable and incontrovertible truths. As Fleck points out (23), a major feature of exoteric knowledge is its apodictic nature and he suggests that "owing to simplification, vividness and absolute certainty it appears secure, more rounded and more firmly joined together". This feature, though, is by no means manifested to the same degree in all forms of popularisation. Depending on the audience being addressed, the purpose of the communication and the main characteristics of the field, the degree of controvertibility and detail being presented may vary. Secondary school textbooks and press articles about new discoveries, for instance, present knowledge as much more apodictic than do many accounts written for professional practitioners or fellow scientists. Similarly, researchers seeking assistance from other specialists or recognition of their contribution for general intellectual goals need to elaborate and justify their arguments and present a substantial amount of detail if they are to convince their audiences. This dimension can be termed the degree of controvertibility of arguments and conclusions.

These two dimensions can be treated as varying independently of each other and different types of popularisation distinguished by the degree to which they manifest each one. Textbooks in the natural sciences today, for example, tend to present knowledge in an incontrovertible manner with relatively little elaboration of the detailed argument behind the conclusions being drawn or of the conditions under which they might not be valid. Assertions are stated flatly with few if any qualifications and doubt is hardly ever entertained. The vocabulary and symbol structure in which this knowledge is communicated are quite technical, of course, and considerable use is made of formal symbols. In contrast, Nobel prize lectures and mass media presentations of scientific knowledge tend to rely upon discursive, everyday terminology and simplify arguments considerably. Little circumstantial detail or background is presented to encourage the audience to make up its own mind; rather, assertions are stated as incontrovertible and certain. In a third type, arguments are justified in greater detail, as when researchers seek to convince other powerful groups, including scientists, of the merits and validity of their work, yet the degree of technical precision and formalisation of symbols is relatively low because audiences are heterogenous and/or research procedures are not highly standardised and esoteric. Finally, a high degree of justification of arguments and technical, formal presentations of them is found in intra-scientific popularisation across specialist boundaries. The efforts of the neurophysiologists to communicate to other biologists and biochemists are an example of this form (Bunders and Whitley). These differences betwen forms of popularisation are summarised in Table I.

Table I.   Types of popularisation.

Degree of formalisation and technical precision

		Low	High
Degree of Controvertibility of Arguments	*Low*	Discursive accounts of certain knowledge as in, e.g., mass media presentation of high status science.	Technical accounts of certain knowledge as in textbooks.
	High	Discursive accounts of conclusions presented in considerable detail and with extensive reasoning, as in many human sciences seeking general recognition.	Technical accounts of detailed conclusions and reasoning as in, e.g. general review articles for other scientists and professionals.

Contexts and Consequences of Forms of Popularised Science

Having distinguished between forms of popularisation in terms of these two dimensions, I now turn to consider the major circumstances in which they are likely to develop and some of the ways in which they can affect research strategies and intellectual standards. Since popularisation is conceived here as the process of communicating knowledge from the context of its production and validation to a wider, different context some obvious contextual factors which affect the form taken by popularisation processes and their consequences are: the nature of the audience addressed, the nature of the knowledge production system and the major relationships between them.

Audiences can be distinguished in terms of two main features: their size and heterogeneity. Large, autonomous audiences cannot be assumed to have a high level of technical competence or interest in scientific knowledge. They are therefore typically addressed in everyday terms with vivid imagery and diffuse, discursive linguistic structures. The obvious example of this form is mass media representation of major scientific finds which simplifies and reconstructs knowledge for the general public. The presumed lack of extensive education and familiarity with scientific reasoning in very large audiences also means that popularisation is apodictic and shorn of detail. Knowledge is presented as certain, important and incontrovertible, typically tied to concerns and issues which are likely to be close to everyday experiences or the widest possible public, as is exemplified by the attempts of journalists to explicate Einstein's theories in the 1920's (Biezunski).

Heterogeneity is perhaps even more important since quite small audiences can vary considerably in terms of their intellectual interests and competences. Clearly, where audiences have very different backgrounds and degree of familiarity with the particular field, they will not all understand knowledge which is presented in a technical manner in a highly formalised language. High level scientific advisory groups, for instance, rarely have much competence in all the fields they are concerned with and so are usually addressed in ordinary language terms with relatively few technical details being presented. Similarly professional service groups who have not been trained in the basic discipline, but rather have had a varied set of educational experiences, will be addressed in ordinary language in a relatively diffuse and discursive manner.

The more heterogenous audiences are, the more simplified and apodictic popularisation is likely to be. Since at least some groups will be unfamiliar with the goals and methods of the research, detailed elaboration of the arguments and reasoning won't assist the communication process. Instead, scientists and other popularisers will tend to emphasise general overall purposes and consequences of their work so as to appeal to all groups. The knowledge will be presented in a simplified form when heterogeneity is high because common interest in the way the conclusions were arrived at cannot be assumed, and validity standards differ among the audiences. Where these are homogenous though, arguments can be presented in greater detail since common backgrounds can be presumed and knowledge expressed in their language. Parapsychologists seeking approval from psychologists, for example, have to express their findings in the conventional form in the latter field and present their arguments in some detail following the standards of the dominant audience. Similarly, the neurophysiologists seeking help from specific groups of specialists in other fields had to adapt their knowledge to the interests and terminology of particular audiences (Bunders and Whitley).

In considering how the nature of the knowledge production system affects forms of popularisation, two important characteristics are: the degree of standardisation and formalisation of work procedures and symbol systems on the one hand, and the general social prestige and scientific standing of the field on the other. Where research is conducted with a variety of procedures that are not standardised across research sites and groups, and communication of results and ideas is expressed in everyday terms and discursive language, the degree of technical precision and formalisation of language in popularising results cannot be high. Thus, in many human sciences, and in other fields before their procedures became standardised and formalised, communication to non-specialist audiences is discursive and non-technical. Furthermore, the boundaries between specialists and other audiences are not strongly drawn or policed in these fields so that popularisation is not always sharply distinguished from contributions to collective intellectual goals, and, indeed, attempts to make such distinctions may lead to major disputes, as in recent debates in English literature.

The greater the social and scientific prestige of a scientific field, the more popularisation is likely to be apodictic and incontrovertible. The degree to which arguments need to be justified and presented in detail is lower than for fields which are less central to dominant scientific values. Parapsychologists and other deviant scientists, for instance, have to present much more detail and substantiate their claims to a greater degree than if they were simply communicating the results of the orthodoxy (24). The more central and widely accepted are the standards governing validity judgements in a field, the less need do researchers have to elaborate their arguments and present circumstantial detail when communicating their knowledge to outsiders.

These two sets of characteristics of scientific fields are clearly connected to their relationships with audiences. A major component of these relationships is the degree of cognitive commonality or, inversely, cognitive distance between knowledge producers and their exoteric audiences. This is obviously dependent upon the extent to which esoteric technical symbol systems are used to communicate task outcomes within the field, and also affects the extent to which popularisation can be expressed in technically sophisticated language. Where an audience is similar in interests, skills and knowledge to researchers, it is easier for them to understand technical terms and the more likely are they to share intellectual goals and approaches. If research is conducted with highly standardised and formalised procedures, then popularisation to cognitively close audiences will tend to be relatively precise, use technical vocabulary and expressed in formal language.

The emergence of many different audiences for scientific knowledge, with varying degrees of technical sophistication and interest in particular problems, has resulted in the degree of cognitive distance between researchers and audiences differing considerably between particular instances of popularisation. Equally, the wide variety of intellectual goals pursued by scientists in state and university research organisations, and of combinations of research skills, has meant that cognitive distance may be considerable on some dimensions, such as basic intellectual training, yet be relatively low on other dimensions, such as problems and intellectual concerns. Boundaries between specialist groups can be highly fluid, then, and need not encompass every aspect of research. Popularisation in these sorts of scientific fields is clearly a different sort of activity from communicating research results to a lay audience, as the comparison of neurophysiologists' communication to fellow biologists (Bunders and Whitley) with Davy's lectures at the Royal Institution (Yearley) illustrates. The dimension of cognitive distance between researchers and their audiences, which incorporates differences in intellectual background, research skills and intellectual goals, is an important variable for distinguishing between contexts of popularisation since it refers to the extent of common experiences, competences and interests between specialist scientists and their audiences.

A second major dimension characterising relationships between knowledge producers, validators and non-specialist groups is the degree to which the audience controls major resources, material and non-material, and so researchers are dependent upon its opinions and decisions. Clearly the more important an audience is to a group of researchers, the more they have to demonstrate the validity and importance of their results to that audience in terms which follow its standards and goals. Thus popularisation has to fit in to the audience's framework and concerns rather than simply expressing the researchers' priorities and approaches. The modification of intellectual goals and priorities in communicating research plans to lay administrators of funding agencies is an instance of this. Even if researchers are partly engaged in simply "relabelling" their projects to obtain funds, the need to dress their work up in different forms to suit current fashions amongst particular audiences has an impact on what work is done, and how it is portrayed, as Green's discussion of the "criminal chromosome" indicates.

The degree of dependence of researchers upon particular audiences is obviously linked to the social and scientific prestige of the field. Where the overall status of scientific knowledge is high and the more central a particular area is to current conceptions of science, such as physics for much of this century, the more its standards of validity and significance will be generally accepted and so the less need there will be for scientists in that area to justify their claims to external audiences or to present elaborate reasoning for their conclusions. Thus, where researchers are not especially dependent upon the particular audience being addressed, they can express their ideas in apodictic and incontrovertible form. In contrast, scientists working in more peripheral and marginal fields are unable to insist upon their own performance and significance standards being sufficient guarantors of truth status and importance without further arguments being elaborated. Therefore, in communicating their research results to more prestigious and powerful audiences they present evidence that dominant procedures have been followed and explicate how their conclusions were arrived at and why they are significant in terms of the audiences' criteria. Social scientists trying to demonstrate their scientific respectability by using experiments and statistical analysis, or mathematical model building, are obvious instances of this.

In summary, a low degree of technical sophistication and justification of arguments in the popularisation of scientific knowledge occurs when there is considerable cognitive distance between scientists and their audience, and scientists have a high degree of autonomy in setting and applying competence and significance standards. Mass media reporting of major discoveries are examples of this situation. Greater technical precision and formalisation of language coupled with a high degree of simplification and incontrovertibility arises when cognitive distance is lower but scientists are relatively independent of the audience, such as communication to students. Ordinary language presentations which go into considerable detail occur when dependence on the audience is higher and it is either quite cognitively distant and/or research procedures are relatively diffuse and informal. Finally, more technically sophisticated and formal forms of popularisation combined with extensive arguments and details are manifested when the degree of cognitive distance is low, the field has quite standardised and formalised research methods and it is relatively dependent upon the audience for access to resources, especially scientific prestige.

Turning now to consider some of the consequences of the popularisation of scientific knowledge, many accounts focus on the uses made of its prestige and truth value by social movements and interest groups. Blondel, for instance, describes how Claude used the apodictic quality of popular science, and its demonstrable ability to control natural phenomena, to support his technocratic ideology and political ambitions. Similarly, Goldstrom examines the use of popularised "laws" of political economy as instruments of social control. These consequences are obviously dependent upon scientific knowledge being socially prestigious and generally accepted as exemplifying truth. For science to be effective as a legitimising tool for non-scientific goals, its standards and procedures have to be considered the dominant means of generating and guaranteeing true, incontrovertible knowledge. Furthermore, the power of invoking "science" as the guarantor of universal truth is increased when it is acknowledged to be the preserve of highly trained and self-regulating intellectuals who produce esoteric truths apart from the mundane world but which have demonstrable consequences for the control of that world. The appropriation of scientific knowledge by popularisers for extra-scientific purposes, then, depends on its having a distinct, established identity as the icon of truth which is discovered by autonomous communities. This almost "sacred" character of science seems essential if it is to function as an aid for social movements.

In addition to this function of popularisation, there are several consequences which are important for particular scientific fields and intellectual approaches. These can be summarised as: (a) consequences for the overall social prestige and status of individual fields, approaches or programmes outside the sciences, (b) consequences for the intellectual prestige and importance of individual fields, approaches or programmes within the sciences and (c) consequences for the status and importance of particular problem areas, approaches or strategies within individual scientific fields.

The first set of consequences or functions of popularisation of scientific knowledge have been widely recognised by scientists and others seeking funds and other resources from lay agencies and groups. Davy's lectures at the Royal Institution were, among other goals, intended to gain social support and recognition for the usefulness and importance of Geology (25). The annual meetings of the British Association for the Advancement of Science were seen by its early leaders as occasions for promulgating a particular view of scientific knowledge and hierarchy of the sciences among powerful groups in British society (26). The decision of some physicists to participate in MGM's film after the war is explained by Reingold partly in terms of their wish to gain support for their science. Similarly, Green suggests that some cytogeneticists sought wider publicity for their work among medical doctors and the general public as a means of increasing their prestige and resources.

To achieve this goal, popularisation has often emphasised the practical utility of scientific knowledge, particularly its military and economic uses. In addition, however, the general social standing of particular sciences can also be increased by their consonance with dominant ideological views and goals of major social groups. The ability of economists to restrict the notion of rationality and rational action to their models of market behaviour seems to me to have been a major factor in their relative superiority over other social sciences in the view of significant sections of the public. Economics also illustrates another point about popularisation and social status: fields which successfully claim their similarity to the dominant model of knowledge and truth in a society are more likely to be accorded prestige than those which seem to be deviant and challenge that model. This remains the case even when, as with economics, a field's claims to practical utility appear less than convincing (27).

The second and third sets of consequences are more important and notice-able when science has become institutionalised as the dominant form of understanding and controlling the environment and when scientists have a substantial amount of control over the allocation of resources, the standards according to which research results are judged correct, and research skills are assessed, and the criteria by which the significance of results and fields are evaluated. The scientific standing of a field or approach to research becomes more critical to scientists when they depend upon this for preferential access to research resources and for their social status. In many ways, popularisation of research to influence general scientific views about its correctness and importance is as crucial, if not more so, than influencing the general public. While Watson's *The Double Helix* was ostensibly addressed to the general educated public for instance, its attempt to influence scientists' conception of research and how it should be organised and controlled was at least as significant, according to Yoxen.

Popularisation of results and conclusions will generally only increase the scientific standing of a field or approach within the sciences when it conforms to current standards of scientific knowledge and validity and makes a substantial contribution to overall scientific goals. To convince the scientific establishment of the significance and correctness of a particular problem area, general communication of its achievements to non-specialists not only needs to demonstrate technical control of cognitive objects but also has to show how they resolve major intellectual issues. Thus popularisation of scientific ideas in such intermediate publications such as *Scientific American* or *New Scientist* often claim general implications and their relevance for broader scientific concerns. Higher order values and conceptions of scientific styles are often invoked in these endeavours to re-orient and re-direct evaluation standards. Television programmes about the "secret of life" and the great advances achieved by molecular biologists were not only addressed to the lay public but also attempted to re-direct scientific opinion in favour of a new definition of "life" and biological phenomena and a new way to study them so that existing hierarchies and programmes were devalued (18). In this case, of course, scientists could legitimate their goals by claiming high scientific status from their use of physical and chemical techniques and concepts.

In a sense, all successful popularisation of scientific knowledge has consequences of the third kind mentioned above because it renders what is provisional and changeable relatively apodictic and certain. The presentation of results and conclusions to non-specialist audiences necessarily involves taking them out of the intellectual context in which they were generated and removing much of the contingency and circumstantial detail which qualified their truth status. Successful communication to influential outsiders thus heightens the status and certainty of particular claims and programmes. While this is perhaps especially noticeable in those fields which have a number of competing intellectual approaches and divergent strategies, such as many human sciences, it is also significant in more monolithic areas as Cloître and Shinn point out. The creation of certainty and strong cognitive order from the contingency and controversy of knowledge production and validation (29) through popularisation is an important factor in arriving at a scientific consensus on the relative merits of particular research groups, problems and strategies. Just as the removal of "modalities" from research reports in journal science is a major weapon in scientific conflicts within fields, so too the generation of certainty among non-specialists is important for those seeking to direct the development of a particular field, as the case discussed by Bunders and Whitley illustrates.

These consequences of popularisation are clearly more likely to be achieved when the audience addressed is influential in setting or applying scientific standards, such as a disciplinary elite which controls access to academic jobs through judgements about the work of research, and when what is being communicated follows their standards of competence and significance. Given the substantial scientific control over criteria for assessing truth claims, and the importance of contributions for general intellectual goals in the contemporary sciences, popularisation of research results directly to non-scientific audiences which do not follow dominant intellectual standards is unlikely to achieve these consequences, as the examples of Velikovsky and the more "practical" social sciences demonstrate. Obviously scientists in fields which require material resources from outside agencies need to popularise their ideas successfully to officials and agency committees, but they need to follow current intellectual standards and values in doing so. Approaches which appear to deviate from general expectations about what scientific knowledge should look like, and from the standards entrenched in more central fields, are difficult to popularise either to a general scientific audience or to non-scientific publics in societies where the natural sciences set truth standards.

Since science is popularly supposed to produce incontrovertible truths, public display of strong disagreements about fundamental issues is unlikely to convince a large audience of the correctness of individual programmes and approaches. The recent outbreak of serious disagreements between eminent economists has equally been deplored and raised doubts about the scientific status of the field in a manner reminiscent of the 19th century (30). Endemic conflicts and disputes in a field seem to make most attempts at popularising any one approach as definitive doomed to failure as outsiders are tempted to deny validity to all truth claims, as of course did Kuhn in his characterisation of the social sciences as "immature" (31). The presentation of particular results, then, not only needs to adhere to dominant intellectual standards and expectations but also to follow social norms of private controversy and public consensus if it is to be successful in communicating certainty to non-specialists.

Conclusions

In conclusion, the popularisation of scientific knowledge is seen here as a major aspect of relationships between groups of knowledge producers and validators and wider publics. As such it is contingent upon the emergence of particular groups of intellectuals controlling standards for assessing validity claims and research competence through the allocation of the reputations that are socially prestigious. As the empirical natural sciences grew in prestige and ability to control substantial resources, their intellectual standards came to dominate general conceptions of knowledge and truth and, at the same time, separated the production of scientific knowledge from the educated public so that research became an esoteric activity. The popularisation of scientific knowledge then became a means of claiming legitimacy for many social movements and interest groups, and also part of scientists' claims for social support and legitimacy as a separate group of autonomous intellectuals. By successfully combining claims to universal validity and social utility through popularisation, they laid the foundation for the present domination and expansion of the sciences.

This expansion and enlargement of the scientific labour force and of the problems dealt with by the sciences has led to popularisation becoming as much an intra-scientific as an extra-scientific matter. In many cases, to gain access to necessary resources, to gain major reputations across specialist fields and to gain assistance with broad problems spanning particular skills, popularisation of ideas, approaches and results to other groups of scientists has become essential. Thus the term needs to be broadened to include all communication to non-specialists which involves transformation. The forms that such communication take and their consequences for intellectual development vary according to the sort of field involved, the audience addressed and the relationships between them. In this introductory paper I have suggested a preliminary framework for comparing and contrasting these forms, the circumstances in which they develop and their consequences for different groups. The papers in this book illustrate many of the relations and connections mentioned here and collectively demonstrate the need for a broader view of popularisation than that presented in the traditional approach.

Notes and References

1. 'Popularisation Within the Sciences: The Purposes and Consequences of Inter-Specialist Communication', in this volume. In referring to contributions to the present book in this paper, I shall simply cite the author(s) name in the text.
2. As discussed in E. Yoxen, 'Giving Life a New Meaning: The Rise of the Molecular Biology Establishment', in N. Elias *et al.* (eds.) *Scientific Establishments and Hierarchies*, Sociology of the Sciences Yearbook 6, Dordrecht: Reidel, 1982.
3. See, for example, the discussions in E. Katz and P. Lazarsfeld, *Personal Influence*, Glencoe, Illinois: Free Press, 1955; E. Katz, 'The Two-Step Flow of Communication', *Public Opinion Quarterly* **21** (1957), 61–78.
4. The reform of the secondary school system in many countries in the late 18th and 19th century, and related reform of teacher training and the universitites, provided the basis for intellectuals to control access to jobs and set standards of intellectual competence. This is argued in more detail in R. Whitley, *The Intellectual and Social Organisation of the Sciences*, Oxford University Press, 1984, ch. 2. See also: R. Collins, *Conflict Sociology*, New York: Academic Press, 1975, pp. 487–492; C. E. McClelland, *State, Society and University in Germany 1700–1914*, Cambridge University Press, 1980, chs. 4 and 5.
5. As in T. S. Kuhn, *The Structure of Scientific Revolution*, second edition, University of Chicago Press, 1970; 'Second Thoughts on Paradigms' in F. Suppe (ed.) *The Structure of Scientific Theories*, University of Illinois Press, 1975.
6. As characterised in many papers of Merton. See: R. K. Merton, *The Sociology of Science*, University of Chicago Press, 1973, ch. 13.
7. As in Kuhn, *op. cit.*, 1970, note 5.
8. See, for instance, K. Knorr-Cetina, *The Manufacture of Knowledge*, Oxford: Pergamon, 1981; B. Latour, 'Is it Possible to Reconstruct the Research Process?: Sociology of a Brain Peptide' in K. Knorr *et al.* (eds.) *The Social Process of Scientific Investigation*, Sociology of the Sciences Yearbook 4, Dordrecht: Reidel, 1980; H. Martins, 'The Kuhnian "Revolution" and its Implications for Sociology' in T. J. Nossiter *et al.* (eds.) *Imagination and Precision in the Social Sciences*, London: Faber and Faber, 1972; E. Mendelsohn, 'The Social Construction of Scientific Knowledge', in E. Mendelsohn *et al.* (eds.) *The Social Production of Scientific Knowledge*, Sociology of the Sciences Yearbook 1, Dordrecht: Reidel, 1977.
9. For a discussion of some recent literature on this and related points, see: R. Whitley, 'From the Sociology of Scientific Communities to the Study of Scientists' Negotiations and Beyond', *Social Science Information* **22** (1983), 681–720.
10. As elaborated in P. Winch, *The Idea of a Social Science*, London: Routledge and Kegan Paul, 1958.
11. This has been extensively discussed in the context of trans-cultural notions of rationality and explanation. See, for instance, the papers in B. Wilson (ed.) *Rationality*, Oxford: Blackwells, 1970 and Steven Turner, *Sociological Explanation as Translation*, Cambridge University Press, 1980.
12. L. Fleck, *Genesis and Development of a Scientific Fact*, University of Chicago Press, 1979, p. 111.
13. Latour, *op. cit.*, 1980, note 8.
14. Yoxen, *op. cit.*, 1982, note 2 and E. Yoxen, 'Life as a Productive Force', in L.

Levidow and R. M. Young (eds.) *Science, Technology and the Labour Process*, London: CSE Books, 1981.

15. See, in particular, K. Knorr-Cetina, *op. cit.*, 1981, note 8; B. Latour and S. Woolgar, *Laboratory Life*, London: Sage, 1979.

16. For an account of how the early leaders of the British Association for the Advancement of Science used its Annual Meetings to promulgate a particular conception of science and knowledge, see: J. Morrell and A. Thackray, *Gentlemen of Science*, Oxford University Press, 1981, ch. 5.

17. See the discussion by M. Mulkay, 'Some Aspects of Cultural Growth in the Natural Sciences', *Social Research* 36 (1969), 22–52.

18. See, for instance, D. Allen, *The Naturalist in Britain*, London: Allen Lane, 1976; R. Porter, *The Making of Geology*, Cambridge University Press, 1977.

19. Exemplified by the many recent empirical studies of laboratories and controversies as well as by historical accounts. In addition to the works cited in notes 8 and 18, see also: H. M. Collins, 'Stages in the Empirical Programme of Relativism', *Social Studies of Science* 11 (1981), 3–10; K. Knorr *et al.* (eds.) *The Social Process of Scientific Investigation*, Dordrecht: Reidel, 1980; R. Whitley, 'Types of Science, Organisational Strategies and Patterns of Work in Research Laboratories in Different Scientific Fields', *Social Science Information* 17 (1978), 427–447.

20. C. Jungnickel, 'Teaching and Research in the Physical Sciences and Mathematics in Saxony, 1820–1850', *Historical Studies in the Physical Sciences* 10 (1979). On the institutionalisation of physics as a distinct field and its changing nature, see: J. L. Heilbron, 'Experimental Natural Philosophy' in G. S. Rousseau and R. Porter (eds.) *The Ferment of Knowledge*, Cambridge University Press, 1980; R. H. Silliman, 'Fresnel and the Emergence of Physics as a Discipline', *Historical Studies in the Physical Sciences* 5 (1975), 137–162.

21. As emphasised by, among others, Knorr-Cetina, *op. cit.*, 1981, note 8 and Latour and Woolgar, *op. cit.*, 1979, note 15. See also the discussion in R. Whitley, *op. cit.*, 1983, note 9.

22. Scientific fields are considered as particular kinds of work organisations in which research is controlled and coordinated through the competitive pursuit of public reputations for contributions to collective goals in Whitley, *op. cit.*, 1984, note 4, ch. 1. Thus reputational organisations are seen here as constituting the primary social units of knowledge production and validation.

23. Fleck, *op. cit.*, 1978, note 12, pp. 111–119.

24. On the parapsychologists' battles for respectability, see: H. M. Collins and T. J. Pinch, 'The Construction of the Paranormal: Nothing Unscientific is Happening', in R. Wallis (ed.) *On the Margins of Science*, Keele, Staffordshire: Sociological Review Monograph No. 27, 1979; S. H. Mauskopf and M. R. McVaugh, 'The Controversy over Statistics in Parapsychology 1934–1938', in S. Mauskopf (ed.) *The Reception of Unconventional Science*, Boulder, Colorado: Westview, 1979.

25. As well as Yearley in this volume, see: M. Berman, *Social Change and Scientific Organisation*, London: Heinemann, 1979, chs. 1, 2 and 3.

26. Morrell and Thackray, *op. cit.*, 1981, note 16.

27. On the restricted and "arithmomorphic" nature of economics, see: N. Georgescu-Roegen, *The Entropy Law and the Economic Process*, Harvard University Press, 1971, ch. 11; T. W. Hutchison, *Knowledge and Ignorance in Economics*, Oxford:

Blackwell, 1977, chs. 3 and 4; P. Jenkin, *Micro-economics and British Government in the 1970s*, Manchester University, unpubl. Ph.D thesis, 1979, ch. 2; H. Katouzian, *Ideology and Method in Economics*, London: Macmillan, 1980, chs. 3 and 7. I discuss some of the peculiarities of modern economics in chs. 5 and 6 of my *Intelectual and Social Organisation of the Sciences*, Oxford University Press, 1984. See also, A. S. Eichner (ed.) *Why is Economics not Yet a Science?* London: Macmillan, 1983.

28. Yoxen, *op. cit.*, 1982, note 2.
29. Emphasised by Collins, Latour and others referred to in notes 8, 15 and 19.
30. See, for example, the papers in D. Bell and I. Kristol (eds.) *The Crisis in Economic Theory*, New York: Basic Books, 1981; also: P. Deane, 'The Scope and Method of Economic Science', *The Economic Journal* 93 (1983), 1–12.
31. Kuhn, *op. cit.*, 1970, note 5, pp. viii, 12, 42–43.

PART I

EXPOSITORY CONTEXTS AND KNOWLEDGE TYPES

EXPOSITORY PRACTICE

Social, Cognitive and Epistemological Linkage

MICHEL CLOÎTRE

Laboratoire d'Hydrodynamique et Mécanique Physique – ERA CNRS 1000
ESPCI, Paris

and

TERRY SHINN

Gemas – ERA CNRS/Paris

Two models of science have by and large coloured recent discussion of popularization. The Mertonian model affirms that science and non-science are clearly demarcated. Both the form and the content of statements articulated within the sanctum of the scientific community are seen as radically different from propositions advanced elsewhere. Here, popularization is depicted as possessing attributes entirely different from those of science proper. By contrast, the relativist model denies this demarcation. The attributes of science and non-science are claimed to coincide. In a sense, popularization becomes ubiquitous, for, according to this analysis, the categories and levels of cognition are strictly determined by social agency alone. In this paper, doubts are voiced as to whether either of these models adequately describes or accounts for the complexities of contemporary expository practices.

This study's purpose is twofold: in the following pages we will first attempt to demonstrate that, although several components common to intra-scientific exposition also occur in articles intended for the lay public, the properties of these components change appreciably as one moves from specialist scientific papers to writings for a heterogeneous scientific audience and to articles in the daily press. There seems to exist then a sort of expository continuum in which the same set of key parameters occur in each of

Terry Shinn and Richard Whitley (eds.), Expository Science: Forms and Functions of
Popularisation. Sociology of the Sciences, Volume IX, 1985, 31–60.
© *1985 by D. Reidel Publishing Company.*

the expository practices. In part one of this paper, we will examine three sets of parameters, argument, image and referent with respect to their particular configuration in four categories of scientific texts: specialist, inter-specialist, pedagogical and popular articles. On the basis of this, we construct an expository typology.

The second argument to appear in this paper is that expository practices play an active role in the knowledge production process. The transfer of knowledge from one expository genre to another affects cognitive content. On the one hand, knowledge elaborated by a researcher in one expository frame bears an imprint of that frame even after the researcher has transferred the knowledge to an alternative frame. On the other, the process of transferring knowledge from one expository frame to another frequently casts light on the shortcomings and potential of the knowledge in question. The first of these effects is generally associated with individual behaviour, the second with collective behaviour.

Finally, all of the expository material examined in this study, with the exception of four items in the daily press, were prepared or published between 1980–1982 by scientists conducting research in a university laboratory in the areas of fluid physics, mechanics and physical chemistry. During this time, one of the authors of the present paper regularly sojourned in the laboratory in the capacity of an historian and sociologist of science. The other author was a bona fide member of the same Laboratory, undertaking research on turbulent flow. During the period in question then, the two authors either engaged in or carefully observed the process of exposition, and they were particularly privileged to view not only the end product, but also the complicities, debates, ambitions, disappointments and satisfactions surrounding expository science.

1. Argument, Image and Referent

The typology of the expository material presented here suggests one way in which categories of scientific texts can be differentiated in terms of the arguments, images and referents that they contain. This typology's framework is not derived from any theoretical reflection, be it sociological, philosophical or linguistic on the structure of expository texts. On the contrary, it was adduced only subsequent to the scrutiny of a considerable expository corpus, and the selection of the parameters was hence posterior and empirical. The research for this paper is largely based on the publications of scientists conducting research related to fluid physics, physical chemistry and mechanics. The analysis is therefore only specifically valid for macroscopic physics and the strength and possible meaning of this typology for other disciplines can only be assessed after comparable research has been undertaken.

One of the most conspicuous and incontestable criteria for differentiating expository material is referent. Some 80% of the themes encountered in the texts examined for this study are reducible to five referents. (a) Phenomenon; that is the "physical world" in terms of matter and the relations between said matter. (b) Experimental protocol and technique; this includes methodology, instrumentation and the operation of instruments. (c) Research in neighbouring fields; that is, research akin, either in terms of protocol, interpretative representation or phenomenological focus, to that reported in the article in question. (d) Historical accounts of former research. (e) Industry, which entails technology and general economic factors.

As depicted in our typology (see Table I), the abundance of phenomenological and protocol references and the dearth of historical and industrial considerations clearly distinguish specialist writings from other scientific genres, and particularly, from the popular press whose referential characteristics are symmetrically inversed. For their part, inter-specialist texts share much in common with specialist papers, with the proviso that the latter concentrate much more on protocol than they do on neighbouring fields, the former focusing more on broad research issues. In the case of "being popular" authors rely heavily on historical referents, while in addition, integrating industrial themes. The historical referent also figures importantly in pedagogical texts where it is combined with moderate use of references to phenomena, protocol and research in neighbouring fields. So, in some respects, the referential logic of pedagogical texts is twofold, divided between the specialist end of the spectrum on the one hand, and the popular, on the other.

A far more subtle parameter, imagery, similarly pervades all of the writings examined for this paper. Five types of imagery are particularly in evidence: (a) Graphs; that is, geometric plots containing numerical or symbolic information pertinent to research results. (b) Icons; this refers to the "natural" representation of objects as seen by an uninitiated observer. (c) Schemas;

TABLE I

	Referent					Imagery					Argument		
	Pheno-mena	Exp. prot. and tech.	Res. in neigh. fields	History	Indus-try	Graphs	Icons	Sche-mas	Reified imagery	Meta-phors	Restrictive-ness	Quantita-tive	Qualitative
Specialist	←	←	—	→	→	←	→	←	—	→	←	←	→
Inter-specialist	←	—	←	→	→	—	→	—	←	→	—	—	—
Pedagogy	—	—	—	←	→	—	—	←	←	→	—	—	—
Being popular	→	→	—	←	←	→	←	←	→	←	→	→	←

they depict selected and often structural features of objects and processes, providing a descriptive focus on a part of said events. (d) Reified imagery; this is the individual mental representation of material, forces, theoretical entities, etc. that escape the domain of percept. This representation is fully personal, yet not arbitrary, since it is circumscribed by the regularities attributed to the phenomena in question. (e) Metaphoric imagery; metaphors (1) are entirely word-based and they operate on the basis of multiple referents and the existence of ambiguous relations between them. Their meaning is socially determined.

The symmetry found in the referential parameter tends to collapse in the case of imagery. To begin with, contrary to conventional wisdom, metaphors only occur alone in popular articles. In the same manner, iconic representation is restricted to this genre. Specialist texts, for their part, are characterized by a profusion of graphs. Intense reification appears in those instances where researchers seek to transgress disciplinary boundaries, as is witnessed in the images frequently used in pedagogy and inter-specialist writings. Finally, schemas are employed for pedagogical purposes to demonstrate the operation of experimental material and lastly, to depict basic structures of phenomena to a lay public.

The concept of argument is doubtless the most elusive of our three parameters. Despite the risk inherent in attempting to treat the problem, we nevertheless advance a simple trichotomy which appears to elucidate, at least to some extent, scientific exposition. (a) Restrictiveness (2); it consists of: (i) the degree to which problems are circumscribed in order to achieve a systematic and rigorous analysis and (ii) the degree to which the propositions are tightly bound to one another. (b) Quantitative argument; this refers to statements based on numerical values or highly rule-bound symbolic relations. (c) Qualitative argument; such argument is rooted in intuition and subjective perception.

Argument-based differentiation of expository texts evinces some of the same characteristics associated with the referential parameter. Quantitative argument and the property of restrictiveness sharply differentiate specialist and popular texts. But contrary to what could be concluded by a hasty examination of the types of arguments contained in specialist and popular literature, restrictiveness and quantitative thought are not necessarily linked to one another. In the case of inter-specialist texts, acute restrictiveness is paired with quantitative arguments which, in turn, are accompanied by qualitative thought. Finally, pedagogical texts contain moderate amounts of the three forms of argument. As will be seen below, this is a consequence of several paradoxical structures within this genre.

In the remainder of Section 1, we will provide a detailed examination of our four categories of expository material in the light of these analytic parameters. Examples of each expository type will be studied at length in order to cast light on the relationship between the parameters of the typology and to understand better the circumstances which surrounded their emergence in different types of texts and their specific organization.

Intra-Specialist Exposition

Specialist texts are located at one pole of the expository continuum. As revealed by our typology, in this category of exposition, the parameters systematically exhibit extreme values: high notations appear six times, low rankings five times. This polarized configuration gives rise to an acute textual dichotomy which is a manifestation of basic underlying paradoxical ambiguities. Specialist articles then, while conforming to the canon of "scientific orthodoxy", also include intellectual and social components less commonly associated with this category of texts.

This appears with particular clarity in an article entitled 'Utilisation de la diffusion Rayleigh forcée à l'étude d'écoulements laminaires et turbulents' (3) published in the *Journal de mécanique théorique et appliquée* in 1982. The authors and, to a lesser degree, the review's editorial staff accorded the article great importance from the outset. The paper's length, 23 pages, permitted the inclusion of considerable detail, both in terms of experimental material and protocol, and in the description and discussion of results. The article was also singular since it proposed a view of the subject at hand, the behaviour and structure of turbulent flow, which was generally alien to many French physicists working in the field, and suggested a new experimental technique for observation and measurement little known and infrequently used in France. The article contains five sections of approximately equal length: 1. Introduction, 2. The experiment, 3. Measurement of speed gradients, 4. Diffusion, 5. Conclusion: perspectives and appendices.

As regards its expository characteristics, however, it contains two principal parts, the point of divergence occurring in the introduction of Section 3. Yet the notion of "divergence" is inadequate to portray the nature and, above all, the severity of what transpires at this juncture. The article possesses in effect two axes, which in terms of argument, referent, and to a lesser degree imagery, are extremely distant from one another. These two axes are not remotely complementary, or even vaguely supplementary. They emerge as quasi anti-nomies, perhaps asserting altogether different messages or radically different shadings of the same message, and apparently addressing different publics or at best speaking to various sensitivities within a single heterogeneous audience.

The purposes of Sections 1 and 2 is clear and indisputable. The subject, laminar and turbulent flows, is set out. The problem, the behaviour and prop-erties of their component structures, is defined; a description is provided of the experimental material, its construction, the interfacing of particular ele-ments and its operation. This portion of the paper possesses a number of characteristics which give it a certain internal coherence and cohesion, and, equally important, distinguishes it from the second half of the article.

First, the limiting conditions which demarcate the phenomena under study from other classes of objects and from other types of phenomena within the same class are clearly stipulated. The experimental equipment and procedures are described in elaborate detail. Difficulties with the experiment are men-tioned and problems of approximation in measurement and potential errors in interpretation are specified. Considerable qualitative information is intro-duced but these qualitative data supplement the quantitative, and, hence, act as a support mechanism rather than as an independent vehicle for the trans-mission of understanding.

Second, the article contains a wealth of images. It seethes with schematic designs of the experimental set up and its operation. In the case of this article some reification occurs when the authors discuss the evolution of the tracers submitted to different types of flows. Such reified imagery is fundamental to the solution of problems particularly because it confers presence, vivacity and immediacy to elements, such as theoretical entities, which otherwise remain illusive and operationally non-functional.

Third, the experimental instruments and protocol figure as the quasi sole referent throughout Sections 1 and 2 of the article. References to all subjects other than the research at hand are carefully and systematically excluded from discussion.

The tenor of Sections 3, 4 and 5 of the article contrasts sharply with the mood and thrust of Sections 1 and 2. Discussion revolves around a presentation of the recent results obtained with the experimental set up. Or does it? The second half of the paper contains graphs giving some results of the experiments described above. But despite the fact that turbulence and particularly the authors' research in the domain is ever present, the interpretation of the measurements in terms of the geometry of turbulence somehow seems not to constitute the underlying argument and referent of the discussion. Here, they appear to figure simply as an alibi, which carries a message never rendered explicit.

In this part of the text, the restrictiveness and quantitative properties of the argument, which were observed in Sections 1 and 2, tend to collapse. In tune with this state of affairs, topics are repeatedly introduced and subjected to terse comment before being abandoned and then reinjected into the discussion at the most unexpected moment. "Argument" in terms of a logical-linguistic image-based progression towards the constitution and elucidation of a puzzle, is largely lacking as is a "mode of reasoning", if what is meant by the latter is a semi-logical sequential or systemic integration of thought processes with respect to cerebral operations related to events. The following example illustrates the situation: the final page of the article contains a particularly lengthy equation which, while technically correct, is not woven into the fabric of the composition. It is a loose end, and although it properly transcribes singular phenomenological events into another language mode, in the context of the present article the exercise is pointless, at least from a narrowly cognitive perspective. The flimsiness of the argument is suggested by the frequent introduction of the conditional mode: "one should be able to see", "this should permit an improved measurement of", "this could lead to the resolution of the problem". In fact, this language seems to enshroud a vague project or personal hope or aspiration.

Finally, if rigour and reasoning are lacking, Sections 3, 4 and 5, are checkered with extra-phenomenological referents. The authors insist on the excellence of the experimental technique designed in the laboratory. They affirm that it deserves recognition and could be reproduced elsewhere with immense profit to study a remarkable range of problems: for instance, "to analyze the behaviour of suspensions and polymer solutions". In addition, as the authors discuss their own work, they also refer fleetingly to research carried out in other laboratories. This implies that their purpose is to forge assent for their propositions and to acquire scientific legitimacy through association with men and laboratories whose achievements are generally uncontested. Here, although those references to research in neighbouring fields occur with medium frequency as indicated in our typology, they constitute a strategy for extending laboratory influence and for soliciting community acceptance.

A sampling of specialist articles strongly suggests that the expository dichotomy presented above constitutes a permanent structure of this scientific genre. Two conclusions can be drawn. First, the analysis of the bifurcating quality of specialist articles shows that while social strategies for acquiring assent occupy a prominent place in this genre, it is systematically accompanied by an equally pronounced concern for the veritable analysis, description and theory of the phenomena under investigation. If our hypothesis regarding this category of literature is correct, scientists are stretched unceasingly between three poles.

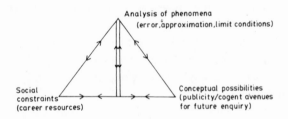

Fig. 1.

The underlying point here is that scientists' behaviour corresponds more closely to "dynamic-state conduct" than it does to "static-state conduct". The result is the formulation of propositions some of which are narrowly phenomenological, others of which satisfy social demands, and the remainder reflect a group of propositions which are vague and have, as their referent, either purposes of "marketing" or carefully pondered avenues of future research. This analysis suggests that the conclusions of Mertonian sociologists and relativists are both valid with respect to specialist literature. Yet, in this particular instance, their propositions are not necessarily exclusive.

On a deeper analytic level, we are moved to ask the question whether our interpretation of the dynamics of journal-based specialist exposition does not introduce a need to reexamine what is conventionally intended by the concept "scientific specialization". In fact, the classical criteria on which specialization is founded, the criteria of common subject matter may be dramatically incomplete, if not fully inoperable. The deeper meaning of specialization seems rather to lie in the establishment of technical (4) and representational communities. For instance, in the paper published in the *Journal de Mécanique*, the hydrodynamicians to whom the article was in part addressed, were familiar with cumbersome experiments employing wind tunnels, water channels, etc. By contrast, the article was based on micro-experimentation using optical techniques initially developped for condensed matter physics. In fact, the divergence between these two technical communities is blatant and serves to inhibit communication and understanding rather than to further it. In addition, research revolves around the construction of a range of phenomenological representations, and the selection and analysis of one of these representations. In the above cited example, several groups of physicists examined the same highly specialized domain, turbulent flows. Yet, in spite of this, their representation differed radically. Some represented the phenomenon in terms of statistics of phenomenological quantities measured in a flow and then related to physical mechanisms. Others represented it in terms of the dynamics of instantaneous geometric structures visualized "directly". A last group attempted to predict the evolution of a turbulent flow by means of a set of fundamental equations. One sees here that the establishment of such representational and technical communities provides the nexus for both tacit and explicit understanding. In the light of this, the concept of specialization pales considerably, if what is meant by specialization is limited to a subject matter. This notion of technical and representational communities will be reintroduced in Part 2 of this paper.

Inter-Specialist Exposition

Two salient features distinguish inter-specialist texts from the other expository categories studied here. As indicated in our typology, this sort of text contains many references to both phenomena and research in neighbouring fields, and depend heavily on reification. Although somewhat different at first sight, several forms of scientific texts fit into this expository frame; these include review articles, some books and even Ph.D. theses.

Perhaps because of the high degree of theoretical integration common to physics, doctoral theses in this discipline, although they are intended as specialist documents, constitute an important vehicle for trans-disciplinary exposition. In their thesis form, statements advanced by doctoral candidates are intended for a small public. To a certain extent, they almost stand as an individual's modest, and hence very incomplete and even sometimes partial view of a narrow scientific problem. Yet, at the same time physics theses revolve around the development of a personal view of phenomena; a precise appreciation of this fact is crucial to understand the link between intra- and inter-specialist exposition.

The personal dimension is evident in the proclivity to interpret complex concepts and phenomena in terms of images which, while preserving the integrity of the phenomena, allow a ready and quasi palpable grasp of the event under study. Translating illusive parameters and formally expressed theoretical entities into a concrete personalized representation involves two techniques. When the subject matter is directly observable, advanced students often portray the nomenclature of science through schemas (nouns = objects and verbs = processes) which are used equally to depict phenomena or the operation of the instruments employed for measurement. But more importantly, in the case of the highly abstract and occasionally esoteric concepts expressed in mathematical formulae, the candidates call on reification to endow formal terms with a physical substance. The following citation taken from a dissertation (5) illustrates the process of reification. "What does the term w_i w_j s_{ij} signify in the case of homogeneous isotropic turbulence? ... The expression encompasses rotation and straining of the vorticity $\vec{w}$ under the action of the velocity gradient field $\bar{\bar{s}}$."

The salient point that emerges here is that thesis students wield a range of imagery and image-linked argument which allows them to bestow substance on phenomena that otherwise remain mere mathematical relations or disembodied instrumental data. On another level, the length of theses permits an exhaustive development of arguments: experimental instrumentation, approximations, protocol and results, as well as calculations, are elaborated much more than can ever be achieved in the longest of articles. Finally, a physics thesis contains basic references to the fundamental concepts of many specialist domains and brings together representations, techniques and data from a broad range of fields.

Because of this, in the discipline of physics, dissertations are perhaps more fundamental to the functioning of the total community than is often recognized. While specialist articles are seldom sufficiently elaborate to permit further research on the basis of them alone, the contrary is true for dissertations. In the case of specialist articles, serious work requires personal exchanges between the concerned parties which may take the form of visits, letters or phone calls. They are in this respect a "sign-board" which furnish the details that enable scientists to determine whether direct contact with the author is warranted. Dissertations, though, communicate adequate information to allow researchers to continue the line of enquiry without recourse to the doctoral candidate. But more importantly, they constitute a vehicle for a particularly transparent style of exposition. This means that while researchers turn to dissertations for specialist purposes, scientists from diverging fields also often consult them. They are thereby able to inject themselves into the student's line of reasoning and thus gain access to another realm of specialization. In this way, dissertations act as trans-specialist avenues.

Inter-specialist texts, as they appear in books or articles, resemble dissertations. Phenomena, research in neighbouring fields, and reification remain the focal point of interest. Although authors seek to assert a point of view derived from their own research, their personal work does not generally occupy an inordinate portion of the paper, thereby allowing ample space for a fair-minded presentation of alternative or competing perspectives. Inter-specialist articles contain abundant references to the research conducted in a multitude of laboratories and across a breadth of areas. They likewise deploy considerable imagery, each major research avenue receiving description through the medium of schemas, and above all reification. As in the case of dissertations, this allows scientists from diverse fields to grasp, from the sanctuary of their own specialities, sufficient information and arguments to benefit from the text.

The specific parameters of this class of literature are highlighted in a recently written paper which examines the problems connected with sol-gel transition (6). The authors' announced purpose is to evaluate the pertinence of the percolation theory for the study of gelation and to signal some of the concept's constraints. The text begins with the mention of a group of models which have been employed to study the phenomena and which have, to some extent, proven successful. The authors quickly point out, however, that these analyses only apply to specific categories of gelation or to highly demarcated varieties of material. The next procedure is to set forth in some detail the principle chemical and physical mechanisms involved in different sorts of gelation. One of them is designated for the basis of discussion since it both embraces a range of substances and partially subsumes other modes. It thus constitutes a strategic selection. The case for a percolation-based understanding of the sol-gel transition is then presented, but with the proviso that, at its present stage of development, the theory's application to the phenomena continues to encounter difficulties. The source of the inadequacies are stipulated and the paper concludes with a mention of other possibly promising theories in the domain. Particular attention is drawn to the "kinetic theory" which, if proven relevant to sol-gel transition, would weaken considerably the claims of the percolation theory.

Throughout this article, the writers conspicuously associate themselves with some of the most prominent specialists in the domain, but such references serve an intellectual purpose since they are integrated into the argument and into the demonstration associated with it. Here, they are not tantamount to simple name-dropping because authors also acknowledge the foibles of their theoretical preference, and even admit the strengths of rival interpretations. Equally essential, the writers make it clear that although many facts are known with respect to sol-gel transitions in the present state of research, the underpinnings of these facts, and the relations between them remain nebulous. They specify that current argument in the domain amounts only to "interpretation", and they acknowledge the shades of epistemological status of interpretation when research is still only in an intermediate phase.

Pedagogical Practice

In our typology, pedagogical texts are characterized by abundant historical references and the frequent use of reification. Most other subparameters fall in the intermediary range; as will be suggested in Section 2, this configuration enhances the possibility that knowledge initially presented in other expository categories can be transferred with some ease towards pedagogy, and the converse. We have particularly studied two types of pedagogical papers. The first one consists of precise texts which propose experiments that can easily be conducted by students in laboratories and that can aid them in acquiring understanding of a given theory. In the second type of article, the object is to give precision to a concept or a phenomenon whose previous ambiguity has blemished otherwise sound teaching. While pedagogical texts of the first sort display many of the expository characteristics common to the first half of the article in the *Journal de Mécanique*, the second variety of pedagogical documents presents a profile hitherto unexamined. In this subsection, we will therefore concentrate our attention on the latter category.

Of the utmost significance, this genre is replete with the historical referent. In the article, 'Attention aux tensions superficielles!' (7), this referent occupies roughly one third of the text. The entirety of Section 1 is completely given over to history and historical allusions frequently crop up throughout the remainder of the document. In particular, the work of Young, Gibbs and Jurin is described and commented on in turn. Young's result concerning the equilibrium of a bubble located on a plane is first evoked. The authors then turn to the contributions of Gibbs in the domain of multi-phasic systems in equilibrium. They indicate to their readers that Gibbs' analysis involves three conditions: (a) relative to temperature; (b) to chemical potential – the exchange of matter in different phases; (c) to purely mechanical considerations. Lastly, they examine Jurin's result. Jurin who studied the problem of a free fluid rising in a capillary, demonstrated an equality between the weight of the fluid and the surface tension of the liquid-air interface, calculated along the capillary circumference. The account of surface tension advanced by the authors in their article is often maladroit and cryptic and from a narrative standpoint frequently unsatisfactory. While the writers' interest lies in the mechanical component of the phenomena, they nevertheless digress from the object repeatedly as when they describe the thermic and chemical attributes of systems in equilibrium. Allusion to work such as Gibbs' is largely irrelevant, since the specific point of this pedagogical paper is that, with respect to their physical meaning, surface tension forces must be calculated in terms of the surface of the interface and act in terms of the perimeter of this interface.

But exactly what role does history play in this article and in others like it? One response is that it represents a convention and provides a vehicle for narrative. Such an analysis certainly contains more than a modicum of truth. In our opinion, however, it corresponds to something much more complex and fundamental than this. Our observations of the laboratory in which this paper was written indicate that historical referents are not a mere technical convenience or ritual. On the contrary, they resound throughout the laboratory as scientists go about their daily activities. This historical framework is invoked when they discuss past errors. It is equally used when scientists reflect on how problems, which have resisted analysis to date, might be more effectively pursued in the light of contemporary understanding or technical advances. In effect, history comprises an underlying feature of scientific work, and this is reflected in the fact that, while it emerges as a paramount characteristic of pedagogical literature, it is in varying degrees present in all expository modes. Scientists seem to think partly through the historical referent and they are often keenly conscious of the path taken by the concepts that interest them. Because of this, they appear aware of the pitfalls awaiting the unattentive and also of the non-linear properties of scientific thought, both individual and collective.

As implied above, the pervasive intrusion of history into pedagogical texts proves a basic problem. It often hinders a reader's attempt to isolate the ambiguity being subjected to correction. Yet why is this so, given the privileged place it occupies in research operations? Although great prudence is required here, we advance the idea that this situation is possibly a consequence of scientists being torn between a diachronic and synchronic approach to problem solving and problem exposition. On the synchronic level researchers seek to set forth problems and to resolve them in terms of a panoply of contemporary referents. On the diachronic level, the scientists' questions and procedures are conditioned by the perception of the past. The pedagogical imperative undercuts this dynamic. While performing analytic operations of research, scientists dip generously into the past and filter history in accord with the needs of their particular problem. In the case of pedagogical writing, this selection is breached.

This trait does not, however, tarnish the originality and in many ways the effectiveness of pedagogical publications. In the case of 'Attention aux tensions superficielles', while the authors' key pedagogical contribution — that is, the need to conceive of superficial tensions in terms of total surface forces — remains opaque throughout much of the article, near the end the objective nevertheless emerges with irreproachable clarity thanks to a physical grasp of factual material which is achieved through reification. The writers treat the question of the admissibility and the inacceptability of certain chains of reasoning. With respect to Jurin's problem, the two solutions — where one calculates the surface tension either from the perimeter interface or its surface — give the same mathematical result. Since the arguments had not been rooted in a physical understanding each line of reasoning was equally defensible or vulnerable. Henceforth, however, certain chains of reasoning, in this example those based on the liquid perimeter interface, are untenable. The authors' demonstration indicates that it is not germane here and that admissible arguments revolve only around total surface forces. In this clarification of the type of reasoning to be retained, the authors elucidate not merely the problem surrounding surface tension, but they also signal a tested and rigorous path which, in certain limited conditions, can be extended outward to other domains.

The importance of reified imagery should, by this juncture, be thoroughly established. Its applications to pedagogy even exceed what is revealed in this particular article. Indeed, advanced students as well as professional scholars frequently turn to texts written in the first half of the 20th century precisely because reification comprises a dominant expository vehicle. Richardson's exegesis of turbulent behaviour, universally recognized as one of the very best, inspired the little poem (8):

> Big whirls have little whirls
> Which feed on their velocity
> And little whirls have smaller whirls
> And so on to viscosity

Yet while these words may seem to some only amusing and perhaps even silly, they nevertheless go some way in painting a picture of the physical behaviour of the relation between the specific variables involved in turbulence. And again in the domain of turbulence, the books of Taylor and Prandtl (9) are continually consulted with profit because of the wealth of terms and relations they propose which can easily be transferred into individual images of complex phenomena — phenomena which are otherwise only expressed as esoteric mathematical relations. In the same vein, it is worth noting that many specialists in solid mechanics are, at one point, often nurtured on geology textbooks. The language and iconic representations of geology prove excellent preparation for the development of the reified imagery needed by this group of physicists in their work.

Being Popular

Here, we will examine two subcategories of exposition: (a) the daily press and (b) *La Recherche* which is a broadly circulated "semi-professional" monthly review somewhat analogous to *Scientific American*. Both the numerical mass of publications and their variety produce a situation where the physiognomy varies considerably from one text to another and, because of this hetero-geneity, we intend to examine parallel sets of underlying structures.

As in the preceding categories of texts, phenomena continue to be the focus of attention, but there is a subtle shift in the way that they are treated. In fact, they become a subject of discussion rather than solely an object of exegesis. In popular exposition, the process of treatment moves from the phenomena outwards towards other sets of concerns, while in the cases of intra- and inter-specialist documents and pedagogy, the movement is funneled towards the phenomena. In many ways, the bend and thrust of argument is modified by the referents contained in a given popular article. Indeed, this category of literature incorporates many more referents than has been en-countered in the other sorts of publications: history, technology, economy, politics, etc. Finally, there are frequent allusions to scientific disciplines other than the one directly involved in the text. Taken together, the specific argu-ment profile and the referential system manifest in this type of literature result in an expository form analogous to a news format. Items, such as recent discoveries, the extension of a body of understanding to a new domain, and inventions and innovations are flashed to a public which ingests them. In a rather oblique way, popular literature is tantamount to the treatment of a subject about which it is more crucial to know that something has occurred than it is to know the minutiae of the occurrence itself. Here, knowing is more relevant than knowledge proper.

In *Le Monde* and its like, scientific articles convey some notions of the nature of the phenomena being considered. The text almost always contains a quantitative dimension. The concepts of quantitative limit-conditions, error and numerical approximation occur with relative regularity. Such articles are equally rife with allusions to orders of magnitude which, in the case of these documents, are always infinite, infinitely large or infinitely small: "it measures ten billionths of a meter in thickness" (10) or "the central nervous system includes one hundred thousand billion neurons" (11). These infinite orders of magnitude remain disconnected from everything a reader can identify, or can identify himself with. Here, they merely serve to impress the reader and to boggle his sense of proportion rather than to provide a new, more complex and significant scale of proportions. Elucidation of phenomena also revolves around the use of metaphors. Although metaphorical components are only syntactic and semantic, the outcome is nevertheless the production of images. Yet, in terms of their analytic potential, metaphoric images diverge radically from analogical imagery (12). While analogy operates through deconstruction and comparison (*a* is like *b*) where similarities and limitations are always stipulated, in metaphor significance is generated through a process of fusion and even con-fusion (*a* is *b*). Take the example (13), "the LEP is a huge hammer for pounding matter" — for the uninitiated reader, what relatively clear and useful meaning does the metaphor provide?

We designate the knowledge derived from such metaphors as "degenerated knowledge", that is to say, knowledge which is so constituted that the nature and relationships of its component elements totally preclude an unequivocal, or even, a coherent "multivocal" grasp of the phenomena. Degenerated knowledge is so distended and distorted, with respect to the initial phenomenological referent, that no mental operations based on the metaphors alone enable a reader to retrieve the phenomenon in question. Degeneracy appears particularly strong in the articles of practising scientists where metaphors evince the qualities of a "word-game", producing nonsense. In such cases, it represents a strategy for justifying the importance of science in contemporary culture and for acquiring broad-based social approval, and not a cognitive device. (For more on this, see Green in this volume.)

While this degeneracy impedes an appreciation of a phenomenon itself, the presence of an elaborately developed extra-phenomenological referent cluster gives such daily press articles a high degree of coherence and renders them useful. The phenomenon is transformed into news by coupling it to a set of concerns: technology, economy, politics, health, etc. It is systematically represented as "revolutionary" or "potentially revolutionary", and as holding out a modicum of hope for mankind. For instance, in 'Biotechnology: The Bacteria Factory', taken from *Libération* (14), the author indicates that highly specialized microorganisms can be cheaply and easily reproduced by genetic manipulation in order to serve man's changing and increasing needs.

A host of French companies, among them Elf Aquitaine and Transgene are working feverishly to produce lines of useful and effective microorganisms to undertake a range of tasks which extend from energy production to pharmaceutical innovations and the creation of new substances. The market, evaluated at one billion dollars by 1987, is also coveted by several American firms, and the French will have to mobilize fully to share in the handsome profits that await the victor of this international contest.

One sees, unfolding here in quick succession, a kaleidoscope of referents: politics (international competition), economics (market conquest), technology and pharmacology. Each referent is tightly knitted to the others to demonstrate the importance of genetic manipulations, both with respect to contemporary life and to life in the future. The phenomenon itself, however, remains shrouded in complete mystery.

Given these characteristics of daily press articles, is it legitimate to place semi-professional scientific journals like *La Recherche* in the same category rather than in inter-specialist literature? Texts in *La Recherche* include a wealth of information about the phenomenon under examination. It falls into two main categories, that contained in the text proper and that associated with the many schemas, graphs, and their captions. If these two sorts of information are complementary, they are also divergent. With respect to imagery and captions, the salient features of the phenomena under study are described minutely. Yet, despite this transparent and direct approach, the representation of the research topics remains stylized and emerges only as an ideal type. The phenomena are not presented as integrated problems but as subjects about which certain features are known or are in the process of being learned. Although these captions overflow with detail, the phenomena are not depicted in all of their pertinent manifestations and ramifications. Thus, the issues of limit conditions, errors and approximations are seldom broached. Quantification is likewise lacking which, in turn, suppresses the possibility of reification.

An article in *La Recherche* (15), which treats the structure of flame, highlights this type of expository practice. In one caption, the authors discuss a schema that illustrates flame instabilities.

Introducing a small sinusoidal perturbation on this interface ... we now consider the changes induced on the flow .... The velocity of the burned-gas is deflected by a mechanism which is similar to Descartes' law giving the deflection of a ray of light at the interface which separates two media of different optical indices.

On the basis of the information provided, most readers would not find it easy, and perhaps not even possible, to produce the appropriate form of the velocity deflection equation. The characteristic lack of equations and incomplete data make imagery through reification an arduous task indeed. Even more significant, the authors then abandon this facet of their demonstration. The line of reasoning is not extended to the remainder of the article and not pushed to its logical bounds.

By contrast with the schemas and captions, the text proper focuses on the relationship between the phenomenon as subject and other subjects. Three principal types of referents appear. The importance of recent findings are measured against their historical interest and the difficulties they posed for past generations of scientists. References to research in neighbouring or even distant scientific disciplines constitute another referential source. In the article on the flame, the authors specifically indicate that their findings are of particular significance to the study of thermodynamics and other processes entailing transport phenomena. In much the same vein, the article insists that the study of flame has been accompanied by improvements in diagnostic techniques and hence many fields have benefited from the growth of knowledge in a narrow sphere. Finally, each *La Recherche* article consulted for this study contains several allusions to the technological advantages derived, or to be derived, from the research project at hand. In the case of "La Flamme",

It would be erroneous to think that only the concern to understand better the properties of a flame guides the researcher in his work. The need to optimize the effectiveness of industrial burners has become a major preoccupation during this energy saving era.

The expository profile connected with *La Recherche* probably stems from a three-fold concatination of circumstances. Researchers are quite naturally engrossed in their own research projects. Their purpose is both to signal the specificities of their particular achievements and to proclaim that they are pertinent in a broader arena. Justification for work that is original in conception, carefully reflected on and exactingly executed, provides another underlying current. Yet the simultaneous presentation of a work as well as its scientific and extra-scientific implications can, in part, be resolved through presenting the phenomena at hand in a somewhat stylized and idealized form.

Here the factors (a) individual pride and consciousness, (b) the compulsion to justify, and (c) the propensity for idealization (which after all is not entirely dissimilar to the process of phenomenological modelling) come together to shape *cognitive news*. Here cognitive news is not news of cognition, but rather about cognition. This information about new cognitive shifts constitutes the substance of *La Recherche* articles and, although the paths so indicated are frequently only obliquely signposted, many readers nevertheless grasp the essential message. Most readers we consulted say that they read the journal neither to grasp a point in particular nor for the purpose of nourishing their own research projects; rather they consult *La Recherche* to see what new things are happening. Thus, *La Recherche* is not useful as a tool of phenomenological exegesis, and, for this reason, it is not an inter-specialist document. It is instead a scientific notice-board.

2. Cognitive Trajectories

The expository categories contained in our typology are more than artefacts of the knowledge production process for, under certain conditions, they play an active role in knowledge development. Although the precise nature of the relationship between exposition and cognitive growth remains illusive, some of its properties are nevertheless discernible. Indeed, the parameters of argument, imagery, and referent, as well as audience expectations, spawn distinct cognitive criteria and norms for each category of expository text. Consequently, not all sorts of propositions, representations or intellectual allusions are equally admissible in every category of exposition. What is acceptable in one genre is often deemed inappropriate to another, even though no analytic contradictions occur with respect to the phenomenon under consideration. In the light of this, it is particularly important to note that the transfer of knowledge claims from one expository category to another constitutes a key stage in cognitive production.

We propose to examine two cognitive trajectories. First, it sometimes happens that research ideas, experiments, projects, etc. born under the "aegis" of one expository category, never come to fruition. This is not necessarily due to an inherent deficiency in the project. It often results, instead, from a failure to fit the properties associated with a phenomenon, which are presented in terms of one expository category, into the framework and norms corresponding to another expository genre. In this situation, the parameters of argument, imagery and referent are "crystallized" at a preliminary phase of investigation, and are thus not readily adaptable to the criteria of other expository types. In sum, analysis becomes imprisoned by the logics of a particular expository mode. Secondly, some ideas, results, etc. which are judged ill-suited for treatment under one expository category, or on the other hand, are viewed as meriting extended systematic treatment, are consciously transferred to another expository genre for analysis in terms of an alternative, albeit complementary, set of parameters. Whether the initial idea is eventually retained or not, the very process of transfer often provokes crucial questions and open vistas. We label this trajectory, "deviation". Although these two cognitive trajectories are acutely different, they both point to the importance of exposition in the research process. In the remainder of this paper, we will briefly examine these trajectories of "crystallization" and "deviation". Although this treatment is far from exhaustive, it will demonstrate the dynamic character of the parameters contained in our typology.

Crystallization

Crystallization occurs in every expository category and, seemingly, in roughly equal proportions. Whether its causes are epistemological, psychological or social, it inhibits the expansion of knowledge by reducing the trajectories along which cognition can travel. Instead circulating freely, from one expository genre to another, cognitive mobility is impeded or blocked. In the following example, an apparatus, initially developed by a sculptor working in kinetic art and which had not been used previously for research purposes, was put on exhibition to demonstrate a recent concept to the general public. We will show how crystallization, which in this case occurred in "being popular", affected the depth and breadth of the analysis of phenomena, inhibited the transfer of knowledge towards specialist exposition and sturted the development of the project.

The exhibit in question was one of many erected in a large suburban shopping centre, on the occasion of the 1981 Société Française de Physique Congress. It contained two elements: (a) a large iconic representation of water pouring from a tap, which, in fact, acted as a metaphor intended to evoke a turbulent system. (b) a pendulum, called a chaotor, having three independent axes, at the end of each were attached small fluorescent balls which could assume either periodic or chaotic motion. The chaotor's purpose was to illustrate a concept advanced recently by the two mathematicians Ruelle and Takens, that disorder can be produced by three degrees of freedom, contrary to the Landau's representation which calls for an infinite number of degrees of freedom.

The public was fascinated by the fluorescent effect but clearly understood nothing of the concept at hand; indeed, a practised eye would have been needed to distinguish between the periodic and chaotic motion of the balls. In addition, the correspondence between the chaotor and the drawing remained totally enigmatic. In fact, the metaphor contained in the drawing embodied a confusion since the turbulence associated with the jet from a tap obeys the Landau's theory while that of the chaotor is related to the Ruelle and Takens' concept. This example illustrates the dangers that accompany the uses of metaphors, for the lay public and scientists alike. At the end of the Congress, the exhibit was dismantled and taken back to the laboratory, the chaotor was then reassembled, becoming a basis for laboratory work.

The ensuing work suffered acutely from the effects of crystallization which occurred around two poles. First, the chaotor's status was that of an autonomous technique possessing intrinsic value, and not that of an agent for investigating a given class of phenomena. Secondly, the narrowly mechanical representation of disorder, present in the exhibit, continually coloured the researchers' perception of the problem under study. In this instance, crystallization was reinforced by the laboratory's past involvement in mechanics research. These two poles had a pronounced impact on the attempts to analyze the physical phenomenon at hand. As a matter of fact, the chaotor shown on the exhibit was never integrated into a fully elaborated research program. On one level, the apparatus concerned here was not conceived in terms of a careful analysis of the experimental and technical requirements of a given category of phenomena. On a second level, while some superficial improvements were proffered on the machine, for instance its capacity to produce visual signals, these improvements failed to take into account the technical exigencies of the experiment proper, such as the linkage of the three axes. Thus, the chaotor emerged as an object of study in itself rather than as a pertinent experimental tool woven into a defined and carefully articulated research initiative.

A first consequence of this crystallization process was the blockage of cognitive flow in the direction of specialist exposition (see Fig. 2). In effect, a blinkered concern with the apparatus and the mechanical representation of disorder associated with it, temporarily masked the fact that fruitful research in the same class of phenomena, albeit in different forms, predated the chaotor's study. In addition, the chaotor-based results proved less precise than those derived through non-mechanical procedures, essentially because of the failure to take into account the effects of friction on the operation of the device. Indeed, numerical simulations and analogies stemming from electronics were yielding particularly precise and exciting results in the sphere of disorder. Yet, since the potential for phenomena analysis was considerably impoverished, the cognitive trajectories which could have led towards

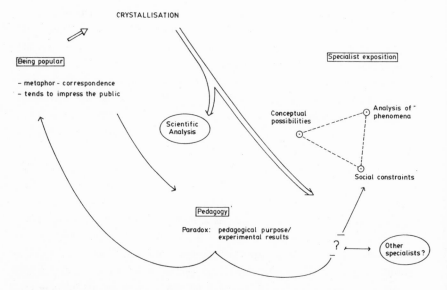

Fig. 2. This schema summarizes the effects of crystallization on the research process in the case of the chaotor's study, which is described in the text. Two sorts of arrows have been drawn:

- main arrows (→) show the cognitive trajectories along which knowledge is transferred (being popular → pedagogy → being popular) or blocked (pedagogy −/ /→ specialist exposition).
- double arrows indicate the phases of the research process which are affected by crystallization (scientific analysis, transfer towards specialist exposition).

specialist exposition were severed. In the same vein, crystallization prevented the development of a new research focus. On the one hand, no initiative to construct a device adapted to the study of a clear cut and original problem was undertaken, for example, the mechanical study of n degrees of freedom. On the other, the selection of an alternative representation, which could have opened the path towards other specialists, also failed to occur.

Finally, in our example, the only direction which knowledge generated by the chaotor study could take, led towards pedagogy (16). This was possible principally because, unlike in specialist and inter-specialist texts, the parameters associated with this expository genre tend to fall in the intermediary range. The mechanical representation of disorder depicted by the chaotor, although not analytically fruitful, nevertheless appeared as a departure from the past. Moreover, the historical perspective of pedagogical texts allowed the juxtaposition of this new approach with that of other important stages of research on chaotic systems. In the same vein, the possibility of seeing optically the generation of several oscillatory regimes monoperiodic, biperiodic, chaotic nourished reification. As things were, however, the pedagogical objectives were not fully accomplished; and, since no insights suitable for specialist exposition were gained, the only available cognitive trajectory led back to being popular. In fact, the experimental device is currently planned for exhibition in France's new National Museum of Sciences and Industry.

Deviation

In deviation, as in the case of crystallization, cognitive trajectories do not necessarily allow an indiscriminate flow of knowledge from any one category of exposition to all others. The direction of cognitive transfer conforms to the requirements of the parameters elucidated in our typology. In deviation, cognition is intentionally shifted from one expository genre to another with the idea in mind that the expository standards and criteria of the alternative category are more felicitous for the growth of the idea at hand. In effect, scientists recognize that, under certain conditions, the characteristics of notions, techniques, results, etc., evoked or logically implied in one category of exposition C_0, do not conform to the exigencies of that expository category, and therefore cannot be effectively elaborated in C_0. As a consequence, the idea, notion, etc. is transferred from C_0 to C_1, in the light of the arguments, images and referents of C_1. Intuitions, ideas, problems are then defined, elaborated or tested in the hope of eventually introducing them back into the category C_0 or into another. In many instances, the inklings which become the objects of deviation, first appear in specialist and inter-specialist texts, while their development takes place within "being popular" and pedagogical writings, where the expository parameters tend to be more conducive to unfettered exploration.

In the following example, we will examine some of the effects of deviation, its underlying mechanisms, and its consequences for the expository categories involved. The specialist article, 'Utilisation de la diffusion Rayleigh Forcée à l'étude d'écoulements laminaires et turbulents' (17), discussed in Section 1 of this paper, contains the description of a new technique for studying hydro-dynamic flows and reports some experimental results. In the text, the authors recommend the use of their experimental device in a broad range of sub-disciplines. The importance of this technique for the authors was reflected by the fact that, inside the laboratory, research on its refinement constituted a long term focus of endeavour. It consisted of using a new type of photo-chromic dye as a tracer, which was excited by incoherent light and detected by means of photography. This upgrading was intended to overcome some of the instrumental limitations described in the article.

Yet, the allusions to the new technique are unstructured, equivocal, and tend to constitute more a suggestion than a concrete project. Indeed, as presented in the article, these ameliorations have the status of "conceptual possibilities" (see Fig. 1). In this particular instance, this status is a conse-quence of the fact that work on the new technique was at a preliminary stage. As a result, the propositions that could be advanced by the researchers with respect to the innovation in question did not fit the requirements of specialist exposition.

Reflections on the new project were, however, fully admissible under "being popular" exposition. In an article entitled 'Ecrire dans l'eau' (18), the scientists boast of the merits of the initial experimental apparatus, but, at the same time, the potential features of the new technique are continually superimposed on the discussion. In this example, deviation is expressed by means of metaphors which punctuate the article: "writing in water", "ink is not indelible", "a writing and reading exercise". Indeed, given the fact that, at this preliminary phase of the technique's development, researchers were exploring several complementary options simultaneously, yet not exhaustively, "being popular" which is essentially a sign-board that something, not necessarily definite, is in the process of happening, constituted the most appropriate nexus of exposition. Yet, and at least as important, while in being popular such degenerate knowledge associated with metaphors is a device for the dissemination of news about science to the lay public, in the case at hand, this type of knowledge also has a critical cognitive function. In effect, it constitutes a free-wheeling epistemological mode where questions and answers are touched upon and cleared of the exigencies associated with specialist or even inter-specialist texts.

As the project gradually matured, the deviation mechanism continued, incorporating other expository modes. The study of the various components on which the new technique was based, and their construction, gave rise to fresh images, arguments and referents which, in turn, influenced cognitive trajectories during deviation. In the present case, articles appeared in both pedagogical (19) and inter-specialist journals (20) yet, notably, not in the specialist press. Within the laboratory, the scientists, at one point, used the newly invented apparatus as a device for teaching advanced university students. Discussions of this pedagogical practice nourished the emergence of expository parameters which spurred the scientists to pen a text intended for pedagogical purposes. Yet, at the same time, thoughts were not ripe for specialist exposition since the results were inferior, or at least no more than comparable to those achieved routinely with the initial apparatus.

Deviation is even more acute in a text which appeared in an inter-specialist review. In effect, growing understanding of the new apparatus and of its utilization, the development of specific and exact criteria for comparison with its forerunner, and finally an enhanced grasp of the new device's potential applications, directed the cognitive trajectory towards interspecialist exposition which is characterized, among other things, by emphasis on research in adjoining fields and moderate concern for protocol. Again, however, the project was not consistent with the specialist requirements because of basic difficulties with the resolution of the optical data, the collection of meaningful information and finally the test of the technique. Thus, as we saw in this case of deviation, the characteristics associated with each type of exposition are not simply artificial devices for delimiting expository categories, but they also constitute active agents which interact with one another, so affecting the research process.

3. Conclusion and Remarks

In this paper, we have suggested that scientific exposition occurs along a continuum where categories of texts are not completely separated from one another. The traditional argument that scientific popularization is somehow radically different from other classes of science associated texts, thus tends to collapse. Our study indicates, for example, that, without exception, every type of writing reflects its authors' social drives, be they enhanced professional recognition or a search for allies in support of a pet idea. Yet, the presence of this admittedly important social register in every expository genre should not be interpreted as signifying that all sorts of texts are essentially the same. On the contrary, analysis of content-structure, namely argument, imagery and referent, reveals that in some critical respects, they are also very dissimilar. For their part, specialist texts largely revolve around tightly reasoned discussions of experimental limit conditions, instrument precision and the relevance of results. Scientific popularization on the other hand, operates as a conduit for informing scientists and non-scientists of recent discoveries and advances, and as a platform for viewing scientific events against a backdrop of non-scientific interests and concerns. Finally, as regards the research process itself, popularizing offers a cognitive space where, as yet fragile and unstructured projects, can be reflected on, free from the epistemological constraints that characterize other expository modes to differing degrees, and free from an acute risk of professional embarrassment. Yet, beyond their respective particularities, these two expository modes also converge in areas of utmost importance, as both examine subject matter and couch their messages in terms of quantitative dimensions and schematic imagery.

In the case of inter-specialist and pedagogical texts, social desiderata are less ubiquitous or, at least less acute, then they are in specialist and popular articles. Or, is their presence only less transparent? At this juncture of our investigation, it seems however that authors' concern for "self marketing" or for "marketing" of concepts is inclined to decrease in texts that contain synthetic treatment of questions or that are exploratory in a tentative and broad-ranging sense. However, this observation is merely preliminary and the social and cognitive causes of such a tendency remain obscure. In contrast, this study offers considerable proof that both pedagogical and inter-specialist texts depend on reified imagery as a major device for analysis and communication, and that they exhibit identical forms of argument. Inter-specialist texts are singular in that they quite logically involve multiple references to research in neighbouring fields while, for their part, pedagogical works are prone to place an emphasis on history. The use of the historical referent is also common in popularizing and this is noteworthy since it again demonstrates that the popular genre is a full-fledged part of science-related exposition and not distinct and isolated as has been frequently claimed.

Finally, we have suggested that exposition entails much more than the communication and eventually the legitimation of results and ideas. The presence of specific, albeit overlapping, parameters for each expository category reveals the existence of particular niches in which different types of argument, imagery and subject matter, and even degrees of validation, occur. The attempts of scientists to recast knowledge in order to transfer it from one expository category to another tend to shed light on the inadequacies and potential of the ideas and results at hand, and to provide information useful for further analysis. Seen from this perspective, exposition is a dynamic agent in the research process. For instance, in "crystallization", the adherence of researchers to the parameters of a single expository genre curtails possible cognitive trajectories leading to other genre and thereby impedes knowledge development through restricting the representation or techniques to which the phenomenon is subjected. Somewhat conversely, in deviation, a broad range of avenues is open between different categories of exposition, which allow researchers to communicate on a multitude of levels. In sum, deviation constitutes an active system of cognitive networking which serves as a lubricant in the research process. Of course, it is recognized here that the characteristics of expository categories and their relationship with one another are influenced by the social and intellectual organization of science (21). Be this as it may, it seems reasonable to believe that most mature disciplines possess an expository typology similar to the one set forth in this paper, and that expository practice affects the growth of knowledge by means of cognitive trajectories.

Notes and References

1. A. Ortony, *Metaphors and Thought*, Cambridge, Cambridge University Press, 1979. W. A. Leatherdale, *The Role of Analogy, Model and Metaphor in Science*, University of New South Wales, Oxford, 1974.

2. C. F. A. Pantin, *The Relations Between the Sciences*, Cambridge: Cambridge University Press, 1968.
3. M. Fermigier, M. Cloître, E. Guyon, et P. Jenffer, 'Utilisation de la diffusion Rayleigh forcée à l'étude d'écoulements laminaires et turbulents', *Journal de Mécanique théorique et appliquée* **1** (1982), 123–146.
4. W. Schrum, 'Scientific Specialities and Technical Systems', *Social Studies of Science* **14** (1984), 63–90.
5. M. Cloître, '*Étude expérimentale du champ de gradients de vitesse dans un écoulement de Poiseuille turbulent*', Thèse 3e cycle, Université Paris VI, Déc. 1982.
6. B. Jouhier, C. Allain, B. Gauthier-Manuel, and E. Guyon 'The sol-gel Transition', *Annals of the Israel Physical Society* **5** (1983), 167–185.
7. E. Guyon, J. Prost, C. Betrencourt, C. Boulet, et B. Volochine, 'Attention aux tensions superficielles', *European Journal of Physics* **3** (1982), 159–168.
8. E. Guyon and L. Petit, 'From the Draining of a Bathtub to the Turbulent Cascade', *European Journal of Physics* **2** (1981), 32–36.
9a. G. K. Batchelor, *Scientific Papers of G. I. Taylor*, London: Cambridge University Press, 1963.
9b. L. Prandtl, *Guide à travers la Mécanique des Fluides*, Paris: Dunod, 1952.
10. Maurice Arvonny, 'Basses températures et effet Josephson. Le Quiteron: un composant électronique pour les ordinateurs de demain', *Le Monde*, 1 June 1983, p. 16.
11. J. L. Martin, 'La mystérieuse chimie de notre cerveau', *Ça m'intéresse*, 25 March 1983, pp. 11–15.
12. R. Tourangeau and R. J. Sternberg, 'Understanding and Appreciating Metaphors', in *Cognition* **11** (1982), 203–244.
13. D. Leglu, 'Physique des particules: la cérémonie de l'anneau', *Libération*, 13 September 1983, p. 14.
14. D. Leglu, 'Biotechnologies: les bactéries à l'usine', *Libération*, 8 September 1983, p. 13.
15. P. Clavin et E. Guyon, 'La flamme', *La Recherche* **9** (1978), 954–963.
16. O. Viet, J. E. Wesfreid, et E. Guyon, 'Art cinétique et chaos mécanique', *European Journal of Physics* **4** (1983), 72–76.
17. 'Utilisation de la diffusion Rayleigh forcée . . .' *op. cit.*
18. 'Ecrire dans l'eau', *Bulletin de l'Amicale des Anciens Élèves de l'ESPCI*, June 1980, pp. 29–31.
19. E. Guyon, P. Jenffer, A. d'Arco, et M. Cloître, 'Sur une mesure en laboratoire de travaux pratiques de diffusivités thermique et massique', *European Journal of Physics* **2** (1981), 193–199.
20. A. d'Arco, J. C. Charmet, et M. Cloître, 'Nouvelle technique de marquage d'écoulements par utilisation de molécules photochromes', *Revue de Physique Appliquée* **17** (1982), 89–93.
21. R. Whitley, *The Intellectual and Social Organization of the Sciences*, London: Oxford University Press, 1984.

POPULARISATION WITHIN THE SCIENCES
The Purposes and Consequences of Inter-Specialist Communication

JOSKE BUNDERS
The Free University, Amsterdam

and

RICHARD WHITLEY
Manchester Business School

Introduction

During 1983 two major symposia were held in the Netherlands on the subject of popularisation of scientific knowledge (1). The fundamental concern of both was the inability of scientists to communicate about their work to the public at large that sustained their research enterprises. Generally, popularisation was seen as being external to the research process and as an activity requiring different skills from knowledge production. In particular, scientists were said to lack empathy with lay audiences which was seen as crucial to effective popularisation. The conclusions of these symposia can be summarised as follows:

(a) scientists do not undertake effective popularisation because they feel too much distortion and simplification would be required;

(b) scientists do not have the essential skills for popularisation which are different from research skills, and

(c) scientists do not undertake popularisation because it does not lead to high scientific reputations and prestige which mediate access to rewards.

These conclusions are widely held by many scientists and administrators and can be characterised as the "standard view" of popularisation. They are echoed by much work in the sociology of science which generally views

Terry Shinn and Richard Whitley (eds.), Expository Science: Forms and Functions of Popularisation. Sociology of the Sciences, Volume IX, 1985, 61–77.
© 1985 *by D. Reidel Publishing Company.*

popularisation as a low status and subsidiary activity for ambitious scientists
(2).

This "standard view" of popularisation stems from a conception of the
scientific community as a cohesive, autonomous, "paradigm bound" entity
which generates esoteric knowledge that is only communicated to non scientists with great difficulty. These non scientists are viewed as a mass of undifferentiated and unorganised people whose distinguishing common feature
is simply their lack of participation in the knowledge production and validation process. Thus the "popularisation problem" is viewed as the Herculean
task of transferring true knowledge produced by a highly organised and
systematic activity to a large, vague and indeterminate audience. Not surprisingly, this "problem" then seems impossible to resolve.

Once the scientific community is conceived in a less monolithic, more
differentiated way, and non scientific audiences are analysed further as
distinct groups which vary in their proximity to, and interest in, scientific
knowledge, this standard view of popularisation becomes clearly untenable.
Not only are these two entities more complex in their internal structure than
the standard view suggests, but the sharp dividing line between them becomes
rather indistinct as knowledge production is construed as a socially organised
activity which has been differently structured in different historical periods
and in different scientific fields (3). The sharpness and firmness of social and
intellectual boundaries between scientific knowledge production and lay
audiences have varied historically and vary today across the sciences as the
papers in this volume bear witness. Recent studies of research laboratories
and research programmes (4) have shown that non scientists, such as lawyers,
civil servants and foundation officials, as well as researchers from other fields,
often participate in the development of research strategies and the interpretation and evaluation of research results so that scientists have to communicate
their ideas, expectations and interpretations to a wider audience than their
immediate specialist colleagues. The constitutive role of a variety of audiences
in the construction of knowledge objects and research results in the public
sciences (5) means that exposition directly affects what research is done and
how it is conducted; thus changes in audience structure and goals affect
scientific interpretations and norms as de Vries and Harbers show. Popularisation, then, is a more complex and broader notion than the standard view
suggests.

In this paper we extend the concept of popularisation to incorporate the translation of ideas and results into different frameworks as researchers seek to communicate them effectively to other scientists who are not directly involved in the same area or who use different approaches and techniques. There seem to be two major kinds of such intra-scientific popularisation: disciplinary and inter-specialty. In disciplinary popularisation scientists communicate their results and approaches to colleagues with similar skills and intellectual identities, but who are working on different problems. Because the "discipline" is often the dominant unit of labour market control and skill certification in the sciences (6), researchers have to convince this general scientific audience of the intellectual significance of their work for disciplinary goals. This means that they have to ensure that their innovations "fit in" to the current orthodoxy and are seen as relevant to others' concerns. The more radical and deviant such innovations are, the more they have to be "translated" and transformed into concepts and terms which make sense to the discipline as a whole. Where the particular problem area is not central to the discipline, such translation is likely to be difficult and leads to different interpretations of results.

Secondly, the need to obtain the cooperation and assistance of researchers and others with different backgrounds and interests in much contemporary science — especially that conducted in organisations with multiple, broad objectives — has encouraged, if not required, many scientists to translate their work problems and outcomes into forms which other specialists can understand and see the point of. Communication to a small group dealing with the same narrow topic with the same techniques is often not sufficient for obtaining the necessary information to resolve intellectual problems or gain resources and so researchers increasingly have to "popularise" their work to scientists from other fields to complete research projects satisfactorily. This sort of popularisation involves the appreciation of others' problems and interests and an ability to demonstrate links between one's results and those of the audience, as will be elaborated later.

In sum, we suggest that the three major conclusions of the 1983 symposia should be modified by the following points:

(a) the ability to convince scientists and others outside one's immediate problem area of the importance and worth of one's strategy and results is a key skill in gaining scientific prestige.

(b) scientists frequently have to translate their ideas and results into other languages and frameworks in order to gain assistance from other specialists to resolve major problems.

Thus, popularisation, in the sense of translating ideas and results to audiences beyond the immediate specialist group, is an important element in scientific work today and in the development of a successful scientific career.

These points will be elaborated and illustrated through a discussion of a particular case study in the rest of this paper. This case highlights the importance of gaining the cooperation of specialists in other fields for conducting research in the contemporary biological sciences and so the increasing necessity of being able to "popularise" one's topic and approach to researchers with different background and interests sufficiently effectively to obtain their positive commitment. As will be demonstrated later, this involves more than simply obtaining materials and technical apparatus; it requires the transfer of knowledge and skills in such a way that they can be used effectively. Thus, the active involvement of other specialists is frequently essential to deal with particular sub problems and so gaining such involvement through successful popularisation is often critical. In considering popularisation of one's research topic, approach and results to other researchers, then, three distinct audiences can be identified: (1) the disciplinary and/or specialism "dominant coalition" (7), (2) long term, i.e., throughout the project or programme, collaborators from other fields and (3) specialists from other fields whose contribution is important for particular parts of the project.

In the next section we summarise the major developments in the case study, which was a neurophysiological research project investigating the behaviour of neuro-endocrine cells in certain snails, and discuss the translation of novel, deviant metaphors into more acceptable terms as the group tried to communicate with the first of these audiences: fellow neurophysiologists. The third section analyses the difficulties and transformations involved in communicating with the other two sorts of audience, and the need for new skills to be developed which enabled scientists to transcend the social and intellectual boundaries of their narrow specialism.

Material for this case study was gathered by the first author from direct observation, interviews, publications, informal conversations with members of the interdisciplinary working group, attending lectures and discussions with scientists from other fields over a two year period. In the following account, all the quotations come from the leader of the neurophysiological research group.

The Development and Communication of Deviant Metaphors in a Neuro-Physiological Research Project

As part of a broader study of the biological functions of neuro-secretion in lower animals, involving histologists, electron microscopists and endocrinologists, a small neurophysiological research group consisting of one Professor, two PhD students and two technicians was set up in 1976 to study the behaviour of neuro-endocrine cells in a snail, *Lymnea Stagnalis*. The two other groups in the project comprised: one Professor, one lecturer, three PhD students and three technicians in endocrinology-physiology and one Professor, one lecturer, two PhD students and three technicians in electron microscopy/histology.

Neuro-endocrine cells have both an endocrine function, i.e., they produce messages in the blood as hormones, and a neuronal function, i.e., electrical messages (action potentials) run through their fibres. These cells occur in all animals but it is usually difficult to investigate them because of their inaccessibility and small size. During the course of this research project the biological functions of two of the snail's neuro-endocrine systems were clarified: one, consisting of approximately 100 cells, initiates ovulation whilst a second system regulates growth. The central research questions for the whole interdisciplinary group then became: how do neuro-endocrine cells work and how is their operation regulated? The specific concern of the neurophysiological sub-group was: how does the electrical control mechanism in the neuro-endocrine cell system, which regulates the production of ovulation — stimulating hormones, actually work?

In attempting to deal with this question, four distinct models were developed in the following sequence:

(1) a system of motor neurons linked to an external command system,
(2) an integrated system of motor neurons and command cell,
(3) a system of neurons which are capable of being locked and bolted,
(4) a system of neurons which can be locked and bolted by means of a clock mechanism.

These models will now be discussed in greater detail.

The first model is derived from the standard neurophysiological picture of the neuron which views the system as a set of neurons waiting for an input (via a synapse) and then passing this input on quickly by means of action potentials to other neurons. This view of neurons, however, was too general. It was made more specific by concentrating on a special class of neurons: the motor neurons. These, like the neuro-endocrine cells being studied, are involved in the last step of a series of processes leading to a tangible effect in the organism, such as the contraction of a muscle in the case of motor neurons, and the ovulation of a number of ova in the case of the neuro-endocrine cells. Thus the neuro-endocrine cell system was seen as producing hormones when commanded to do so by an external command system, following the currently accepted view. In order to trace this command system, snails were stimulated electrically in many places but no normal action potentials were observed and so this model seemed incorrect. In the words of the leader of the neurophysiological group:

If you looked at them in a normal, standard fashion then they were just a bunch of cells which didn't do anything.

After some time, the sub-group realised that the production of the ovulatory hormone followed stimulation of the cells within the 100-cell system rather than stimulation of external cells and so they abandoned the normal model of motor neuron systems and focussed their attention on the cell system itself.

You could apply the electrical stimulus into the system itself. That was when we knew there had to be a structure in the system itself. It could do it all by itself. This was different from the usual systems. This particular motor neuron system seemingly contained elements that are normally external to neuron systems. We found that hard to believe. It was difficult to accept that this was the case.

The search for command cells within the system led to some morphologically deviant cells being found which seemed to affect linkages to other cells. However the concept of command cells was subsequently abandoned completely because the sub-group established that ovulation behaviour could be induced from every cell in the neuro-endocrine system and not just the morphologically deviant ones. The result led to new concepts and metaphors being suggested which were quite different from those current in neurophysiology. The central metaphors were: bolt, lock and clock.

So we thought: "Hey – it seems like a bolted door: you can open it if you've got the key, but first you've got to undo the bolt, or it won't work". The way we saw it, there had to be two things in these cells: you needed a key to set them off, but you could also bolt them. This picture also gave us an indication of the times involved. The bolt is a long-term thing and the key is quick. . . .

Whilst experimental research using this model of a system of neurons capable of being locked and bolted was being conducted, a considerable literature on the subject of "bursting" pacemaker neurons appeared. These cells alternate between a few seconds of activity, evoked by a "firing pattern" produced by the cell itself, and a few seconds of inactivity. Comparison of these "bursters" with the neuro-endocrine cell system led the sub-group to formulate the fourth model mentioned above in which the system of neurons could be locked and bolted by a clock mechanism. In this model the periodic "firing" of the bursters was seen as the ticking of a clock and, just like a clock, each burster has its own mechanism to keep it ticking.

Then we thought: this bolt is something regulated by a clock. This implied automatically that it's inside the cells themselves, for that's the basic idea of a clock timer. A clock is a good model because it gives out a time signal. Now's the time to ovulate and no questions asked . . .

The ticking mechanism was the periodic opening and closing of the ion channels already roughly identified. Since clocks not only have their own internal mechanisms but also can be set externally, this model allowed for the possibility of processing influences from outside the neuro-endocrine system. This was a necessary feature because external influences affect the duration of the cycle, i.e., the clock's speed, and so the frequency of ovulation.

It is clear from this summary of model development that metaphors play a crucial role in these scientists' attempts at understanding neurophysiological processes and that changes in their understandings were constituted by changes in the metaphors used to express them (8). In communicating their views through the formal publication system, however, the sub-group had to modify their "deviant" metaphors so that they were less controversial and easier for other neurophysiologists to assimilate.

If you've got a metaphor which deviates a lot from the norm, then it's difficult to hide it away in your story. Then the writing gets difficult: then you get the question "Whatever are you asking that question for? Your story doesn't hold water. And that's a difficult problem to solve . . . ."

So, for instance, the three different possible cell states (locked and bolted, locked and unbolted, unlocked and unbolted) were described as distinct "states of excitability" and the strong discontinuities in cell activity were redescribed as gradual variations.

You've got to express the results given in some framework, so you distort them until they fit into something. Now we don't do that so consciously, but we just use the standard formalisation normally used in electrophysiology. The use of metaphors necessitated some alterations in these standard formalisations. But that didn't mean the whole system collapsed. The only thing was, for these cells you needed a couple of extras so you could understand, and so we could stay within the bounds of what was generally permitted ....

In seeking to generalise their findings to other systems the group had to convince their colleagues of the viability of the "state of excitability" model as described for one neuro-endocrine system of one snail for other cell structures.

This model was only valid for one cell system under certain conditions ... of course, ovulation is something that's got to happen at a certain moment, and half an ovum's out of the question. So in this respect I think that the metaphor fits ....

Such generalisation was limited by the fact that the metaphor left many questions unanswered even for this specific neuro-endocrine system.

The model falls short in the way the system functions relative to the exterior. We don't know exactly as yet how that works. The whole metaphor was meant to describe that bunch of 100 cells and, if you add others, then you can invent anything you like, such as whose job it is to draw the bolt, and so on. But the simple way didn't hold true, and then your metaphor isn't worth so much any more ....

In coping with these difficulties, the sub-group compared their results with other published work on snails and extended the metaphor to other neuro-endocrine systems in the snail.

Now I'm using the model in looking at other cells. I use it as a reference point for research because it's all we've got ... it gets us doing experiments − if it then proves to be true, then you've shown that it's generalisable ....

The demonstration of the suitability of the model for another neuro-endocrine system of the snail is, however, only a small step towards showing its validity for neuro systems in higher animals such as in human brains. Despite this, some thought was given to such generalisations.

If the model holds true for growth hormone cells, it's hardly generalised because that's also a neuro-endocrine system . . . I do feel, however, that parts of the model's outline could be valid in a more general sense . . . .

It happens so often in brains that systems should be able to be switched off for a bit. That's quite usual. If everything in the brain is working at once, then it's utter chaos. So it should be possible to switch off systems completely, so they don't do anything . . . . That'd be of great importance for ordinary neurons in general as well. As yet, this idea still is not commonly accepted, but that's the way I see it . . . .

In this section we have briefly described the processes by which the sub-group of neurophysiologists developed new, deviant metaphors and models for understanding the behaviour of one neuro-endocrine system. As their work proceeded and they had to communicate their ideas to other researchers, the sub-group had to modify their ideas so they "fitted in" with those being used by neurophysiological and other colleagues. To gain acceptance, and high reputations, they had to demonstrate the relevance of their research for the work of other neurophysiologists dealing with different problems, and so communicate effectively to them (9). We now turn to their popularisation of their work to scientists from other fields.

Popularisation of Ideas and Results to Scientists in Other Fields

As mentioned above, there were two sets of specialists from other fields who were important audiences for research ideas and results: those who were involved in the same working group throughout the project and those who were needed for collaboration on particular sub-problems which arose at different times. First, we will discuss the reactions of the endocrinologists and histologists in the interdisciplinary work group. Second, the different interactions with other specialist groups at different stages of the research will be analysed.

With the other members of the interdisciplinary research group, i.e., endocrinologists, histologists and electron microscopists, communication was facilitated by their common focus on neuro-endocrine systems, but hampered by their different intellectual backgrounds.

It's extremely difficult, you have to exert yourself in order to be able to understand the other person, what he's talking about, what his main interest are . . . .

Some of the problems encountered in such inter-field communication can be illustrated by the discussions on the metaphors and models used. It proved impossible in the end to construct a common model.

It's very difficult to make up a model that pleases both of us. I once said it's as if we were two sculptors each working on either side of a piece of rock. Every now and then we look at each other and find what the other is doing is insane . . . so far we haven't been able to construct a coherent image . . . .

Vexation and anger were often the reactions to metaphors like bolt, lock and clock.

To an endocrinologist it means nothing, it's even repulsive. . . . He thinks it's wrong, it creates a wrong image. Of course, to an endocrinologist it's of no use . . . .

In this instance, however, it did prove possible for antagonism to be followed by some understanding and appreciation.

It's a matter of mutual understanding which grew because they realised we were achieving something. That we could show something about the system that had never been seen before . . . .

This understanding grew after the neurophysiologists had obtained some positive results and the endocrinologists and histologists had accustomed themselves to the way in which the neurophysiologists formulated and tackled their problems. As it developed, the scientists in the whole group became firmly convinced that the progress of research on a biological system was considerably facilitated by inter field cooperation.

Less continuous contacts with scientists from other fields during the research project proved straightforward when dealing with technical questions — because most techniques were highly standardised — or with acquiring materials but difficulties grew when questions of intellectual approach and interpretations were involved.

On a technical level, everyone wants to give advice. Questions on how to make electrodes, how to apply them to the cells, that's always plain sailing . . . and that's the way it always goes, no problem getting the substances, but what you can do with them, that's something you have to find out on your own . . . .

Obtaining useful information about the substances for the project raised considerable difficulties largely because pharmacologists and pharmacochemists needed to have some insight into neurophysiological problems and ways of tackling them if they were to be able to provide the right kind of information. As a way of generating this insight, talks were organised from time to time but these had a rather cool reception for quite a long period.

People simply would not react when you'd tell them a story, or they would say the research was nice, that's all you get ... they don't react to the things you think are important ... they want to elaborate on something which you think is a detail ... .

Gradually the neurophysiologists realised that there were a number of barriers blocking effective communication. These arose from fundamental differences in fields of interests and from an apparent lack of any mutual benefits for the audiences' research from such contacts. Medical researchers, for instance, seemed to be exclusively interested in the general properties of certain systems rather than specific ones. They were also uninterested in possible relationships between the particular properties being studied and the whole organism.

Every organism has something general and something specific. As a biologist, you have to be alert to this. A medical scientist couldn't care less, not even if he studies a rat. You can't generalise without seeing the specific and casting an occasional glance at the entire organism.
They don't do that in general ... the effect is that medical scientists do show interest in the fact that there are dopamine-receptors on a membrane, but they don't care on what kind of membrane in other words, in what kind of system they occur. ... But I think it's necessary to keep an eye on that constantly. It wasn't there for nothing, it was doing something there; and it will show general characteristics, but also specific ones. Besides, I feel it could be a purpose to understand a total organism, because it's very special that such an organism should survive, that it should exist. We biologists are being accused of reaching for the sky, but this fundamental interest is something I would expect from all medical scientists, something they really ought to have ... .

In contrast, biochemists and biophysicists were not expected to have an interest in the organism as a whole. As was clear from the beginning, differences here concerned the extent to which reduction is meaningful.

Biologists always come up with a coherent totality. Physicists and chemists object that this does not make you any the wiser, that biologists do so out of impotence. On the other hand, we say that people are reducing down to the impossible, to the meaningless. The nice thing is to stay in between. Without reduction you can't work, but you shouldn't lose sight of the whole. And in order to reduce you can use metaphors. I don't see any other way to do it. Usually you call it a model ... .

The lack of overlap in problem formulations and so of intellectual interests also tended to restrict communication to a polite minimum.

They simply couldn't see what could be in it for them, which they told us very frankly ... whether they're interested in your results depends on whether they can fit it into something they themselves have experienced during the research. In fact, this interest does not develop until there is an overlap in a certain field.

The gradual realisation that talks and discussions had to be connected to the interests of the audiences if they were to be useful led to changes in presentation.

You can try to be flexible. If you want response, it makes sense. Sometimes it works a little, and sometimes it doesn't because you're still stuck to the biological system you are working with. You can try to compare systems, but that's always difficult ... the best thing is to get on a track by coincidence, as was the case with dopamine receptors.

Attempts were made to find out what other scientists considered important in their own fields and conscious efforts made to link these to the subjects of the talks. Detailed accounts of the neurophysiologists' own experiments were limited in favour of comparisons of problems and approaches between fields.

When popularising for scientists, you have to link up directly with something right in the middle of their own field. If you do that, you can get them to cooperate with you. ... What I really want to know is what inspires them ... then I see if I can make a story out of this agreeing with what we want.

Apart from an increased interest in the neurophysiological research, this new approach resulted in everyone rapidly understanding which topics were of mutual interest as well as which were not. In some cases this led to concrete cooperation on projects.

He said, I'm interested in this and acknowledges that we have other interests besides. That there are different views on what kinds of things you would like to know. As you go along, you have to discuss this, or split off part of the project and let him take it. That's a healthy thing to do, because you yourself of course have to keep following your own main field of interest ....

The development of this novel approach to communicating one's ideas and problems to different audiences was quite a difficult process, akin to acquiring a new skill. The ability to undertake this sort of popularisation was regarded as an important component of scientists' research skills which was difficult to learn and which should be more emphasised during research training.

I find it a bit impractical to have to do it this way. I also think it's difficult, but you can learn it. It's a skill you can develop. . . . It wasn't part of my training, and I never realised it had to be done this way. . . . It would be really good if it was raised during one's training . . . .

In addition to this rather laborious process, common interests were sometimes identified through more adventitious encounters such as by car-pooling.

And then someone in the car said: yes, but we are working with snails, and they have simple nerve systems. After that, we just experimented one afternoon. That was fun, and then it grew as if by itself . . . .

As well as acquiring the necessary materials and information for the research projects, these contacts broadened its scope and led to comparisons with results of experiments based on different techniques.

We were now constantly comparing things we had measured at the membrane level to what they had seen on an entirely different level. That's inspiring . . . .

They also reinforced the feeling that the neurophysiologists were working on an interesting scientific problem.

Soudijn came up with this 4 amino-pyridine, but what was much more important was his reaction. I was very pleased by the way he reacted, simply showing interest in the system we were working on. That was important, it gave me a kick. In science, there's always this background fear that you're working in a remote corner on something utterly insignificant from a scientific point of view. It happens so often; especially in biology, it's hard to find out whether or not you're working on something important . . . .

By eliciting information and interest from other groups of scientists, then, this group reduced the level of strategic task uncertainty about their project and broadened its appeal to wider audiences. Successful communication of its goals and results was, therefore, an integral part of implementing the research strategy and legitimating its significance as well as being essential to its technical realisation.

Conclusions

This brief case study emphasises the importance of translation processes for presenting results to a wider scientific audience. Thus translation processes are not only characteristic of popularisation for the general public but are also an integral part of everyday research practices. Nevertheless this does not necessarily imply that scientists are always capable of applying the skills required for inter-scientific popularisation to translations for the general public. As the neuro physiologists observed, many translation processes occur subconsciously since scientists are thoroughly familiar with, and firmly believe in, the dominant metaphors used to express the central concepts of their field. The more metaphors diverge from these central concepts, though, the more scientists have to pay attention consciously to translation processes as they seek to convince fellow specialists of the significance of their results. This conscious attention to translation processes is even more marked, of course, when contacting scientists with different interests and intellectual backgrounds. As we have seen, however, this sort of popularisation is by no means easy for many scientists and requires the development of new skills which enable them to transcend specialist boundaries. So it is not too surprising that communication to the general public is perceived as being very difficult in today's highly specialised, esoteric sciences.

The need to tune in to the problems, concepts and interests of their audiences in order to gain intellectual assistance and support meant that the concepts and metaphors of the neurophysiologists were transformed. As Fleck suggested: "communication never occurs without a transformation, and indeed always involves a stylized remodelling which . . . intercollectively yields fundamental alterations" (10). Such transformations can result in the main question being lost sight of as it is adapted to a variety of audiences and the underlying research strategy fragments. Less dramatically, perhaps, it also often results in new glosses being put upon one's results which comulatively alter their meaning. As Latour has pointed out (11):

Every time JR or W writes an article or answers an interview or discusses with one of his colleagues, creditors or competitors, they build up a new version of how analogs are linked to one another.

Many of the results of this case study are characteristic of neurophysiology. The high degree of technical standardisation — and thus relatively low technical task uncertainty — enabled communication on technical matters to be quite easy while it proved much more difficult to obtain useful information for strategic and substantive questions (12). The considerable dependence on information from scientists in other fields is also a general feature of much bio-medical research which is not so prevalent in other sciences. However, while the importance of inter-field communication may vary between sciences, following the degree of strategic dependence and limitation on reputational control of significance standards in the field, the sort of translation processes described here do occur elsewhere, as the papers by Cloître and Shinn, Yearley and others in this volume indicate, and, arguably, perhaps should be more common if broader intellectual innovation is to be encouraged. In any case, the more research organisations are oriented to multiple goals and audiences the more specialised research skills become and are required to be combined to deal with general problems which are not the province of any single field, the more critical will these processes be for the successful completion of research projects and the more important will it become for scientists to communicate effectively to colleagues with different backgrounds. This case study clearly demonstrates the importance of being able to understand other groups' interests problems and approaches for such communication. Such understanding involves more than simple cognitive recognition of others' goals; it also necessitates some emotional identification, or empathy, with them if common ground is to be established and useful information gained. While this point is commonplace in many other activities, the intensified competitive pursuit of reputations for intellectual innovations has encouraged specialisation, as large numbers of knowledge producers seek to differentiate their work from that of others to such an extent in the public sciences that many scientists are not competent at appreciating others' concerns or approaches. This increasing inability to communicate to other specialists has, of course, also meant that communication with non scientists has become very difficult for many researchers. Where intra-scientific communication skills have been improved, on the other hand, we would expect greater facility in translating ideas and results to non scientific audiences to develop.

Acknowledgement.

We wish to acknowledge the considerable assistance of Theo de Vlieger and Wim van der Steen.

Notes and References

1. The symposium on 'Scientific Illiteracy' was held on the 10th of March 1983 and the symposium on 'Science as Common Property', on 27th of April 1983.
2. See, for example, S. Blume, *Toward a Political Sociology of Science*, New York: Free Press, 1974, p. 226 and W. O. Hagstrom, *The Scientific Community*, New York: Basic Books, 1965, pp. 34–35.
3. This view of scientific knowledge has, of course, become much more widely accepted in the past decade or so, at least in the European sociology of science. As well as the previous volumes of this *Yearbook*, see: M. J. Mulkay, *Science and the Sociology of Knowledge*, London: Allen and Unwin, 1979 for a general survey of this literature. A more critical account is in: R. Whitley, 'From the Sociology of Scientific Communities to the Study of Scientists' Negotiations and Beyond', *Social Science Information* 22 (1983), 681–720.
4. Such as those by Callon, Knorr and Latour and Woolgar. See, for instance, M. Callon, 'Struggles and Negotiations to Define What is Problematic and What is Not: the Sociologic Translation', in K. Knorr *et al*. (eds.) *The Social Process of Scientific Investigation*, Sociology of the Sciences Yearbook IV, Dordrecht: Reidel, 1980; K. Knorr-Cetina, *The Manufacture of Knowledge*, Oxford: Pergamon, 1981; B. Latour and S. Woolgar, *Laboratory Life*, London: Sage, 1979.
5. "Public" in the sense of relying predominantly upon public communication of task outcomes for the coordination and control of research, as distinct from relying primarily on personal control or formal, standardised rules. See: R. Whitley, *The Intellectual and Social Organisation of the Sciences*, Oxford University Press, 1984, chs. 1 and 2 for a more extended discussion.
6. Scientific disciplines are thus viewed here as units of labour market definition and control rather than as units of knowledge production and validation. These latter are termed scientific "fields" in which research is coordinated through the competitive pursuit of public reputations for contributions to collective intellectual goals. This view is developed further in R. Whitley, *op. cit*., 1984, note 5.
7. Or scientific "establishment" which controls the standards by which intellectual contributions are assessed for their correctness and significance. On scientific establishments, see: N. Elias *et al*. (eds.) *Scientific Establishments and Hierarchies*, Sociology of the Sciences Yearbook VI, Dordrecht: Reidel, 1982.
8. As claimed by R. Boyd, 'Metaphor and Theory Change: What is "Metaphor" a Metaphor for?' in A. Ortony (ed.) *Metaphor and Thought*, Cambridge University Press, 1979. See also T. S. Kuhn's comment entitled 'Metaphor in Science' in the same volume. In referring to the importance of metaphors in the development of this research project we do not wish to engage in the long running philosophical discussions about the roles of metaphors, analogies and models in knowledge production, but simply to emphasise their significance in reflecting and constituting intellectual change in much scientific research.
9. Intellectual innovations, that is, have to be coordinated with the work of other groups if they are to be considered significant contributions to collective intellectual goals as opposed to mere idiosyncracies. In some sciences, these audiences are fairly homogeneous and stable so that standards are clear cut and widely shared. In most biological fields, though, the variety and equivalence of audiences are

relatively high so that significance standards and intellectual goals are multiple and diverse. See: R. Whitley, *op. cit.*, 1984, note 5, ch. 6.

10. L. Fleck, *Genesis and Development of a Scientific Fact*, Chicago University Press, 1979, p. 111.

11. B. Latour, 'Is it Possible to Reconstruct the Research Process? The Sociology of a Brain Peptide', in K. Knorr *et al.* (eds.) *The Social Process of Scientific Investigation*, Sociology of the Sciences Yearbook IV, Dordrecht: Reidel, 1980, p. 64.

12. That is, there was much more uncertainty about the theoretical significance of research results and the importance of particular problems and strategies than there was about technical matters. Compare: Whitley, *op. cit.*, note 5, 1984, ch. 4.

REPRESENTING GEOLOGY

Textual Structures in the Pedagogical Presentation of Science

STEVEN YEARLEY

The Queen's University of Belfast

Introduction

Although it might not generally be thought of in this way, the teaching of science has represented a form of popularisation in at least two senses. On the one hand, science has frequently been imparted as a constituent of polite culture or as wholesome and edifying knowledge so that science education and popularisation have directly overlapped (1). On the other, because teachers of science have to provide an entry for newcomers into the esoteric character of scientific knowledge, it can readily be argued that at least the initial stages of a scientific education comprise a type of popularisation. The purpose of this paper is to identify some of the principal systematic features of the pedagogical exposition of science.

In a number of recent studies analysts have argued that images implicit in texts of various sorts — including newspaper reports, official documents and scientific writings — play a decisive role in promoting the persuasiveness or credibility of these texts (2). It is the objective of the present study to ascertain whether regular images of science occur in the pedagogical presentation of science and to evaluate, within the limits of this paper, the role and effect of these images. The principal empirical focus of the study is the lecture course on geology delivered in the first two decades of the nineteenth century by Humphry Davy at the newly-formed Royal Institution of London (3).

Any claim about the practical significance of implicit models in the teaching of science should be based not on general résumés of science courses but on detailed analyses of the content of particular lectures, classes and so on. Accordingly, the analyst is confronted with the conflicting demands of minute

Terry Shinn and Richard Whitley (eds.), Expository Science: Forms and Functions of Popularisation. Sociology of the Sciences, Volume IX, 1985, 79–101.

examination and representativeness. In this study the demands of detail have been granted precedence and it is necessary at this point to justify the selection of Davy's lectures. There are a variety of reasons for this selection: firstly, because of Davy's historical stature the study could readily be defended in its own right as an historical exercise. Secondly, and also at a pragmatic level, copies of Davy's lectures exist and are readily available so that my analyses may be checked. A full set of lectures for 1805 has recently been published in a modern edition and the manuscript notes of these lectures, together with two other, partially complete sets, have survived (4). There is also a published account of notes taken at the lectures in 1811 by an Edinburgh scientist named Allan (5). It is to be doubted that as full a transcription of any science lectures of such significance could be found. Thirdly, a comparison between Davy's lecture texts and his more formal publications on geology will allow the images of science which are peculiar to his pedagogical presentations to be identified and may permit the recognition of any stylistic idiosyncrasies. Finally, the fact that the Royal Institution was founded at about the same time as the earlier Mechanics' Institutes (indeed Carlyle described it as 'a kind of sublime *Mechanics' Institute* for the upper classes' (6)) means that it may be possible to compare any images of science found in the lectures with the results of other studies of the curriculum of Mechanics' Institutes (7).

Davy had moved to the Royal Institution in 1801 and, together with his other duties, developed his longstanding interest in minerals and geology (8). Although he had learned geology chiefly from followers of the Huttonian or 'Plutonic' theory, he was also familiar with the opposing 'Neptunist' writings (9). The former theory, briefly expressed, proposed that the earth had been undergoing gradual change over vast periods of time. Powered by the earth's heat and volcanic energy, these small modifications ensured that the continents were always being renewed and re-created. According to Neptunists, however, the continents had been formed and moulded by the actions of water and chemical precipitation in the not too distant past. On this interpretation, geological processes were regarded as relatively rapid but intermittent. Once in London Davy figured prominently in the group of young men who were to form the Geological Society of London in 1807 (10). He lectured on geology in 1805, 1806, 1808, 1809 and in 1811. These lectures were advertised for a general audience and were a popular and regular feature of the Institution's public face. By 1811 he had modified the lecture

course and it was considered worth paying £750 for him to repeat it in Dublin
(11). Davy left the Royal Institution in 1812 but continued working with,
among many other achievements, trips to experiment on Vesuvius (12). He
remained predominantly abroad for his last years, writing about science and
religion in a more philosophical vein. His writings in geology are scattered –
in works on chemistry, in lectures and addresses, notebooks and miscellaneous
papers, and in his philosophical reflections (13).

While the need to deal with a whole lecture course precludes the kind of
fine-grain analysis employed, for example, in conversation analysis, the
method adopted still owes much to semiology and ethnomethodology. The
notion of ethnomethodological indifference provides a valuable heuristic, for
rather than directing initial attention to possible relations between elements
of the lecture texts and extra-textual features, I shall examine how general
claims made in the text – say, about the nature of science – are borne out
in the rest of the lectures (14). Thus, for methodological purposes the text
will be read literally to see how consistent the textual images are. As in ethnomethodological studies of rule following, one begins with a rule proclaimed
by participants and one studies how that rule is enacted and invoked in the
light of participants' avowed reasoning (15). Only when the immanent basis
of the text has been disclosed can one start to examine the broader correlates
of the images drawn on in the text. Hence the analysis will consist of comparisons between the implicit view of science and scientific evaluation detected
in Davy's lectures and in his formal writings on geological science. Then the
literal coherence or consistency of the image of science found in the pedagogic texts will be examined. Only then will it be appropriate to consider
how this pedagogic presentation of science can be explained, and how it is
related to the social and historical context within which Davy taught.

The Character of 'Science' in Lectures

Davy certainly talks about the concept of science (and of geology *qua* science)
a great deal in his lectures. Thereby, one could say, he presents a picture of
science by characterising its features, the exemplary careers of good scientists,
and the lapses perpetrated by poor scientists. In order to allow for the possible influence of Davy's idiosyncratic views about the nature of science, this
lecture-view of science must be compared with any image of science broadcast

in his formal publications. In the following analysis, images and invocations of science have been detected by a close reading of the published version of Davy's complete set of 1805 geology lectures (in conjunction with an examination of the MSS), and a similar study of the set of four formal papers which deal chiefly with geology (16). These latter comprise two papers of 1808 announcing new experimental discoveries and including discussions of their significance for geology; a paper of 1822 on the natural production of minerals; and a paper of 1828 describing research on volcanoes.

An examination of these formal papers shows that they contain very few references to science itself, and nowhere is science described explicitly in the affirmative part of a sentence. Indeed the opening of the paper discussing the aëriform matter in crystal cavities declares that there 'are few enquiries in natural science more calculated to awaken our curiosity' then those concerning geological phenomena (17). In this case a degree of familiarity with the nature of science is imputed to the reader. Equally general is the comment that the new facts uncovered by Davy will 'open many new views' to the 'sciences kindred to chemistry' (18). However, what the reader is to take scientific to mean is spelled out by this association of new facts with the extension of science and the contrasting claim that speculation would be 'easy' (19). This opposition is employed elsewhere also: rather than subscribe to the predominant, speculative views on geological topics, Davy relates how he had (20):

often, in the course of [his] chemical researches, looked for facts or experiments, which might throw some light on this interesting subject, but without success, till about three years ago . . . .

Again, on another occasion it is Davy's newly uncovered facts which (21):

shew that a step nearer at least has been attained towards the true knowledge of the nature of the alkalies and the earths.

This same sense of persistence and of dependence on strictly observational/ experimental work is to be found in his paper on volcanoes. He stresses how (22):

since 1812 [he has] endeavoured to gain evidence respecting [the agency of volcanic fires] by examining volcanic phaenomena of ancient and recent occurrence in various parts of Europe.

Similarly, the information which he attained on Vesuvius (and despite the broad claim above, this is the only volcanic site mentioned in the empirical core of his paper) came from *numerous* trips *close* to the lava itself where *experiments* were conducted (23). Thereby, his information on volcanic operations contains the facts on the 'actual products of a volcano in eruption' which will persist '[w]hatever opinion may be ultimately formed or adopted on this subject' (24).

Whilst each of these four formal texts could no doubt be subjected to further textual analysis (perhaps in terms of their sequential arrangement and so on (25)) it is already possible to draw out some systematic features. There is an implicit image of science which pervades the texts: it is an image of a science firmly founded on close, precise factual observation. The gathering of facts may be arduous but the rewards are great for facts offer an understanding of how the world actually is constituted. Factual knowledge is enduring and cannot be gainsaid by 'opinion'.

This implicit image — and it is literally implicit since science is given nothing but the vaguest ostensive definition in these texts — is not merely an incidental adjunct to Davy's scientific articles. Rather it appears to form the interpretative background against which Davy is able to justify the judgements and evaluations made in his texts. Thus it is in the light of these empiricist background assumptions that it makes sense to present hypothetical thinking as tentative. For example, concerning his proposals about the causes of volcanic activity Davy says 'I venture to hint at these notions: but I do not attach much importance to them . . .' (26). And it is also in the light of this implicit epistemology that Davy is able to put forward favourable evaluations of 'good' laws and theories. In this way too Davy is able to pass unfavourable judgements on Neptunian ideas because they conflict with established, 'good' laws: he claims that Neptunian histories of the earth are contrary to 'the laws of chemical attraction' (27). Good laws and theories are presented as arising from factual observations in an unproblematic way, and the closeness of this relation is often expressed by grammatically identifying observation as the agent which extends knowledge, as in 'new discoveries may throw [new lights] upon this subject' (28). On the other hand, poor theories are presented as speculative and at a distant remove from facts (29):

If the idea of LEMERY were correct, that the action of sulphur on iron may be a cause of volcanic fires, sulphate of iron ought to be the great product of the volcano; which is known not to be the case.

In such cases, the facts are made to pronounce their condemnation of falsity and groundless theorising.

Positively affirmed facts, on the other hand, are provided with a textual endorsement. They are generally supported either by the presentation of some form of warrant for knowledge (such as the details of experimental procedure; elaborate personal testimony; or citation (30)) or are given some internal, textual validation. As examples of the latter, I include comments such as (31):

Geologists are generally agreed, that the greater number of the crystalline mineral sub-stances must have been previously in a liquid state.

Similarly, the claim (cited above) that iron sulphate is 'known not to be' the chief product of volcanic activity also invokes the generalised knowledge of the relevant scientific community. Such internal, textual warrants appear to operate in place of more extensive, evidential warrants (32).

In summary, therefore, in Davy's formal scientific publications (or at least in these four geological examples) science is implicitly presented as dependent on painstaking factual observation. In other words, these texts draw exten-sively on what is known as the empiricist repertoire. True knowledge and 'good' theories proceed from facts and the incorrigibility of such facts is given a textual basis. Although this view of science is implicit, it is not merely incidental. Rather, it figures as a central interpretative resource in the pre-sentation of evaluations and judgements in the text and occasionally serves as the basis for textual warrants in which the aggregated knowledge of the scientific community can be invoked to endorse judgements. This image of science plays a central role in organising the argumentation of the text, and in ordering the conflicting interpretations which hold sway beyond the text. Contrastingly, the lectures contain relatively many references to science itself, and, as I shall show, a rather more complex set of characterisations of scien-tific knowledge.

Initially, the explicit concern with the nature of science appears easy to understand, almost self-evident. Davy was offering an introductory course on geology (a 'task which . . . has never before been undertaken, and it is one connected with much labour and with many difficulties' (33)), and could expect to have to explain the nature of geology and, to some people, the nature of science itself. He had to establish, one might say, the character of the discourse. At the beginning of the first geological lecture Davy describes how (34):

the same object may be examined with the most opposite views and considered under many diversified and beautiful relations. It is on this fact of our nature . . . that the great extent and progression of science and philosophy depend.

Science involves a particular way of looking at the objects of creation, and geology, as a specialised science, is concerned with certain aspects only of objects. Indeed, modern science has led to (35):

a new creation, as it were, of facts . . . of facts as much superior to mere speculations as things can be to words. . . . [Scientific] knowledge is like a river which, unless its springs are constantly supplied, soon becomes exhausted, and ceases to flow on and to fertilize.

These explicit references to the nature of scientific knowledge feature far less frequently after the two introductory lectures. Subsequent weeks' lectures are devoted to specific topics and allow fewer animadversions of a general character. It is therefore of interest to examine how well this early picture of science is carried through, and how essential it is to the audience's reception of the succeeding material. I shall now turn to a more detailed examination of invocations of science and scientific knowledge.

Early on, Davy considers the value of lectures, in terms of how much worthwhile knowledge can be conveyed, given the peculiarities of scientific knowledge. He acknowledges that (36):

Some few arguments are now and then brought forward against the efficacy of public instruction. It is urged that superficial and general knowledge often tends to produce pedantry . . . [This] charge of pedantry . . . can only be applied to the half-taught in manners, as well as in science; and, in such a refined period as this in which we live, it is scarcely possible that such a folly can flourish . . . .

That persons who are only *beginning* to attend to the principles of science often overrate their acquirements and abilities, cannot be denied; but this is a circumstance of very little importance and seldom of much permanence.

Hence, Davy cannot be proposing to impart only a superficial knowledge because that would be contrary to the utility of public lectures. Accordingly, scientific knowledge must be susceptible of terse presentation. Yet, he equally stresses the enormity of the knowledge generated by science, the role of 'labour' and 'exertion' in science, and the actual incompleteness of knowledge ('All human knowledge is necessarily imperfect' and '[science] is still unfinished')(37). In the need to strike a balance between culpable ignorance and mankind's inevitable ignorance, a certain tension in the conception of science is disclosed. It is at once readily learnt, yet won by labour; it is singularly complex, yet can be acquired by attendance at lectures. These contrasts suggest that Davy's actual use of science's characteristics requires detailed analysis.

The introductory lectures are followed by a lengthy historical account of the topics covered by geology, occupying sessions two through four. On many occasions Davy attributes advances in geology to 'observation and experiment', to 'devotion to experiment', or 'an undefatigable spirit of investigation' (38); all of which are in agreement with the observational interpretation of science advanced in the earlier sections (for example: 'attainment of the knowledge belonging to these highly interesting subjects is founded almost wholly upon observation, for in a few cases only can instruments of experiment be applied' (39)). Seen from this point of view, the tortuous progression of geological knowledge, requiring three lectures to document, looks rather baffling. *Pace* Davy's introductory comments, ignorance can be persistent. Furthermore, the history is much occupied with speculations, systems and theories, and when Davy emphasises the distinctness of modern geological views he refers to (40):

[former] systems and . . . doctrines relating to nature [which], when compared with the truth and theories of modern time, appear as the vain toys and amusements of children when contrasted with the useful occupations and pursuits of men.

Here the importance of modern *theoretical* knowledge seems to be stressed. Yet, the role of theories was scarcely mentioned in the introduction; the history appears to evoke and depend upon a view of science for which the audience has not, strictly speaking, been prepared.

A wide variety of factors is called upon in the historical account. Davy suggests how the health of science is dependent on societal features: science requires a degree of patronage; the prevalent religious beliefs must not be inimical to science; and methods which favour objectivity must be introduced into learned debated (41). Aberrant figures afford temporary set-backs, but barring the disintegration of civilisation, the growth of science is natural.

Thus, throughout the recounting of this history, an image of science is being developed. Science is Christian, beneficial to mankind, and historically cumulative, but these overall characteristics are so general that their distinctive relationship to any external political objectives is hard to descry. On close examination, a more striking feature of the view of science developed is its dual character. The textual image is not only more elaborate than in formal papers, it is also less homogeneous.

Amongst the features of science most commonly called upon by Davy's history is its dependence on the contribution of outstanding individuals. Hypatia preserved geological knowledge in Alexandria 'being, as it were, a single brilliant star in a night of clouds and obscurity' (42). Roger Bacon and Albertus Magnus usher in a scientific renaissance virtually unassisted, and the period between them and the seventeenth century is related only in terms of the achievements of individual minds, each with a particular genius and corresponding attainments (43). Thus, Roger Bacon (44):

evidently studied nature and the productions of the earth with the views of a philosopher, but his knowledge was so superior as to be unintelligible in the age in which he lived.

Indeed, '[t]his great man . . . was himself persecuted as an enchanter' (45). Similarly, Becher ('with the sound judgement of a true philosopher') was 'driven from Germany by envy and persecution' (46). Advances in knowledge are attributed to the genius of singular men, who were sometimes misunderstood and who quite outreached their age. They were thoroughly distinct from the common citizens. Consequently, if science is to progress, the conditions under which genius can flourish must be sustained (47). So necessary is this special 'endowment', that the elder Pliny, despite the fact that 'he beheld things in their obvious form' and 'possessed the highest degree of industry and an ardour in the pursuit of knowledge which no difficulties could repress' and was withal a 'minute observer', was 'still deficient in the great characteristics of . . . a philosophical spirit'. In fact, he was '[e]ndowed with none of the high elements of reason, . . . nor [was he] a man of genius' (48).

On the other hand there is a less exclusive historiography operative as well. Sometimes, Davy suggests that it is 'the times' which govern the state of science. For example (49): ·

The spirit of science and that of Mahometanism, like the good and evil principles of
Zoroaster, were incapable of being reconciled.

More explicitly, it was because the 'public was prepared to receive them' that
Francis Bacon's teachings were adopted (50). It was not Bacon's contribution
to the stock of geological knowledge, but the *general* implementation of his
method which really counted, for (51):

The pursuit of the new methods of investigation, in a very short time, wholly altered the
face of every department of natural knowledge, but their influence was in no case more
distinct than in the advancement of geology and chemistry.

No genius, accordingly, is requisite for the methodical advancement of science.
This viewpoint would seem to be in agreement with his introductory emphasis
on the ease of geology, and its simple dependence on observation.

Immediately after the description of Baconianism, however, Davy reverts
to his former story. Hooke is cited as one of the first persons to apply Bacon's
teachings to the theory of the earth, yet his scientific successes are attributed
to 'his genius [which] was too powerful and too active to be limited' to the
extension of chemistry and mechanics alone (52)! On Davy's own testimony,
such talents had frequently sufficed, in the absence of Baconianism, in
furthering science. Neither are the achievements of subsequent characters
plausibly linked to Bacon's instauration: the successful scientists are con-
tinental (like Leibniz) and no connection is revealed in the text between them
and Bacon, whereas the English scientists (Burnet and Whiston) are credited
with meagre contributions. At one stage Davy repeats Bacon's claim that the
scientific method is a great leveller, yet when accounting for specific advances
in knowledge perpetually refers to genius.

I suggest that this tension between a scientific elite and the indifferent
mass of people who must look to method, is intimately connected to the
uneasy division, mentioned earlier, between theory and observation. For
example, a decisive stamp of Hooke's genius was that it allowed him such
insight that in 'many principal parts of theory he had anticipated the modern
plutonic philosophers' (53). The discussion of Hooke is deeply concerned
with questions of theory: Hooke's 'hypotheses' and 'speculations' are intimately related to the 'great laws of the globe considered as a part of the
planetary system'. Similarly, his ideas are praised for 'boldness'. Indeed in the
whole section on Hooke, there is no reference to observation or its cognates.

And this is how Davy makes scientific knowledge accountable immediately after the introduction of Bacon's revolutionary insistence on the view that 'all the sciences could be nothing more than expressions of facts' (54). Given that Hooke's brilliance is made accountable in terms of theoretical advancement without a textual insistence on observation, one may simply be led to conclude that Davy was a poor historian and meta-scientist, who should have stuck to science proper. Yet, whatever effect Davy's literary pretensions may have had on the lectures, they were popular enough to be repeated in successive years (55). Equally, his formal papers are not characterised by this dual structure. I suggest that such inconstancy is a systematic feature of accounting for science in a public, pedagogic context.

The duplex imagery of Davy's lectures can be exemplified in further instances. Leibniz receives praise for undertaking a 'general system of geology', and his 'genius' was necessary for such a project since, on such a topic 'high talents [are] ... required ... to produce any philosophical views' (56). No mention of observational endeavour is made concerning Leibniz. Effectively, genius is associated with theoretical advance, whereas observation is exemplified (although not explicitly depicted) as more commonplace. Thus, even the alchemists, paradigmatically wrong in their theoretical views, produced 'facts scattered amongst their absurdities [which] were valuable in the highest degree to the philosophical men who came after them' (57). In the introductory section there is, by contrast, no emphasis on the necessary role of genius; indeed, common observation is depicted as straightforward and sufficient for science. Geology, one is told, 'requires no experience or complicated apparatus' and 'may be acquired without much difficulty' (58). The two factors invoked to account for the most stupendous and crucial aspects of geology's history (theoretical knowledge and genius) are absent from the factual/observational science proclaimed in the introduction.

In this section I have sought to analyse neither Davy's personal beliefs about science nor the view of science which motivated his great contribution to experimental philosophy, but rather the implicit imagery of science which underlies certain of Davy's scientific texts. None of these textual images is totally explicit nor implicit; they have been elicited by procedures similar to those employed in curriculum studies and discourse analysis.

At this stage there appears to be no decisive political rationale for these images. Rather, they seem to be related to local features of the lecturer's task;

he must establish the knowledge as both accessible and worth knowing. The results of this analysis seem to confirm the claim of studies of scientific discourse that scientists are able to invoke varying accounting systems under different conditions. In this instance, conflicting ways of accounting for science occur *within* one institutional discourse. This conflict can, I suggest, be traced to peculiar features of pedagogic contexts; Davy must allow that it is possible to learn science in public lectures — for this a view of science as inherently observational and straightforward is invaluable. Additionally, he must account for the distinctness of present/modern science — for which the major advances in history at a super-observational level are essential. They are handled as the product of genius. So far, however, only the introductory and historical sections of the lectures have been treated. It is now time to turn to Davy's treatment of contemporary science, to see how textual images of science are used in this context.

Imparting the Principles of Scientific Evaluation

In the remaining lectures (five through ten), Davy is concerned with current geological knowledge. On the whole, far less consideration is given to the characteristics of science, although the talk does occasionally refer to science itself. For example, Davy stresses that (59):

by scientific modes of comparison, a distinct arrangement is perceived even in those rudest forms of matter [i.e., in seemingly disorderly veins and in the great variety of types of rock].

By this stage therefore, notions of science are being employed in establishing the acceptability of informational items (in this case a classification of rock types). Both genius and the unproblematic face of observation continue to make their appearance, but they are eclipsed to some extent by informative, geological matters. The text is concerned with evaluating contemporary science, and in elaborating the principles whereby evaluation proceeds. Thus, just as it was illuminating to contrast Davy's avowed view of science with the one evidenced by his historical account, so it will be instructive to compare his espoused principles of evaluation with his textual practice.

Given his early concern with 'fundamental facts' (60) and the quantity of factual material in the later lectures, Davy devotes surprisingly little discussion to the principles by which facts are adjudged. Indeed, only occasionally does any indication appear to suggest that the observation of facts requires the application of principles. One is told that the secondary strata display 'characters which can be deciphered only with difficulty' (61); yet apart from urging caution, accuracy, a general view, and an investigative frame of mind, Davy offers no real principles or guidelines for proceeding (62). On the subject of theories (whose contemporary existence he acknowledges, principally in terms of Plutonism and Neptunism which were outlined above), Davy is somewhat more explicit. Typically, he suggests that theories flourish from drawing analogies, and that they should be constantly referred to facts (63). Moreover, 'it is proper that we should reason from the present concerning the past' providing, however, that 'we reason with a calm understanding' (64). Theories are valued for their fruitfulness and are to be spurs to thought (65).

Formal papers contain virtually no explicit prescriptions of evaluative principles. General synopses of such principles are invoked in statements such as (66):

all the intellectual powers are required to be brought into activity to find facts or analogies, or to institute experiments, by which [geological phenomena] may be referred to known causes.

This is an explicitly introductory comment (taken from the paper's first paragraph), and serves to identify the argument that follows as the 'sort of thing that all scientists agree shoule be done'. A similar role is performed by the invocation of principles in relation to observation – thus (67):

One of the most important points to be ascertained was, whether any combustion was going on at the moment the lava issued from [Vesuvius]. There was certainly no appearance of more vivid ignition when it was exposed to air, nor did it glow with more intensity when it was raised into the air by an iron ladle. *I put the circumstance, however, beyond the possibility of doubt*: I threw some of the fused lava into a glass bottle furnished with a ground stopper . . . and examined the air on my return.

Here, a principle (which might be expressed as 'subject observations to experimental test') is invoked, and used to identify the significance of Davy's test. I suggest that, in formal papers, both implicit and semi-explicit principles of evaluation perform textual functions which contribute to the text's argumentative capacity. In short, such principles are among the textual means of warranting the author's claims, and identifying them as truly scientific.

On turning to Davy's presentation of factual material in the lectures, and to his use of textual warrants and underlying evaluative principles, one remarks how frequently he proceeds through simple assertion. Davy puts forward very many factual, geological claims and my analysis will necessarily be selective. I consider the following examples to be representative of the types of factual claims he makes; but even if their representativeness were to be disputed (and I do not consider that it should be), my contention would stand on the basis of the few examples I shall be able to cite. Thus, it is asserted that 'soft schist is almost always disposed in horizontal layers', despite the fact that the only evidence produced by Davy is a painting of a (possibly imaginary) single landscape (68). In a post-Humean age this can hardly be regarded as rigorous. By contrast in the formal literature scientists generally adopt the resources of the empiricist repertoire to warrant generalisations: using references; by relating them to prior generalisations; or by the use of a comment such as: 'scientists have repeatedly found that . . .'. It is the absence of any warrant which is peculiar in Davy's lectures. Another, similar instance is found on the same page, where one learns that '[p]it coal is always found in secondary countries' (69).

In an analogous fashion, an introduction to the facts and classifications relating to minerals and stratigraphy is effected through illustration alone. Thus, typical minerals are displayed and painted views of coastlines and mountain sections (at cliffs and the like) are offered for inspection (70). The intended sufficiency of this knowledge is indicated by Davy's comment that 'by those who are desirous of acquiring practical information, the specimens may be afterwards examined accurately and in detail' (71). Again, no justification (i.e., no evidential or social account) is generally given in the texts for the introduction of classificatory terms. Granites, schists, serpentines and all the rest are presented as simply constituents of the world. Possibly, single facts are even less frequently furnished with a warrant: the 'mountains [of North America] . . . are few in number and none of [them] can be compared in height to the Pyrenees' (72). The warrantlessness of this assertion is enhanced for the modern reader by its ironic falsity, although what might be regarded as its falsity is not the feature which interests me here. Furthermore, when the fact of the maximum known height of secondary (i.e., fossiliferous) rocks *is* provided with a textual warrant, thus: Mr Deluc found a petrified *cornu ammonis* [i.e., the shell of a sea creature] at [7,300'] in Mount Grenier', the warrant appears rather weak (73). For one thing no reference is given to Deluc's work, and elsewhere in the lectures his views are treated very lightly (74).

Finally, Davy's basic division of rocks into primary and secondary classes (which is enshrined in their allocation to separate lectures – the fifth and sixth) is presented as simply in the nature of things or as the result of the most innocent observation, despite the fact that it was in opposition to the views of many eminent geologists (75). When it comes to handling the classificatory schemes of others, Davy is quick to point out their artifactual status. Hence in criticising Werner's insistence on a distinct class of 'transition rocks', one is told that (76):

> it is more than probable that the acute mineralogist of Freiberg would not have adopted it himself had it not been connected with his peculiar theory of the aqueous origin of all mountains.

Thus, whereas correct, observationally-derived facts are not accounted for in an elaborate way (e.g., Greenough's note-book recollections are allowed to serve as an authoritative report on Etna (77)), erroneous observations are accounted for more fully. Unlike the case of the formal literature, factual truth is infrequently given a textual warrant in these lectures. However, such accounting as there is relies heavily on an inductivist imagery. The same model is employed in treating erroneous claims, and ordering in the text plays a role in this (for example, the error of Werner's 'peculiar theory' had been established already, two lectures previously – 'in theory he has contented himself with stating . . . a mere history of guesses' (78)).

As was illustrated above, Davy does give a little explicit indication of how theories are to be evaluated. Criteria of fruitfulness and investigative utility are also used in the presentation of his own hypothetical/theoretical thought. In discussing volcanoes, he explicitly invokes such a criterion (79):

> On phenomena of so impressive a character it is scarcely possible to avoid indulging in speculation. Some hypothesis must be formed, and the greatest merit that a hypothesis can possess is that of accounting for general appearances.

This explicit portrayal of 'the greatest merit that a hypothesis can possess', which broadcasts a very instrumentalist view of theoretical conceptions (and thus differentiates sharply between facts and theories), is not to be found in the implicit principles by which theories are judged. Typical of the way in which evaluations of theories are implicitly made accountable is this comment on the theory of fossils (80):

All the appearances, all the different facts, show in the most decided manner that the various strata filled with organic remains were covered by the sea at the time of their production. This is the ancient theory which will not be disputed . . . .

While in both cases it is allowed that theories somehow exceed facts, the broadcast view of what the goodness of a good theory consists in, is very different. By the implicit principles, theories are good insofar as they are true — not merely insofar as they are useful instruments. Explicitly, facts and theories are of such different stuff that they are assessed by different criteria. Whereas implicitly, theories are positively evaluated for being literal statements about how the world really is. It is perhaps not going too far to suggest that the equation of genius with theoretical endeavour is an acknowledgement of this implicit view of theories. Only genius can make the timeless, irrevocable (literally 'not disputed') step of identifying a true theory. The difference between the implicit and the explicit versions of how theories are to be evaluated is further illustrated by noting that other past theories about fossils, however fruitful they might be, are consigned to oblivion in Davy's account as simple falsehoods.

Thus, neither the explicit principles of theory evaluation, nor the general guidelines for assessing factual claims, are utilised in the implicit evaluations which comprise the 'business end' of Davy's lectures. Furthermore, as is shown by the practice of teaching simply by a display of rock samples, the audience is not expected to proceed to knowledge through their independent exercise of these principles. Instead, just as in the formal literature, it appears that principles of evaluation are among the means employed to generate textual warrants for claims. These warrants are however used less frequently in the lectures than in formal texts and, correspondingly, more information is presented by assertion. This can readily be attributed to Davy's authoritative position as the teacher, who is already endowed with knowledge (81). The implicit imagery appears to serve the local purpose of presenting informational items as appropriately correct.

Conclusion

It has been proposed that Davy's lectures display an extensive and elaborate set of textual images, both of science and of scientific evaluation. Moreover it has been argued that, by the use of these images, Davy was able to present knowledge as adequately warranted and to display judgements as correctly made in the course of the lectures. Accordingly, the presence of these images should certainly not be seen as incidental to the lecture texts. However, the invocation of these images has not left a consistent impression: by a method of literal reading it has been possible to detect a dual textual arrangement. One component of this dual structure indicates that scientific knowledge is observationally based, straightforward and cumulative. This part of the textual image has, it is suggested, served to demonstrate the learnability, accessibility and utility of science. In turn, these claims might be thought to coincide with (or be tailored to) the objectives of the principal founders of the Royal Institution. Representatives of modernising landed capital, these founders can be said to have had an interest in harnessing the power of scientific knowledge, in sponsoring straightforward improvements for use on the land, and in promoting social order and orderly social change (82). In this way a sociological explanation of the lectures' content could readily be provided. Davy could be regarded as the mouthpiece of these interests or as playing up to their perceived requirements.

Against this direct explanation of the lectures' imagery, it appears that the second component of the textual view of science — which stresses the difficulty of proper observation and the esoteric, specialised nature of scientific competence — would be hard to accommodate within this interpretation. This second image is no less pervasive yet it can easily be seen as dysfunctional for this social group either in its emphasis on the need for genius or its concern for the supreme value of scientific truth. The existence of this duality might be overcome by ascribing it to Davy's confusion. But the popularity of the lectures, Davy's scientific successes, and the absence from the published literature of complaints on this basis all suggest that Davy was unlikely to be simply confused. Hence it appears that the two-fold character is systematic. This impression is reinforced by the manner in which the particular characteristics of both of these implicit images have been shown to depend on which precise aspect of geology Davy was dealing with at any specific point in the lectures. It seems therefore that a textual and contextual explanation of this duality must be sought. Such an explanation has been provided in terms of the demands of pedagogic exposition.

Of course, the general explanation of the identity of these textual images must be sought in historical and personal terms, such as the utilitarian orientation of some contemporary science and Davy's own views on truth and genius (83). But beyond these general considerations, the dual textual images correspond best to the demands of imparting scientific knowledge: these images meet the problems of balancing the specialised nature of science against the demands of accessibility; of honouring both the requirements of the teacher's authority and the 'universal' or 'democratic' character of scientific enquiry; and of weighing the orientation of science towards enduring knowledge with the fallibility of individual scientists. Thus it is the argument of this study that successful pedagogy, and other forms of exposition, may well depend on local resolutions of these kinds of interpretative difficulty — resolutions which are accomplished in part by textual images. In conclusion this study both illuminates Davy's discourse (in ways which sociological and psychological accounts of his lectures have not) and indicates that the sociology of education and of popularisation may benefit from examining the kinds of interpretative difficulty which scientific exposition both generates and must overcome.

Acknowledgements

The cited extracts from *Humphry Davy on Geology: The 1805 Lectures for the General Audience*, edited and introduced by Robert Siegfried and R. H. Dott, Jr. © 1980 The University of Wisconsin Press, Madison and London appear by permission of the publisher.

Notes and References

1. See Steven Shapin and Barry Barnes, 'Science, Nature and Control: Interpreting Mechanics' Institutes', *Social Studies of Science* 7 (1977), 31–74.
2. Roger Fowler *et al.*, *Language and Control*, London: Routledge & Kegan Paul, 1979; Gunther Kress and Robert Hodge, *Language as Ideology*, London: Routledge & Kegan Paul, 1979; Frank Burton and Pat Carlen, *Official Discourse*, London: Routledge & Kegan Paul, 1979; G. N. Gilbert and Michael Mulkay, 'Contexts of Scientific Discourse: Social Accounting in Experimental Papers', in K. D. Knorr

et al. (eds.) *The Social Process of Scientific Investigation*, Sociology of the Sciences Yearbook IV, Dordrecht & Boston: Reidel, 1980, pp. 269–94; Steven Yearley, 'Textual Persuasion: The Role of Social Accounting in the Construction of Scientific Arguments', *Philosophy of the Social Sciences* 11 (1981), 409–435; and G. N. Gilbert and Michael Mulkay, 'Accounting for Error: How Scientists Construct Their Social World When They Account for Correct and Incorrect Belief', *Sociology* 16 (1982), 165–183.

3. See Thomas Martin, 'Origins of the Royal Institution', *British Journal for the History of Science* 1 (1962), 49–63, and T. Martin, 'Early Years at the Royal Institution', *op. cit.* 2 (1964), 99–115, as well as Morris Berman, *Social Change and Scientific Organization: The Royal Institution, 1799–1844*, London: Heinemann, 1978, pp. 1–99. Concerning the lectures see Robert Siegfried and R. H. Dott, Jr. (eds.) *Humphry Davy on Geology: The 1805 Lectures for the General Audience*, Madison & London: University of Wisconsin Press, 1980, pp. xiii–xliv (for the editors' introduction).

4. Siegfried and Dott, *op. cit.*, 1980, note 3. The majority of MS notes are held in the library of the Royal Institution. The exact descent of the MS evidence is disputed; the issue is engagingly controverted in *ibid.*, p. 145 and in A. M. Ospovat, 'Four Hitherto Unpublished Geological Lectures Given by Sir Humphry Davy in 1805', *Transactions of the Royal Geological Society of Cornwall* 21 (1978), 2–9. (Ospovat's article occupies all of Volume 21.)

5. [Thomas Allan] Anon, *Sketch of Mr Davy's Lectures on Geology. Delivered at the Royal Institution, London 1811. From Notes Taken by a Private Gentleman*, 1811 (no other details).

6. Quoted in G. A. Foote, 'Sir Humphry Davy and His Audience at the Royal Institution', *Isis* 43 (1952), 7. In this context see also Martin, *op. cit.*, 1962, note 3; Berman, *op. cit.*, 1978, note 3; and Ian Inkster, 'Science and the Mechanics' Institutes, 1820–1850: The Case of Sheffield', *Annals of Science* 32 (1975), 451–74.

7. See Shapin and Barnes, *op. cit.*, 1977, note 1 and Inkster, *op. cit.*, 1975, note 6.

8. On Davy see: Berman, *op. cit.*, 1978, note 3, pp. 1–99; Sophie Forgan (ed.) *Science and the Sons of Genius: Studies on Humphry Davy*, London: Science Reviews Ltd., 1980; J. Z. Fullmer, *Sir Humphry Davy's Published Works*, Cambridge, Mass.: Harvard University Press, 1969; J. A. Paris, *The Life of Sir Humphry Davy*, London: Colburn & Bentley, 1831 (two volumes); John Davy, *Memoirs of the Life of Sir Humphry Davy*, London: Longmans, 1836 (two volumes); and the editors' introduction to Siegfried and Dott, *op. cit.*, 1980, note 3, pp. xii–xliv.

9. Davy apparently borrowed Kirwan's work from the Public Library in Bristol: see Siegfried and Dott, *op. cit.*, 1980, note 3, p. xx. A recent, thorough account of developments in geology at this time is available in Roy Porter, *The Making of Geology*, Cambridge: CUP, 1977.

10. See M. J. S. Rudwick, 'The Foundation of the Geological Society of London', *British Journal for the History of Science* 1 (1963), 325–55.

11. See Siegfried and Dott, *op. cit.*, 1980, note 3, pp. xiv–xv for further specification. That substantially the same lectures were given is indicated by the MSS of the 1811 lectures where references to 'Ireland' and so on have been crossed through and replaced by 'this country'. Similarly, some illustrative instances (of granite hills etc.) have been altered.

12. *Ibid.*, pp. xxxix –xliv.
13. This variety is reflected in the collection of materials, including some lectures, scattered through the nine volumes of John Davy (ed.) *The Collected Works of Sir Humphry Davy, Bart.*, London: Murray, 1839–40.
14. A defence of ethnomethodological indifference is provided in Anthony Wootton, *Dilemmas of Discourse*, London: Allen & Unwin, 1975, pp. 93–107.
15. See the analysis of a teacher's implementation of a rule in a classroom setting in Hugh Mehan and Houston Wood, *The Reality of Ethnomethodology*, London: Wiley, 1975, pp. 84–87, and the study of scientific rules in H. M. Collins and R. G. Harrison, 'Building a TEA Laser: The Caprices of Communication', *Social Studies of Science* 5 (1975), 441–50. In both cases, examination of the use of participants' avowed 'rules' throws new light on the way in which sense is made of their activities.
16. Humphry Davy, 'The Bakerian Lecture, on Some New Phenomena of Chemical Changes Produced by Electricity . . .', *Philosophical Transactions of the Royal Society of London* 98 (1808), 1–44; H. Davy, 'Electro-Chemical Researches on the Decomposition of the Earths . . .', *op. cit.* 98 (1808), 333–70; H. Davy, 'On the State of Water and Aëriform Matter in Cavities Found in Certain Crystals', *op. cit.* 112 (1822), 367–76; and H. Davy, 'On the Phaenomena of Volcanoes', *op. cit.* 118 (1828), 241–50. One further geological article (H. Davy, 'Hints on the Geology of Cornwall', *Transactions of the Royal Geological Society of Cornwall* 1 (1812), 38–50) has not been included in this analysis because it is neither a research article nor straightforwardly pedagogic. Davy was the foremost scientific honorary member of this society and wrote the piece as a celebratory article at the founding of the journal: on Davy's Cornish connections see Michael Neve, 'The Young Humphry Davy: Or John Tonkin's Lament' in Forgan, *op. cit.*, 1980, note 8, pp. 1–32. In Siegfried and Dott, *op. cit.*, 1980, note 3, an 'Introductory Lecture' for the whole set of courses on science is provided in addition to the introductory geological lecture (number one). The text of this lecture has also been used in the present analysis. It should also be noted that the formal "paper" of 1808a is actually designated as the "Bakerian Lecture". Its status as a lecture does not invalidate the comparisons made in this study because: (a) all papers to the Royal Society were delivered orally in the first instance, (b) Davy had the opportunity to amend the text before publication, and (c) as is argued later, it is the pedagogic function, not the auditory reception of the 1805 lectures which is related to the prevalent forms of accounting.
17. Davy, *op. cit.*, 1822, note 16, p. 367.
18. Davy, *op. cit.*, 1808a, note 16, p. 44.
19. See *ibid.*, pp. 42–43.
20. Davy, *op. cit.*, 1822, note 16, p. 368.
21. Davy, *op. cit.*, 1808b, note 16, p. 365.
22. Davy, *op. cit.*, 1828, note 16, p. 241.
23. From *ibid.*, pp. 245, 242–43, and 245–46.
24. *Ibid.*, p. 250.
25. On sequential arrangement see Yearley, *op. cit.*, 1981, note 2, pp. 430–34.
26. Davy, *op. cit.*, 1808b, note 16, p. 369. See also *ibid.*, pp. 369–70 and Davy, *op. cit.*, 1828, note 16, p. 250.

27. Davy, *op. cit.*, 1822, note 16, p. 368.
28. Davy, *op. cit.*, 1808b, note 16, p. 365.
29. Davy, *op. cit.*, 1828, note 16, p. 248.
30. Respectively: Davy, *op. cit.*, 1822, note 16, pp. 369–70; Davy, *op. cit.*, 1828, note 16, pp. 242–45 and 247–48; and Davy, *op. cit.*, 1808b, note 16, p. 368.
31. Davy, *op. cit.*, 1922, note 16, p. 367.
32. For a study of the role of warrants in arguments see S. E. Toulmin, *The Uses of Argument*, Cambridge: CUP, 1958. In relation to formal scientific writing see also Yearley, *op. cit.*, 1981, note 2; and G. N. Gilbert and Michael Mulkay, 'Warranting Scientific Belief', *Social Studies of Science* **12** (1982), 383–408.
33. Siegfried and Dott, *op. cit.*, 1980, note 3, p. 14.
34. *Ibid.*, p. 10.
35. *Ibid.*, p. 7.
36. *Ibid.*, p. 9 – original emphases.
37. From *ibid.*, p. 7; *ibid.*, p. 9; and *ibid.*, p. 7 respectively.
38. From *ibid.*, p. 34; *ibid.*, p. 27; and *ibid.*, p. 49.
39. *Ibid.*, p. 13.
40. *Ibid.*, p. 33.
41. Respectively: *ibid.*, p. 34; *ibid.*, p. 35 and *ibid.*, p. 40.
42. *Ibid.*, p. 35. On the, sometimes singular, instances which comprise Davy's history the notes provided in Ospovat, *op. cit.*, 1978, note 4, are most helpful.
43. Siegfried and Dott, *op. cit.*, 1980, note 3, p. 36 and pp. 36–39.
44. *Ibid.*, p. 36.
45. *Ibid.*, p. 36.
46. *Ibid.*, p. 41.
47. *Ibid.*, p. 34. On Davy's concern with genius see the essays in Forgan, *op. cit.*, 1980, note 8. See also J. Z. Fullmer, 'The Poetry of Sir Humphry Davy', *Chymia* **6** (1960), 102–26; D. M. Knight, 'The Scientist as Sage', *Studies in Romanticism* **6** (1967), 65–88; and Anne Treneer, *The Mercurial Chemist: A Life of Sir Humphry Davy*, London: Methuen, 1963.
48. Siegfried and Dott, *op. cit.*, 1980, note 3, p. 31.
49. *Ibid.*, p. 35.
50. *Ibid.*, p. 39.
51. *Ibid.*, p. 39.
52. *Ibid.*, p. 40.
53. *Ibid.*, p. 40, as also are the following quotes.
54. *Ibid*p. p. 39.
55. On Davy's literary interests, friendship with Coleridge and so on, see the works cited at note 47. Davy's possible enthusiasm for elegance, whilst making the lectures pleasant to attend, does not explain their literal inconsistencies.
56. Siegfried and Dott, *op. cit.*, 1980, note 3, pp. 41 and 42.
57. *Ibid.*, p. 38.
58. *Ibid.*, p. 13.
59. *Ibid.*, p. 60.
60. *Ibid.*, p. 11.
61. *Ibid.*, pp. 77–78.
62. Respectively: *ibid.*, p. 91; *ibid.*, p. 75; *ibid.*, p. 59; and *ibid.*, p. 60.

63. From *ibid.*, p. 91; *ibid.*, p. 102; and *ibid.*, p. 59.
64. *Ibid.*, p. 102.
65. From *ibid.*, p. 58 and *ibid.*, p. 129.
66. Davy, *op. cit.*, 1822, note 16, p. 367.
67. Davy, *op. cit.*, 1828, note 16, p. 243 – my emphases.
68. Siegfried and Dott, *op. cit.*, 1980, note 3, p. 80. On Davy's use of illustrations and the impossibility of locating the majority of the actual pictures he employed, see the editors' comments in *ibid.*, p. x.
69. *Ibid.*, p. 80. In this case one might say that the lecture's opening few paragraphs (*ibid.*, pp. 73–75) contain the warrant for the information contained in the rest of the chapter, since Davy claims that "[i]t is within the last thirty years that accurate methods of classing different secondary strata . . . have been developed" (*ibid.*, p. 75). However, given that Davy accepts only some of the findings of these methods, this warrant appears too meagre. On warrants see the works cited at note 32.
70. *Ibid.*, p. 82 and *passim*.
71. *Ibid.*, p. 61.
72. *Ibid.*, p. 72.
73. *Ibid.*, p. 75.
74. *Ibid.*, pp. 53–54 and *ibid.*, pp. 99–100.
75. Indeed, his advocacy of the primary/secondary division, conceived in terms of successive formation on naturalistic principles might be viewed as among his most enduring contributions to geology, rather than as a report of what was commonly believed. Again, his discussion of basalt in these terms was controversial and by no means an expression of universal geological opinion – see the editors' comments in *ibid.*, pp. xvii–xliv.
76. *Ibid.*, p. 77.
77. *Ibid.*, p. 119.
78. *Ibid.*, p. 56.
79. *Ibid.*, p. 130. In retrospect this appears to be a shrewd comment for by 1807 he had changed his mind about the cause of volcanic fire; in the 1811 lectures he ascribes volcanic activity to the presence of subterranean alkali metals in volcanic regions. By 1828 he came to doubt this opinion also and tentatively supported the notion of a central fire (Davy, *op. cit.*, 1828, note 16, p. 250).
80. Siegfried and Dott, *op. cit.*, 1980, note 3, p. 99.
81. For confirmatory evidence see the analysis of John Walker's eighteenth-century geological lectures, given at the University of Edinburgh, and of Allan's version of Davy's lectures (see note 5 above) which is to be found in Steven Yearley, *Contexts of Evaluation*, unpub. D. Phil. diss. University of York, 1981, pp. 203–207.
82. See Berman, *op. cit.*, 1978, note 3, especially pp. 32–74.
83. In addition to the works cited at note 8, see Robert Siegfried, 'Davy's "Intellectual Delight" and his Lectures at the Royal Institution', in Forgan, *op. cit.*, 1980, note 8, pp. 177–99. To compare Davy's images with those invoked at other Mechanics' Institutes see the works cited at note 7 and for a comparison with other geological lectures see H. W. Scott (ed.) *Lectures on Geology . . . by John Walker*, Chicago & London: University of Chicago Press, 1966; W. T. Brande, *Outlines of Geology: Being the Substance of a Course of Lectures Delivered in the Theatre of the Royal Institution in the Year 1816*, London: Murray, 1817; J. M. Edmonds, 'The

Geological Lecture-Courses Given in Yorkshire by William Smith and John Phillips, 1824–1825', *Proceedings of the Yorkshire Geological Society* **40** (1975), 373–412; and J. M. Edmonds, 'The First Geological Lecture Course at the University of London, 1831', *Annals of Science* **32** (1975), 257–75.

ATTUNING SCIENCE TO CULTURE

Scientific and Popular Discussion in Dutch Sociology of Education,
1960–1980

GERARD DE VRIES and HANS HARBERS

The State University of Groningen

Although popular science usually is intended primarily to educate, entertain or advise laymen, a popular scientific article may also become part of a public debate and serve political functions. This can even happen unintentionally. A scientist writing about nuclear energy in a newspaper, for example, may perhaps have meant to educate his fellow-citizens only to discover to his embarrassment that some of his audience interprete his contribution as a political statement. Trained and prepared to answer factual questions, he is suddenly confronted with queries concerning values. Particularly in those areas where problems of risk and health are discussed and public controversies arise, scientists may, through their popular expositions, become engaged in normative discussions related to their research work (1).

The interaction of scientific ideas with value systems through the channels of popular science can affect scientific work and alter the concepts of fact and scientific ideals dominant in a scientific community. While in the natural sciences such repercussions of popular expositions of scientific ideas are generally only marginal and long term, in the social sciences they are more direct. In the social sciences, the distance between scientific theories and ideas on the one hand, and the language and thought of laymen on the other is characteristically shorter than in the natural, and most of the medical, sciences. For that reason, we may expect the impact of popular expositions on esoteric research work and discussions among social scientists to show up more vigorously.

To study how the public contributions of social scientists affect their scientific work we analyse in this paper a social science which produced results which were extensively discussed outside the academic world, *viz.* the

103

Terry Shinn and Richard Whitley (eds.), Expository Science: Forms and Functions of Popularisation. Sociology of the Sciences, Volume IX, 1985, 103–117.
© 1985 *by D. Reidel Publishing Company.*

sociology of education. More specifically, we will review the development and the reception of research on unequal distribution of educational opportunities in the 1960s and 1970s in the Netherlands to determine the ways in which scientists attune their interpretations of a social problem to those of their colleagues and to those predominating in their extra-mural audiences.

From the end of the 1950s, the governments of the industrial world have shown, for a variety of reasons, explicit interest in problems of unequal educational opportunity. Large scale scientific research projects were initiated to uncover the social mechanisms underlying the statistics. The *Coleman Report* in the United States and the British *Plowden Report* are well-known examples of the outcomes of these research efforts. Their Dutch equivalent was the *Talentenproject* ('Project on Talents'), started in 1961 and directed by Van Heek, professor of sociology at the University of Leyden. This research project comprised of a series of interrelated subprojects and was executed by a staff group of 11 social scientists. In 1968 the final report was completed and published as a book: *Het Verborgen Talent* (The Hidden Talent) (2).

The inquiry focussed primarily on the barriers between primary and secondary schools; these barriers were supposed to be very strong especially for lower class children. The main causes of unequal educational opportunities were thought to be related to the determinants of choice of a particular type of secondary education for a child and to the factors which affect success at school. The existence of a reserve of talent was postulated − especially in the lower classes. It was expected that sizable numbers of children would be found who were qualified for advanced levels of secondary education but were not attending the appropriate schools.

The *Talentenproject* findings refuted these expectations. The research project found that, whatever their social background, qualified children attended schools suited to their abilities. The anticipated large reserve of available but unused talent from the lower strata of society was not shown to exist. The relatively poor attendance of working class children in secondary and higher education was not brought about by misdirected choices of school type; these children must have lagged behind already in primary school or even earlier. For that reason the focus of research was shifted from the determinants of choice of school to the unequal social distribution of abilities.

From the 1970s onwards, however, the conceptualization of the problem of unequal educational opportunities in projects such as Van Heek's began to be questioned. For example, sociologists associated with the practices of schools and educational policies criticized the implicit pedagogic conformism of the traditional approaches which took the content and the structure of education for granted. As a result of these and other criticisms, empirical studies into curriculum development, classroom practices and the effects of integration and segregation of different types of school have been set up. Moreover, theoretically-minded sociologists questioned the existing social hierarchy for which the school serves as an entrance in both scientific and political terms. A theme already discussed in the classical sociology of Durkheim, Mannheim and Marx, *viz.* the relations between education and society, was reinstated on the research agenda of the sociology of education.

No dominant coherent theoretical framework has yet emerged from this criticism. There is now, however, a general consensus that the narrow approach, represented by the concentration − characteristic of the research of the 1960s − on the problem of unequal educational opportunity has to be superseded by the broader study of the function of education for the reproduction of society. The sociology of education in the latter 1970s and beginnings of the 1980s is marked by a plurality of research styles and theoretical backgrounds involved in a process of rather intensive mutual communication (3).

The Production and Diffusion of the Talentenproject's Results

As the structure of the argument in the *Talentenproject*'s final report *Het Verborgen Talent* reveals, Van Heek's work was inspired by the empiricist's, "received view" of science. In its preface, Van Heek drew his reader's attention to the diversity of the interpretations and explanations available for the unequal educational attainment of children from different social backgrounds. A responsible policy could not be formulated on this confused basis, he argued. The main goal of his project was therefore to scrutinize the validity of the different views. A scientific inquiry would separate the acceptable interpretations of facts from 'mere opinions'. For this purpose, Van Heek enumerated explicitly ten views on educational opportunities. At the end of *Het Verborgen Talent* he contrasted these views with his project's results.

Ten non-scientific views were put on trial: science had to give the final verdict.

Het Verborgen Talent was brought out by a general publisher and in addition to its technical parts, the book also contained chapters suitable for a non-specialised audience. Summarizing his research for the general reader in 1968 in *Sociaal Maandblad Arbeid* (4), Van Heek skipped the technicalities and focussed on the main conclusions, their policy implications and their consequences for popular views on education. Van Heek accepted the necessity to make adjustments in the presentational form of his results for didactic reasons and he eliminated technical jargon and reduced the complexity of his theoretical arguments. He simplisticly supposed that these adjustments would have no repercussions on the validity of scientific knowledge. Moreover, Van Heek did not try to defend his results: he had justified his conclusions before the forum of his scientific colleagues and in his popular exposition he stuck to the elucidation of his findings. In Van Heek's image of science, scientific questions and debates are confined to the social system of science and do not involve external forums. Without further discussion, he supposed that the reception of his results would not contribute to or discount in any way their scientific meaning or validity.

As we see, the concept of science held by Van Heek (and most of his colleagues at the time), was not only founded on empiricist ideas about the *internal* operation of the system of science and the special nature of scientific knowledge, but also implied suppositions about the way scientific knowledge operates *externally*, outside scientific circles, in society at large. The phases of production and justification of knowledge on the one hand, and its dissemination on the other, are thought to be separated not only in time, but sociologically and epistemologically as well. For this reason, we may speak of the *production-diffusion-model* of science and its exposition.

Since the 1960s the received view of science has been criticized by philosophers, historians and sociologists of science. Their critiques primarily assail the empiricist assumptions about the internal operation of science. We should however notice that those who abandoned the empiricist concept of science (and its Mertonian counterpart in the sociology of science), often still accept the production-diffusion model as a good approximation of the dissemination of scientific knowledge outside scientific circles. Moreover, the early reception of Van Heek's work suggests that there are good empirical reasons to do so. The fact is that Van Heek's diagnosis of the problem of unequal educational opportunities was generally accepted. It was taken for granted that what Van Heek had established were 'hard facts'. Their importance was recognized widely and immediately. *Het Verborgen Talent* was reviewed in a variety of scientific journals, as well as newspapers, weeklies, political periodicals and other magazines. Apart from an isolated critical note, all of these reviews were favorable. The results and policy implications of the project's findings were extensively cited and when, in 1969, the Dutch Minister of Education published a detailed report on democratization of education, the *Talentenproject* results were extensively reviewed and used. Knowledge, produced in a small circle of scientific experts, had become diffused and accepted in wide political circles.

After some time, however, more critical reactions appeared. A notable one is Van Kemenade and Kropman's in 1972 (5). Using Van Heek's original data, they made new calculations and argued that there positively was a reserve of talent, a conclusion opposite to the *Talentenproject*'s. Van Kemenade and Kropman's results were derived from a different operationalisation of 'talent' than Van Heek's. The latter had defined this concept as the child's school-capacities, *i.e.*, as the prediction-score for the child's chances of completing secondary education successfully. This score was determined on the basis of test-results, teacher's judgement, the child's age and its father's profession. Especially the last factor, *i.e.*, the father's profession, was considered by Van Kemenade and Kropman to be an unacceptable contamination of the indicator.

Even though the language of the dispute between Van Heek and his critics was that of research technicalities, there was more at stake than a mere question of methods. In staff discussions in the research team of the *Talentenproject*, Van Heek had explicitly argued in favour of including the father's profession in the indicator because this factor was known to affect the child's later performance in secondary school considerably. Arguing along these lines, Van Heek reasoned within the confines of the existing social inequalities and educational practices. The socialist Van Kemenade and his associate Kropman deviated from this position. They concentrated on the child's actual abilities and decided to use exclusively the results of the achievement tests as an indicator of talent. The educational effects of existing social inequalities, for example those associated with differences in parental professional backgrounds, would have to be removed by *e.g.*, compensatory education or the comprehensive school system. Within a new educational system, Van Heek's 'hidden talents' would still get a chance.

The scientific dispute was obviously related to political differences of opinion. In Van Kemenade and Kropman's paper and in a succeeding one by Van Kemenade (6), both published in scientific journals, the connections between science and politics were explicitly discussed.

Van Kemenade and Kropman's 1972 paper reveals the way in which Van Heek's conclusions, perceived and presented as inevitable and factual statements, were derived from specific theoretical and normative assumptions. The *Talentenproject* had been conducted within a specific thought style. Its factual conclusions ('passive connections', to use Fleck's (7) phrase) depended on meritocratic assumptions 'active connections': Van Heek considered social hierarchies of occupations and their status to be fair, provided that the individual's ascent and descent on the social ladder was determined by achievements and abilities, and not influenced by improper factors like power, social background, gender, race or physical disabilities. He supposed the educational system to play a key role in the allocation and distribution of different social positions, and concluded that a fair allocation of positions would result from fair competition and selection in the educational system. In Van Heek's meritocratic perspective, equal educational opportunities imply equal chances of succeeding in a hierarchical society. Neither social inequalities, nor the content and hierarchical structure of the educational system are questioned. Like all meritocrats Van Heek only took an interest in the optimization of selection and mobility with regard to the existing educational system and existing social structures. He therefore confined his study to improper barriers in the transition from primary to secondary education as it existed at the time in the Netherlands.

As soon as we recognize that the *Talentenproject* conforms to a specific thought style, a few peculiarities of the internal history of the project can easily be explained (8). For example, research reports written by one of the permanent members of the staff were systematically ignored in the *Talentenproject*'s final report. This member's conclusions could not be fitted in the main framework, because his reports criticized crucial assumptions of the meritocratic perspective.

The external history of the project and in particularly the reception of

Het Verborgen Talent in non-scientific circles, can be elucidated by pointing to the *Talentenproject*'s thought style as well. Van Heek's perspective on education and society was subscribed to by a variety of political movements in the Netherlands. This was not pure coincidence. The opening sentences of *Het Verborgen Talent* consciously present the book's perspective as a reasonable compromise, balancing preferences for (respectively) conservatism, socialism and liberalism: "Inheritance of privileges, equality and individual achievement are rightly seen as the three basic principles for the occupation of social positions and the recruitment of the members of the different social strata", Van Heek wrote. "A true democracy has to apply these three principles to create an optimal social balance." Translating what is actually a political compromise into scientific terms, Van Heek manoeuvred for position as a scientist in the centre of the political spectrum — thereby making sure that he would also get a hearing outside scientific circles.

We can thus consider the *Talentenproject* to be the esoteric variant of a thought style shared by a thought collective which covered a broad political spectrum. The project started from widely accepted assumptions about education and society, but its mode of argumentation differed from the one common among *e.g.*, politicians. Rules of scientific method played an important role, and technical and methodological considerations predominated in discussions within the research team. Moreover, Van Heek's reputation as a scientist was derived from his methodological competence. Given his esoteric mode of reasoning and the meritocratic perspective he shared with his audiences, Van Heek's conclusions were perceived in both esoteric and exoteric circles as inevitable and as 'facts'.

The reception of the main results of the *Talentenproject* was thus facilitated by an agreement between its theoretical assumptions and the views held in mainstream Dutch politics. In his report to the Parliament on democratization and education, the Minister of Education could accordingly ignore almost all specific and political considerations outside the scope of the meritocratic perspective. "For practical reasons", he wrote, "I'm forced to concentrate on adjustments to the existing educational system. (. . .) Traditional ideas about the structure of society and the function of education continue to provide the foundations of our policy." His proposals, which he admitted were anything but novel, are in accordance with the conclusions of the *Talentenproject*. The wide and high esteem accorded to Van Heek's work and its marginal role in redirecting the foundations of the government's policy on education are closely related.

Like most of his colleagues in the 1950s and 60s, Van Heek used to stress the differences between scientific and political discourse. These lie at the heart of his views on science and its social role. For a short period, Van Heek's views on science and its social role seem to correspond with the actual course of affairs around the *Talentenproject*: an issue formerly debated in political terms had become the object of a scientifically informed public discussion. For both Van Heek and his audience, the *Talentenproject* had demonstrated the capacities of modern social science to play an informing and mediating role in society.

Our discussion so far, however, suggests that this role was enabled by a resonance between the thought style of the inquiry and of the mainstream of Dutch politics. The wide political assent to the scientific conclusions was mobilized by normative means. The practical relevance of Van Heek's conclusions did not derive from his advanced research techniques, but was provided by the meritocratic perspective which he shared with his extra-mural audience. When in the early 1970s the exoteric meritocratic consensus about education and society had vanished, Van Heek's work appeared accordingly both esoterically and exoterically in another light.

Exoteric Pluralism and the Sociology of Education in the 1970s

At the end of the 1960s and the beginnings of the 1970s, important cultural changes started to take place in all Western industrial states including the Netherlands. A broad spectrum of indicators shows these changes to have affected political styles in Western societies. The era of the 'end of ideology' had itself ended (9). From an elite-directed democracy with passive constituencies following their compromising leaders, Dutch politics changed into a system of political parties openly competing within a polarized political culture, each appealing to the electorate in ideological terms. The changes were marked by the fact that in the 1970s each of the major Dutch political parties drew up a new platform to indicate its ideological positions. The former homogeneous political culture had ceased to exist.

In debates about educational affairs too, ideological controversies became important. With general agreement, a number of experimental comprehensive schools had been set up in the Netherlands at the end of the 1960s. Only five years later, the comprehensive school system had turned into an issue for heated political debates.

At about the same time, the Dutch university system underwent rather dramatic changes. The number of students had almost quadrupled between 1955 and 1972 and the traditional system of university organisation, centred round professorial chairs, came under heavy pressure. Considerable numbers of new (junior) lecturers were appointed to meet the increased need for higher education.

The cultural and political changes which took place led to a reactivation of thought styles which seemed to have disappeared completely after the second world war. Partly due to the need to appoint new lecturers, these thought styles — popular especially, although certainly not exclusive, among students — soon had their representatives in the universities. In addition to the meritocratic perspective, socialist, marxist and other alternative views on education and society began to be defended and elaborated. As a consequence, *Het Verborgen Talent* was accorded a different reception. At the beginning of the new era, of course, sociologists of education could not neglect Van Heek's work, because the meritocratic perspective still made its mark on government's educational policies. However, the *Talentenproject*'s conclusions, the 'passive connections' established in the inquiry, had lost their inevitability for all who didn't share the meritocratic thought style. And although after Van Kemenade and Kropman's critique of *Het Verborgen Talent* the book continued to be considered as a 'classic' in Dutch sociology of education, it had changed from a book which stated the facts, into a paradigm of a specific tradition in the discipline.

By the early 1970s, the former general consensus among sociologists of education in the Netherlands, based on their shared meritocratic thought style, had effectively disappeared. In its place emerged a complicated and dynamic system of interacting scientific currents, related to different theoretical backgrounds, philosophical and especially methodological ideas, and political positions. The topic of unequal educational opportunities ceased to be treated as an isolated social problem and was increasingly discussed in relation to more general sociological themes, *e.g.*, the class-structure of industrial societies. Large scale quantitative inquiries lost their primary role, and qualitative methods came into vogue. Theoretical questions became more important and were often – and still are – considered to have greater weight than empirical findings. Explications of foundations – both theoretical and political – began to receive much attention. Disputes among specialists began to appear in scientific journals as well as in party and union media, and in weeklies and cultural magazines.

A remarkable difference with the pre-1970 situation is the appearance of explicitly political arguments in scientific journals. For example, in an established scientific journal the marxist 'reproduction thesis' is rejected, not only because it is scientifically unsound, but also for the political defeatism to which this thesis is supposed to lead. In other ways too, politics and science have become more openly entwined than before. In public debates (*e.g.*, discussions about compensatory education and the comprehensive school system), scientific experts have become opinion leaders. Van Kemenade is only an extreme example. In 1973 he left his university post to become the Labour Party's Minister of Education. Later he became an influential member of the Dutch House of Commons, and held at the same time part-time Chairs in Educational Sciences at the Universities of Amsterdam and Groningen.

It is, of course, impossible to characterize the post-1970 Dutch sociology of education as the esoteric variant of a particular thought style, distinguished from popular and political discussions about related topics by its dependance on specific methods and research techniques and the subtlety of its arguments. For one reason, given the polarized political culture (especially in educational matters) we have to deal now with several exoteric circles. Moreover, it is impossible to formulate a *general* distinction between knowledge considered to be scientific because it meets certain standards of method and rationality, and knowledge external to science. Arguments conceived as 'internally scientific' by a marxist may be beyond the pale for sociologists of different, *e.g.*, positivistic, traditions. The contrary holds as well. The meritocratic social scientist who tried to establish the facts without regarding their historical backgrounds in a class society, was – in a marxist perspective – investigating chimeras. The judgement of where, and by what means, boundaries between esoteric and exoteric knowledge are erected and non-scientific debates thereby separated from discussions among scientific experts, differs between different thought styles. This, however, implies that we have to abandon the production-diffusion model as a descriptive device for the post-1970 role of the sociology of education in the Netherlands. For this model rests upon the assumption that the production of scientific knowledge can be clearly separated from its exposition to non-scientific audiences and this is no longer true. To cover the new era, a new model has to be constructed.

To start off, we should notice that the scientific collectives associated with different styles of thought didn't act as closed formations. Regardless of the differences in theoretical backgrounds, methodological positions and political affiliations that had emerged, intensive mutual communication between specialists continued. They began to meet regularly in the Steering Committee on Sociology of Education and the Association for Research on Education and Social Inequality. With, respectively, about 120 and 90 members, these two organisations cover the esoteric circle of the sociology of education in the Netherlands and its variety of thought styles. Meritocrats, diverse socialists and one communist author published reviews of a book forwarding the reproduction thesis and in a long reply, the authors reacted explicitly to the theoretical, empirical, methodological and political points of critique. Apart from such discussions in the scientific press, experts on education also began to discuss issues in a variety of non-scientific magazines and newspapers. What has often been perceived as a 'crisis' in sociology, the disappearance of the former general agreement on theoretical and methodological questions, has not, then, resulted in a break-down of intellectual communication. However, compared with discussions in the 1960s, the character of communication has changed. In the 1970s, the participants in debates show an explicit awareness of the role of theoretical, methodological and normative presuppositions in scientific work. Theory-ladenness and style-permeatedness of scientific obser-vations and conclusions are explicitly acknowledged. With regard to facts, an explicit relativism or, as Mannheim (10) would have preferred, relationism, emerged among scientists involved in the field. The naive realism which identified the establishment of 'facts' along the lines of general scientific methods and research techniques as 'truth' had vanished almost completely.

Where specialists meet outside scientific circles and participate in public debates about educational policy, a comparable change in attitude can be observed. Van Heek presented in 1968 'the facts' to his lay-audience and pretended to discuss *sine ira et studio* their consequences for popular views on education and society. Only a few years later, this is hardly imaginable any longer. Contributions of sociologists to newspapers, political periodicals, and so on, are explicitly presented as experts' opinions, as informed stands in a public discussion. In contrast to Fleck's (11) remarks on popular (physical) science, references to controversial issues are included in the expositions of results to non-scientific audiences. In exoteric circles relativistic attitudes emerge as well.

In the 1970s, the social sciences have been driven out of the position of the judge who could decide on the validity of popular and political opinions. Instead of this, a kind of jury court has been established, with social scientists acting as proponents of specific views and interests, defending their claims both for esoteric and exoteric forums. From their apparent position *above* politics and culture, the social sciences came down to occupy a position *within* culture and politics.

To cover subsequent developments, the production-diffusion model which covered Van Heek's work and its early reception quite well, has to be abandoned for a *stratified-consensus* model. Where this second model applies, research is typically conducted simultaneously within several both esoterically and exoterically interacting thought styles. Claims have to be forwarded to, and defended in, forums at different levels at the same time. As a result, an awareness of relationism emerges and normative issues are not confined to political debates, but also become subject of esoteric discussions. Disputes about foundations are no longer considered to be the teething troubles of social science: they have become an integral part of 'normal scientific' procedures. In this situation, sociologists tend to live up to the idea of their discipline being a discursive science, *i.e.*, a specific way of discussing issues which are debated elsewhere and in other ways as well. Paraphrasing Clausewitz, one might even claim the social sciences now to be a continuation of politics by other means. The 'by other means', however, has to be stressed. Procedural differences between science and politics continue to exist. Scientific debates are not settled by majority vote. In science one aims for a rational consensus about validity claims. The specialists in the esoteric circle continue to be prepared to argue, to give reasons for their beliefs, and to defend the claims they make in discourses against criticism. In theoretical matters, exoteric circles no longer take scientist's views for granted. Where the stratified-consensus model applies, it is senseless to speak of 'popularisation', meaning exposition of results to non-scientific audiences, clearly separated from production of scientific 'facts'. The content and further development of science is decided by esoteric discussions, as well as their exoteric counterparts.

Conclusions

The changes in Dutch sociology of education we have dealt with concern both the relations of scientists and their non-scientific audiences, and the image of science and concepts of fact and scientific ideals dominant in the scientific community. These changes may be summarized as a transition from a situation covered by the production-diffusion model to one for which the stratified-consensus model applies. Two questions remain now to be answered. Firstly, how are these two models ('logically') related? And secondly, which circumstances can be claimed to have brought about the transition?

To answer the first question, we may consider the fact that, expressed in general terms, both our models describe ways in which science is established as a collective effort, in which scientists co-ordinate their interpretations of phenomena and problems among themselves, and attune these to views (thought styles) predominating in non-scientific circles.

Where (relative to a cluster of problems or phenomena) a *heterogeneous* culture exists, *i.e.*, several thought styles operate, attunement of interpretations has to be assured along different dimensions, *viz.*, theoretical, normative, methodological as well as an empirical one. In this situation, the stratified-consensus model applies. The need to co-ordinate interpretations along several axes is reflected in the variety of discussions we found: theoretical as well as empirical, methodological as well as normative ones. Given the resulting complexity of the co-ordination-problems in this case, no single group of professionals can claim the prerogative to either innovation or selection of interpretations. As a consequence, scientists as well as politicians and policy-makers have to defend their views before a variety of forums. Esoterically as well as exoterically, relativistic attitudes to knowledge-claims can be expected to develop.

In a *homogeneous* culture, where (relative to the problems/phenomena under discussion) one thought style dominates, co-ordination of interpretations is easier to accomplish. Consensus has been assured already along one or more dimensions; shared background-knowledge provides a common theoretical and normative perspective and agreed-upon methodological procedures are available to care for the problems of attuning diverse empirical findings. Here, the production-diffusion model applies. Contrary to the former case, one group of specialists may indeed claim to have the resources (methods, techniques, training) to accomplish the co-ordination problems. Interpretations have to be defended now before this forum of specialists. As a consequence, the esoteric circle is manoeuvred in a position opposed to that of the exoteric circle. Scientific knowledge will consequently be perceived to occupy a position above the general culture. Moreover, because all but the co-ordination of interpretations along the empirical axis is taken for granted, the empiricist image of science offers itself as the natural interpretation of scientific work.

We contend therefore that the production-diffusion model is a special case rather than the opposite of the stratified-consensus model, *viz.*, one that emerges in cases where one thought style predominates both esoterically and exoterically. In that (restricted) situation, traditional ideas about science (including popularisation) keep their validity, which they lose in situations where a plurality of thought styles exists.

This result enables us finally to relate the changes which emerged about 1970 in the content and procedure of Dutch sociology of education to changes in the nature of its audience, especially its new cultural heterogeneity. Of course, it would be too ambitious to speak about causes here, because changes in social sciences are as much a part of general cultural transformations as their consequences. But we can conclude that when Dutch culture became more pluralistic than it had been earlier and new thought styles were introduced in the universities — facilitated by the appointment of new lectures —, the exposition and justification of ideas for scientific as well as extra-mural forums changed.

Acknowledgements

Research supported by a grant from the Netherlands Organization for the Advancement of Pure Research (Z.W.O.). The authors wish to thank John Naughton for his valuable comments.

Notes and References

1. See *e.g.*, L. R. Graham, *Between Science and Values*, New York: Columbia University Press, 1981 for discussion.
2. F. van Heek, *Het Verborgen Talent: Milieu, Schoolkeuze en Schoolgeschiktheid*, Meppel: Boom, 1968.
3. Cf. A. Wesselingh, 'Sociology of Education in the Netherlands: Situations, Developments, Debates', *British Journal of Sociology of Education* 3 (1982), 319–329. Comparable developments in the United States and England are evaluated in *e.g.*, 'Educational Research: A Review and Interpretation', in J. Karabel and A. H. Halsey (eds.) *Power and Ideology in Education*, New York, 1977.
4. F. van Heek, 'Bevordering van doorstroming van kinderen uit sociaal lagere milieus naar het vhmo', *Sociaal Maandblad Arbeid*, (1968) 7/8, 452–465.
5. J. A. van Kemenade and J. A. Kropman, 'Verborgen Talenten? Kritische kanttekeningen bij een onjuiste interpretatie', *Sociologische Gids* (1972), 219–228.
6. J. A. van Kemenade, 'Het Talentenproject, een casestudy van de beperkte waardevrijheid van sociaal onderzoek', *Mens en Maatschappij* (1972), 266–272.
7. L. Fleck, *Genesis and Development of a Scientific Fact*, Chicago: University of Chicago Press, 1979.
8. Cf. H. Harbers, 'Het Talentenproject', *Kennis en Methode* 6 (1982), 290–312 and 7 (1983), 4–34 for further details on the internal history of the project.
9. Cf. *e.g.*, R. Inglehart, *The Silent Revolution*, Princeton: Princeton University Press; for the Netherlands: C. P. Middendorp, *Ontzuiling, Politisering en Restauratie in Nederland*, Meppel: Boom, 1979.
10. K. Mannheim, *Ideology and Utopia*, London: Routledge Kegan Paul, 1960.
11. Fleck, *op. cit.*, p. 113.

THE REACTION TO POLITICAL RADICALISM AND THE POPULARISATION OF POLITICAL ECONOMY IN EARLY NINETEENTH-CENTURY BRITAIN

The Case of 'Productive' and 'Unproductive' Labour

GREGORY CLAEYS

University of Hannover

The popularisation of the new discipline of political economy was, with the fierce debate which accompanied the publication of Darwin's *Origin of Species*, perhaps the most deeply contested development in nineteenth-century intellectual history. From the publication of Adam Smith's *Wealth of Nations* (1776) through the mid-Victorian period, political economy grew to become one of the most important ideological forces in the nineteenth century, welding together a system of morals, a philosophy of government and politics, and an account of the best state for mankind as well as its characteristic economic doctrines, and deeply affecting in the process the rise and development of popular educational institutions and ideas, the evolution of trades' unions, reform and working class movements, the pattern of popular emigration, and millions of individuals' conceptions of how life might and ought to be lived.

In this paper I shall concentrate on a neglected aspect of the relationship between the popularisation of economic ideas (particularly among the working classes) and the evolution of one of its most important early doctrines, which was based upon the distinction between 'productive' and 'unproductive' labour (1). This distinction, which was first clearly stated in Britain by Adam Smith, was adopted by both radical and socialist critics of Smithian and later Ricardian political economy in order to argue that the working classes as 'productive labourers' deserved a larger (or the entire) produce of their labour. It was this distinction which gave a sharpness and clarity to their use of variations on the 'labour theory of value', whose presence in their

119

Terry Shinn and Richard Whitley (eds.), Expository Science: Forms and Functions of Popularisation. Sociology of the Sciences, Volume IX, 1985, 119–136.
© 1985 by D. Reidel Publishing Company.

writings has always been acknowledged in literature on the subject, but never carefully examined (2). Quite a few defenders of the predominant economic orthodoxy recognised this antagonistic, class conscious use of the language of productive and unproductive labour, moreover, and argued that such implications required the rejection of this language and substitution of less ambivalent categories of analysis. Such terminology was hence rejected, at least by some economists, because of its political and ideological associations *as well as* its seeming inaccuracy or inability *scientifically* to assess the quality of 'productiveness'.

In this example we can thus clearly see one aspect of the effects of popularisation upon the expository development of a form of knowledge which claimed for itself (especially in the first third of the nineteenth century) both the accuracy and hence also the authority of a natural science. Here, in other words, the process of popularisation had a clear impact upon the research process itself and upon the theoretical elaboration of the categories of the science. A clarification of this problem hence represents a further step towards a more general examination of the political and ideological context of the popularisation of political economy.

I

In Book II, Chapter 3 of the *Wealth of Nations*, 'Of the Accumulation of Capital, or of productive and unproductive labour', Adam Smith was concerned with the underlying causes of capital accumulation, and was anxious to argue, against the French school of Physiocratic economists, the view that manufacturers were indeed 'productive labourers' (and hence did contribute to a nation's wealth), rather than confining this productiveness to farmers (3). In so doing Smith offered four criteria to distinguish productive from unproductive labour. Firstly, productive labour added value to the materials it worked upon, while the labour of the servant, for example, added to the value of nothing. Secondly, the manufacturer's labour was fixed and realised "in some particular subject or vendible commodity" which, thirdly, "lasts for some time at least after that labour is past". Finally, "that subject, or what is the same thing, the price of that subject, can afterwards, if necessary, put into motion a quantity of labour equal to that which originally produced it." Such objects, in other words, could command as much labour in the market as was used to produce them (4).

These criteria hence excluded a great many occupations whose functions, Smith admitted, might well be described as honourable, useful and necessary. The sovereign, army, navy and judiciary were all unproductive, and "In the same class must be ranked, some both of the gravest and most important, and some of the most frivolous professions: churchmen, lawyers, physicians, men of letters of all kinds; players, buffoons, musicians, opera-singers, opera-dancers, etc." "The labour of even the meanest of these", Smith added, "has a certain value", but that of even the most noble and useful still produced "nothing which could afterwards purchase or procure an equal quantity of labour." (5)

Smith was of course aware that, whatever technical ends the productive/unproductive distinction served, such labels still invoked nontechnical evaluations of the worth of specific activities. The languages of economic and of moral judgment could not be so easily separated. Like David Hume, whose essay, 'Of Interest' had stated that "lawyers and physicians beget no industry, and it is even at the expense of others that they acquire their riches", Smith was certainly aware that the overtones of both the virtuous 'calling' and the sound civic occupation would have resonated in the minds of his readers. Despite his choice of employments to be termed 'unproductive', he could as easily drawn upon Cicero's ancient but familiar list of "perfumers, dancing-masters, and those who supply us with dice or cards", or some others of "all those trades that are pitiful and low, that purvey and cater for the satisfying man's pleasures." Smith's inclusion of lawyers, physicians and the like was of course intended to show that he was not merely engaged in a classical condemnation of luxury trades and their moral effects. But even if Smith primarily intended the productive/unproductive distinction to describe a technical category in his economic theory, he was also doubtless aware that there was a tacit reproof present in classing together "the gravest" and "the most frivolous" professions. When later in the *Wealth of Nations* he admitted that the term 'unproductive' was "a humiliating appellation", it was these sorts of associations to which he was calling attention. Nor did his comparison of unproductive labour with a barren marriage do anything to lessen such implications in a pre-Malthusian era (6).

This coincidence of moral and political with technical language was the chief reason why the productive/unproductive distinction generated such a controversy during the development of post-Smithian political economy. On the one hand a debate continued between British physiocrats and those who accepted the productivity of capital as to the relative value of agriculture and manufacturing to the growth of the economy. Particularly after the turn of the century, this debate came to revolve around the question as to whether an overaccumulation of capital and overproduction of goods was possible in a manufacturing nation, and thus correspondingly whether some form of underconsumptionist explanation might not be the most plausible account for the existence and recurrence of glutted markets (7).

The ideological debate, on the other hand — and to the extent that we can separate it from technical evaluations — took a somewhat different form. That the suggestion of a value judgment was present in Smith's discussion was apparent to one of the most important early teachers of Smithian political economy, Dugald Stewart. "The epithets *productive* and *unproductive*, as they are commonly employed", he cautioned,

being as precise and significant as any which the language furnishes, can scarcely fail to have some effect on the estimate we form of the comparative importance of the two kinds of labour to which we are accustomed habitually to appropriate them. (8)

Stewart went on to suggest that it was "an abuse of language" to bestow the word 'unproductive' upon any species of labour which essentially contributed to the happiness of society, a view which was often to be subsequently repeated. At about the same time in France, too, the economist Jean-Baptiste Say admitted when writing of 'unproductive capital' that "idle and unproductive finery" were most commonly to be found in political despotisms, but nonetheless accused Smith of mistakenly calling the labour of lawyers, physicians and others 'unproductive' because of an error in his definition of wealth, which should have contained some conception of "immaterial products". (9)

In England the ideological significance of Smith's categories was most clearly indicated and vitriolically assailed by a War Office employee named Simon Gray. In a number of works, especially *All Classes Productive of National Wealth* (1817) and *The Happiness of States* (1819), Gray accused Smith of setting up a system of 'Economism' which presumed "to pauperize half the human race" by thrusting all those who worked chiefly with their minds, as well as many other classes, "into the proscribed division of paupers." (10) Smith's unproductive theory, said Gray, was "pernicious in morals and dangerous in politics", and being "calculated to set the various classes of society against each other, as well as to inspire general discontent, and a spirit hostile to subordination among the lower classes", had already led to a climate of disloyalty and sedition (11). In less than twenty years, Gray complained (writing in 1804), "the plausible but false and dangerous ideas of Smith had reached even the illiterate classes." The labouring classes had come to esteem all those who did not work 'unproductive'. Clearly they had not learned this by reading Smith themselves, but through the medium of demagogues, amongst whom Gray later singled out William Cobbett. In effect, all that they knew of Smith's system was "the most dangerous dogma of all . . . the distinction of classes into productive and unproductive, or those which produce wealth and those which consume it." (12) Gray claimed that his own system, which unlike that of Smith and Malthus did not concentrate upon the *material* quality of wealth, but rather on use-value and price (and hence upon services generally) would have the opposite effect in politics and morals, by making "men contented with their lot, quiet and . . . kind, friendly, cheerful, happy." If all classes produced wealth, "every class is found to be useful to the whole", and "classes view one another not as feud-foes, but as friends." (13) This view, we will see, was to prove popular among the Ricardian economists of the 1820s, '30s and '40s.

The writings of the first great purveyors of political economy to the masses also demonstrate an awareness of the ideological significance of the language of productive and unproductive labour. Mrs. Marcet, one of the better-known of the popularisers of Smith, avoided a number of possible problems by creatively announcing that labourers were classed as productive because the rich distributed their capital among them, "who consume it, and reproduce another, larger capital – hence they have obtained the name of productive labourers." (14) In one of her *Illustrations of Political Economy*, the popular writer Harriet Martineau had a dialogue explaining the 'true' meaning of the distinction, and the dependence of the prosperity of the nation upon the existence of unproductive labour (which was also Malthus' main emphasis), prompting her working class character, Hill, to announce apologetically that he was "only sorry I ever understood any reproach by the word *unproductive*: but I shall never fall into the mistake again." (15) Thomas Chalmers, too, while benignly reconciling Christian Providence with the new economic doctrines, entered at length into a discussion of the moral implication of 'productive labour', stating that "we think the political economy of our day bears a hard and hostile aspect towards an ecclesiastical establishment; and we have no doubt that to this, the hurtful definition of Smith has largely, though perhaps insensibly, contributed." (16) As a leading popular theologian Chalmers may well have been defending his own special interest here, as he was doubtless aware that those who lived upon the tythes of the established Church were amongst the 'consumers' ridiculed in the radical press (17).

It is difficult to estimate the extent to which the language of productive and unproductive labour contributed to the progress or increasing sophistication of radical rhetoric before 1800, however. The most important writer in the 1790s to use the distinction in the service of consciously working class ends was the London author John Thelwall. In Thelwall the distinction served as much in a vituperative capacity as in a technical one; the unproductive were "caterpillars and locusts ... blights and mildew" (18). Nonetheless Thelwall was probably the first to address an audience of artisans and labourers by speaking of "the wealth resulting from your productive labour" (19). Far more often than not, however, the use of the term 'productive' in radical writings up to the early 1820s was largely synonymous with 'labourious', 'industrious' and other similarly vague epithets of self-description rooted in variations upon the 'work ethic' as well as upon the position of the labourer in the economy. Hence, for example, Thomas Spence spoke of the "idle classes" as opposed to the "industrious bees" (20). As the anti-Jacobin outcry subsided, however, it would appear that the more technical meaning of the term begins to recur more frequently in radical writings. It is certainly present, for example, in John Bone's *The Reasoner* (1808), Thomas Wooler's *Black Dwarf* (1817), and John Wade's *Gorgon* (1818). In an attack on Malthus, for example, Wooler noted that the former's main doctrine was that "a nonproductive class must exist, in order the produce of the productive classes must be consumed – a proposition not unlike a declaration that caterpillars must exist, lest cabbages should not be destroyed" (21). By 1820 Smith's distinction was so well-known, certainly, as to provoke a London cabinetmaker named James Brodie to describe its author as "that renowned Smith, who we have heard so much about, and who is the great oracle of the discontented" because of the productive/unproductive distinction (22).

II

While a number of post-Napoleonic political radicals made sporadic use of the categories of "that renowned Smith" to describe existing inequalities, it was the early Owenite socialists who first attempted to use the concepts of productive and unproductive labour as the basis for an elaborate and systematic critique of society. In order fully to comprehend the development of this unorthodox side of political economy, and hence to see what it was the Ricardian theorists reacted against, these views must be treated in some detail.

Much of Robert Owen's early social analysis was based, like the Owenite John Gray's, upon the 1814 population statistics and system of classification given in Patrick Colquhoun's *Treatise of the Wealth, Power, and Resources of the British Empire*. Here society was divided into eight classes, mainly by income. The king, royal family and lords were the smallest, followed by the baronets and wealthy gentlemen as well as any others on large incomes. Third came the clergy under the rank of bishops, fourthly the other clergy, free-holders, physicians, lawyers, merchants, bankers and manufacturers livng on moderate incomes, fifthly, small freeholders and shopkeepers, sixthly, the officers, NCO's and pensioners of the armed forces, and seventh, the working classes, larger than all the others united (and Owen was fond of demonstrating these classes with metal cubes, holding up the seventh to show its social strength). An eighth and final class was composed of paupers and criminals (23).

Owen was the first to use this scheme in order to analyse social groups upon the basis of their existing and potential contribution to the common good, a contribution which he estimated largely in terms of their productivity and efficiency. With reference to the three highest divisions Owen couched his criticisms in delicate terms. Of the fourth division he commented that while "many of these are occupied as much as the working classes, and lead a life which requires many sacrifices, and often for little comfort in return", it was still true that "some of them are uselessly, while others are injuriously employed; but none of them are occupied to produce the best results in their avocations or professions." Such classes, thus, were productive but inefficiently so. Of the small freeholders and shopkeepers, one-twentieth of their number and one-hundredth of the capital expended by them would suffice to produce as much wealth under better social arrangements. The army was largely drawn from the working classes, who were thus converted from producers to consumers while injuriously being demoralised by the life of the soldier. In general, too, the working classes were scarcely efficiently employed under the present system, and paupers less so (24).

The Owenite printer George Mudie was probably the first to claim that neither the capitalist nor the master-manufacturer were productive labourers, on the basis of the fact that capital was neither a source for nor a power of production. In a polemic two years later against James Mill's view that all classes were equally useful and contributed equally to production, too, Mudie explicitly denied that this was the case. The working classes alone supported the state, paupers and all other classes. They alone were "really productively employed", not "the masters or employers of the labourers, who do not work themselves". Because labour was the source of wealth, "*all income*, whether it be wages, poor's rates, profits, rents or taxes" was "entirely taken from or paid by the fruits of productive industry, and from no other source whatsoever." It was hence the "actual labourers" in agriculture, trade and manufactures who supported the rest of the population in the country (25).

The greatest populariser of the working class interpretation of the productive/unproductive distinction was the Owenite John Gray, whose *Lecture on Human Happiness* (1825) was widely circulated among both British and American Owenites. Gray initially introduced six categories, firstly, "the three grand occupations of life" (cultivating the earth, preparing and appropriating the products for use, and distributing these) and three others, government, instruction and amusement, and the medical profession. All those who did not belong to one of the first two occupations named (agriculture and industry) were unproductive, and as such "a DIRECT TAX upon the productive classes". Every productive person was in addition deemed a "USELESS member of society, unless he gives an EQUIVALENT for that which he consumes." (26)

After further subdividing the population into 51 categories, Gray stated more precisely his definition of the productive classes, who included only three of these 51 categories: "labouring people, employed in agriculture, mines and minerals", "aquatic labourers in the merchants' service, fisheries, rivers, canals, etc", and "artisans, handicrafts, mechanics, and labourers, employed in manufactures, buildings, and works of every kind". These groups, then constituted "the whole of the productive classes", who produced the entire income of society except for that small proportion (less than 1%) produced by paupers and pensioners. They alone were "productive members of society who apply *their own hands* either to the cultivation of the earth itself, or to the preparing and appropriating the produce of the earth to the uses of life." Dividing the national income by the population of the productive classes, Gray then arrived at the conclusion that while the latter produced goods to the value of £54 millions annually, they received only £11 millions in income, "being but a small trifle", he exclaimed, "more than ONE-FIFTH PART OF THE PRODUCE OF THEIR OWN LABOUR" (27).

Gray next examined each of the 51 social groups separately, with the aim of proving that as much as one-third of the population were "useless members of society". Two criteria were used to determine this: whether any group gave an equivalent for what it consumed (which is akin to Smith's notion) and whether, under the proposed Owenite reorganisation of society into small communities of self-supporting groups, their occupations would be socially necessary. With each of these groups Gray acknowledged that some portion (usually a much smaller number than existed, as in the case of government officials) of the unproductive classes could be deemed to be termed 'useful'. Gray's exclusion of various categories, moreover, was often underlaid by moralistic criteria. The very name of a soldier was "a disgrace to human nature ... which will one day be forgotten". Lawyers "without a single exception" would "ultimately be superseded" in the new world of moral relationships. Physicians were all useful, but their numbers would be greatly reduced when extreme luxury and poverty had been banished. Fashion was "better named *folly*", and sumptuous profusion merely "empty, vain distinction", and hence all classes associated with these would disappear. Lace dresses, in particular, were singled out as the sort of products the future could do without (28).

The centrality of the distinction between productive and unproductive labour in Gray's analysis is hence quite clear. The mere presence of some variety of the 'labour theory of value' in such an analysis is in itself insufficient to characterise injustice in any relationship other than that between the genuine 'idlers' who do not work at all, and the working classes. Upon the sole basis of the claim that 'labour is the source of all wealth' (a slogan frequently echoed in the working class press) virtually every form of labour could claim to add value to a product through assisting its circulation, aiding others who were themselves productive labourers, etc. This was indeed, as we have seen, the principal point of counter-attack against Smith's distinction by Simon Gray and others.

The idea that 'labour is the source of all wealth' could thus only be a coherent statement of working class consciousness if such wealth were specifically defined in material terms. It is this physical quality of wealth, in turn, which underpins the distinction between productive and unproductive labour, and it is, finally, the specifically *manual* interpretation which Gray gives to this physical definition which allows him to isolate so precisely that class which is the creator of wealth — those who fashion the product themselves — while excluding not only those who derive their incomes from rent, profit or interest, but equally those who in an irrational economic system over-populate those occupations where many fewer might prove more efficient. It is only because Gray also acknowledged the existence of 'productive but useless' occupations (such a lace dressmakers) that his plan does not essentially set forth an ideology of the productive classes. The distinction between true and false needs which underlies this view, however, was only infrequently introduced by many of those who did use a variation on this theme, and indeed was eliminated in Gray's own later work.

In its most popular working class form, then, the productive/unproductive distinction indubitably became frequently associated with the claims of manual labourers against capitalists. Writing in 1831, the radical journalist William Carpenter complained that his correspondents seemed to think that mental labour was not a "productive species of labour", and urged them to

endeavour to estimate the influence of science in the direction of labour, and in the production of wealth, and they will not again use the phrase 'working classes' as descriptive only of *manual* labourers, and much less of the poorest class of manual labour, namely that which is destitute of capital.

Here again it was the opposition of the 'idle' and 'industrious' classes which was of greatest interest to Carpenter (29). The London tailor Francis Place, too, was amongst those who actively endeavoured to combat the manualist definition of productive labour. Place wrote a number of articles for the working class press defending his views against the attacks of, for instance, George Ensor on 'unproductive labourers'. In his own recollections about the development of struggles over economic doctrines in the 1820s and '30s, Place also especially blamed Owen for preaching the "right of every man to his share of the earth in common, and his right to whatever his hands had been employed upon." The key to the beliefs of Owen and others, wrote Place, was the view that

Every thing which has been produced is the work of men's hands, that is, has been made by the hands of the labouring portion of the people and of *right* belongs to them. No matter when it was produced or by whose head work as well as by their hands' work it was produced, it all belongs to them because they are the workmen, or in their own language, producers (30).

III

How then was the radical and socialist development of the terminology of productive and unproductive labour related to the development of mainstream (i.e., Ricardian) political economy after the early 1820s? The precise extent to which alterations of Smith's views were a function of their radical usage cannot, of course, be exactly determined, since other reasons were also put forward for rejecting Smith's distinction. Let us first look briefly at these additional reasons as they were put forward by economists writing after the heyday of Smithian orthodoxy.

Ricardo's *Principles of Political Economy and Taxation* succeeded in avoiding much of this controversy by mentioning 'productive labour' only in passing, and refering to it by contrast with "expenditure on luxuries and enjoyments", hence alluding primarily to its use as a means of describing forms of consumption rather than as a category of production (31). 'Productive labour' is not, hence, rejected as a category, as it had been for example by Lauderdale, for whom labour could not be considered as a measure of value (32). The term, rather, is supplanted by an emphasis upon 'productive' and 'unproductive' *consumption*, but in any case according to John Stuart Mill, whose essay "On the Words Productive and Unproductive" was published in 1844, the consequences of an emphasis upon consumption were very nearly the same from the point of view of the science, since what economists intended to show in both categories was that "In proportion to the amount of the productive labour and consumption of a country, the country . . . is enriched: in proportion to the amount of unproductive labour and consumption, the country is impoverished." (33)

This emphasis was to represent one important trend of thought after Ricardo; the latter's chief disciple James Mill, for example, emphasised the categories of "Productive and Unproductive Consumption" in his *Elements of Political Economy* (1826) (34). Another equally important development sought to redefine Smith's conception of wealth so as to extend the notion of productivity to other social groups, which as we have seen was Simon Gray's main emphasis as well. J.-B. Say's correspondence with Malthus on this matter, first published in 1821, for example, substituted the phrase 'productive service' for 'productive labour', and emphasised that the 'immaterial produce' exchanged by doctors, lawyers and soldiers did indeed have an exchangeable value (and hence conformed to one part of Smith's definition). J. R. McCulloch, in particular, defended the view that physicians and others were 'indirectly' productive since their labour allowed others to produce more, arguing further that

It is on this principle that the productiveness of players, singers, opera-dancers, buffoons, etc., depends ... the amusement afforded by these persons – how trifling soever they may in the estimation of cynics and *soi-disant* moralists – create new wants, and by so doing necessarily stimulate our industry to procure the means of gratifying them. They are unquestionably, therefore, a *cause* of production, and it is very likely a truism to say that what is a cause of production must be productive (35).

This conception was also generally accompanied by an expanded definition of wealth, which meant, for example to Longfield, "any of those things which satisfy the wants or gratify the riches of mankind, and which possess an exchangeable value" (36), to Nassau Senior, "those things only, which, directly or indirectly, are made the subjects of purchase and sale, of letting and hiring" (37), or for Scrope, all the "purchaseable means of human enjoyments." (38) At the same time there were frequent defenses of the general *social* (as opposed the more narrowly economic) utility of the various professions in particular; Chalmers for example pointed out that "To the physician, I may owe the continued health of a lifetime – to the lawyer, the preservation of my family estate, along a line of successive generations – to the soldier, the independence of my nation for centuries – to the clergyman, the virtue of the people, and the imperishable good of their eternity." (39) Other writers, however, were careful to stress (as did J. Broadhurst in 1824) that while

It may be said, that the services of soldiers, sailors, and tax-gatherers are full equivalents for the necessaries these classes consume ... The existence of these persons is necessary, but it is not the less an evil . . . the expense of subsidising these persons acts on all classes immediately concerned in the business of production and commerce, precisely the same as if the cost of producing necessaries was increased (40).

IV

Some economists, of course, were prepared to follow Smith's (and later Malthus') material definition of wealth, and even to continue to use Smith's productive/unproductive distinction without alteration (41). Most, however, had by 1850 shifted to some conception of productive and unproductive consumption (42). What, however, is it possible to conclude about the process by which political economy was popularised from the controversy over the categories of productive and unproductive labour? Firstly, as we have seen, the ideological dimension of this terminology did play a major role in leading *some* economic writers to counsel its rejection. This is particularly the case for Simon Gray (whose works however became quite well known), for whom the effect of a distinction in political philosophy was a primary cause for introducing a new and less dangerous set of terms. Most writers on political economy, however, were probably aware that the language of this 'science' was politically-laden, and few if any failed to recognise that the popularisation of political economy was a battle to achieve peaceable class relations, after 1832 in particular between the middle and working classes.

It cannot however be argued that the terminological shift which largely occurred after 1800 took place *solely* for ideological reasons, at least for the simple reason that the degree of 'influence' which such considerations had vis-à-vis the technical dimensions of the debate simply cannot be measured. Without doubt political economy was in this period exceptionally conscious of its political mission, and of the classes affected positively and negatively by its doctrines. Nonetheless, it seems equally clear that an 'indirect' or 'immaterial' increase in national wealth certainly could be attributed to many of those groups described by Smith and his followers as 'unproductive'. Given a different definition of wealth all of those performing services of any kind or even aiding in any manner in the circulation of wealth could be understood as contributing to the wealth of the nation, even if their manual and mental exertions were not aimed at furthering the production of material or exchangeable objects.

Nonetheless it is clear both that the exposition of political economy often took place with a clear consciousness of its social import, and that the most important part of this process was the simultaneous functioning of key aspects of the terminology of economics in both a moral/political and analytical manner. This is not merely to say that writers on political economy saw themselves as moral ministers, in competition with the Church in their specification of the precise virtues (frugality, sexual and hedonistic abstinence, punctuality and dedication to work, etc.) upon which it was believed the progress of society depended. It is also the case that the exhortation to practice these virtues was embedded within the teachings of the economists, and that the ranking of specific virtues varied from one economic system to the next. Indeed, much of the defense of 'unproductive labour' involved the recognition of the Mandevillian paradox that the apparent amorality of slothfulness, dissoluteness and aristocratic inactivity might indeed represent a positive contribution to the nation's wealth and hence well-being, through for example the trade in luxury goods.

Seen from this perspective a significant aspect of the debate over productive and unproductive labour concerned the general interpretation of the 'work ethic', and in this sense the most fundamental assumptions of the debate were certainly shared by its working and middle class participants, even if the criterion of work lacked appeal to more delicate aristocratic temperments. For the Owenite John Gray, as we have seen, an attack upon luxury goods also accompanied a narrowing of the definition of productive labour to manual labourers, while others did admit mental labour into the same category (e.g., William Thompson). This sort of distinction, however, could also be used by or in the name of other classes as well. Spokesmen for the landed proprietors like the eccentric tory radical James Bernard could claim that land-owners and the working classes were productive, while the middle classes were not, insofar as the former created material rather than money wealth (43). The middle classes, too, could descend to constructing essentially physical notions of labour which embodied eminently Protestant virtues in order to defend the 'sacrifice' of immediate enjoyment (in Nassau Senior's characterisation) which wages and profits entailed, while condemning the indecent idleness of the landed proprietor, who exerted no energy and resolved no sublimations in enjoying his rent (44).

Given this very fundamental moral dimension it is not surprising that the popularisation of political economy bore a relatively intimate relationship to the theoretical elaboration of the science itself. The more powerful political economy became, and the more it structured the terms of 19th-century political and economic debates, however, the less its moralising substructure was evident. Up to about 1850, though, it was by no means entirely clear that political economy had gained a genuine hold over important sections of the working classes, though thereafter it can generally be said that this was the case. Up to 1830 in particular, hence, this ascendancy was by no means beyond dispute, and it is thus the first third of the 19th-century when this ideological dimension is most clearly perceptible, and when it can thus be demonstrated to have entered to varying degrees into the elaboration of the theory of political economy itself.

Acknowledgements

I am grateful to Istvan Hont and to the participants of the Conference on Expository Science, Forms and Functions of Popularisation, Paris, December 1–3, 1983, for their comments on earlier versions of this article, and to the Managers of the Research Centre, King's College, Cambridge, for helping to fund the research upon which it is based.

Notes and References

1. For a recent treatment of the foundations of political economy see in particular Istvan Hont and Michael Ignatieff's 'Introduction' to their edition entitled *Wealth and Virtue: The Shaping of Political Economy in the Scottish Enlightenment*, Cambridge: University Press, 1983.
2. For general acknowledgements of the importance of these categories to early British socialist writing see Max Beer, *A History of British Socialism* (2 vols., London: G. Bell, 1929), vol. 1, pp. 194, 213, 239, 248, 250; and Mark Blaug, *Ricardian Economics*, New Haven: Yale University Press, 1958, pp. 141–2.
3. R. K. Webb, *The British Working Class Reader 1790–1848*, London: George Allen and Unwin, 1955, p. 99. On working class education and political economy in this period see also Robin Gilmour, 'The Gradgrind School: Political Economy in the Classroom', *Victorian Studies* 11 (1967), 207–24; J. M. Goldstrom, 'Richard Whately and Political Economy in School Books, 1833–80', *Irish Historical Studies* 15 (1966), 137–46, and *The Social Content of Education 1808–1870, a Study of the Working Class Reader in England and. Ireland*, Dublin: Irish University Press, 1972, pp. 60–1, 71–6, 89–90, 124–6, 170, 178; Richard Johnson, 'Notes on the Schooling of the English Working Class 1780–1850', in R. Dale, R. Esland, and M. Macdonald (eds.) *Schooling and Capitalism. A Sociological Reader*, London: Macmillan, 1970, pp. 44–54, and 'Educational Policy and Social Control in Early

Victorian England', *Past and Present* **49** (1970), 96–119; Jeffrey Marsh, 'Economics Education in Schools in the Nineteenth Century: Social Control', *Economics* **13** (1977), 116–28; D. G. Paz, *The Politics of Working Class Education in Britain 1830–1850*, Manchester: University Press, 1980; Bruce Rosen, 'Education and Social Control of the Lower Classes in England in the Second Half of the Eighteenth Century', *Paedagogica Historica* **14** (1974), 92–105; Harold Silver, *English Education and the Radicals 1780–1850*, London: Routledge and Kegan Paul, 1975, pp. 20–89; Brian Simon, *Studies in the History of Education 1780–1870*, London: Lawrence and Wishart, 1960, pp. 138–43; R. L. Meek, *The Economics of Physiocracy*, London: George Allen and Unwin, 1962, pp. 22, 205, 95, 349.

4. Adam Smith, *An Inquiry into the Nature and Causes of the Wealth of Nations*, Ed., W. B. Todd, 2 vols., Oxford: Clarendon Press, 1976, vol. 1, p. 330.

5. *Ibid.*, p. 331. For discussion see Samuel Hollander, *The Economics of Adam Smith*, London: Heinemann, 1973, p. 147; Mark Blaug, *Economic Theory in Retrospect*, London: Heinemann, 1968, p. 56; Edwin Cannan, *A History of Theories of Production and Distribution in English Political Economy from 1776 to 1848*, London: P. S. King and Sons, 1903, pp. 14–25; Maurice Dobb, *Theories of Value and Distribution since Adam Smith*, Cambridge: University Press, 1973, pp. 59–62; and V. Bladen, 'Adam Smith on Productive and Unproductive Labour: A Theory of Full Employment', *Canadian Journal of Economic and Political Science* **26** (1960), 325–31.

6. D. Hume, 'Of Interest', in *Hume's Economic Writings*, Ed. D. Rotwein, Edinburgh: University Press, 1955, p. 53; Cicero, *The Offices*, London: Dutton, 1923, p. 66; Adam Smith, *The Wealth of Nations*, pp. 330–1.

7. On these questions see in particular R. Meek, 'Physiocracy and the Early Theories of Underconsumption' and 'Physiocracy and Classicism in Britain', both reprinted in *The Economics of Physiocracy*, pp. 313–63. For one of the main statements of British physiocracy see John Gray (no relation to the later Owenite of this name), *The Essential Principles of the Wealth of Nations Illustrated, in Opposition to Some False Doctrines of Dr. Adam Smith and Others*, London, 1797, especially pp. 22, 28–9, 35, 49–52. For a recent general treatment of this topic see Michael Bleaney, *Underconsumptionist Theories. A History and Critical Analysis*, London: Lawrence and Wishart, 1976, pp. 22–61.

8. Dugald Stewart, 'Lectures on Political Economy', *Collected Works*, Ed. Sir William Hamilton, Edinburgh, 1855, vol. 8, p. 269.

9. *Ibid.*, p. 290; J.-B. Say, *A Treatise on Political Economy*, 1803, 6th edn., New York, 1880, pp. 119–20.

10. Simon Gray, *The Happiness of States*, London, 1819, pp. xx–xxi.

11. Simon Gray, *All Classes Productive of National Wealth*, London, 1817, pp. 227–30; *The Happiness of States*, p. xxxvii.

12. Simon Gray, *All Classes*, p. 234, *The Happiness of States*, p. vi, 'Remarks on the Production of Wealth', *The Pamphleteer* **34** (1820), 414.

13. Simon Gray, *All Classes*, p. 236, *The Happiness of States*, p. xxxvii. For material from this period see also Lauderdale, *An Inquiry into the Nature and Origins of Public Wealth, and Into the Means and Causes of Its Increase*, Edinburgh, 1804, p. 37, *Edinburgh Review* **4** (1804), 358–62 (which argues that "all those occupations which tend to supply the necessary wants, or to multiply the comforts and

pleasures of human life, are equally productive in the strict sense of the word, and tend to augment the mass of human riches, meaning, by riches, all those things which are necessary, or convenient, or delightful to man", p. 362); Daniel Boileau, *An Introduction to the Study of Political Economy*, London, 1811, pp. 190–5 (which terms services productive but otherwise strives to maintain Smith's definition), and David Buchanan, *Observations on the Subjects Treated of in Dr. Smith's Inquiry into the Nature and Causes of the Wealth of Nations*, Edinburgh, 1814, pp. 131–7, where Smith's views are upheld against the *Edinburgh Review*.

14. Mrs Marcet, *Conversations on Political Economy*, London, 1816, p. 92.

15. Harriet Martineau, *Illustrations on Political Economy* (6 vols., London, 1832), vol. 1, pp. 51–5.

16. Thomas Chalmers, 'On Political Economy in Connexion with the Moral State and Moral Prospects of Society', *Works*, Glasgow, n.d., vol. 19, p. 350.

17. E.g., *Black Dwarf* 10, no. 1 (1 January 1823), 2.

18. John Thelwall, *The Tribune* (3 vols., London, 1795–96), vol. 1, pp. 36, 130, and *The Rights of Nature Against the Usurpations of Establishments*, London, 1796, pp. 16, 80, 91–2.

19. J. Thelwall, *The Rights of Nature*, p. 91. William Frend (*Principles of Taxation*, London, 1799, pp. 3–4) also uses the distinction in a technical fashion, though his audience was more genteel.

20. Thomas Paine, *Complete Writings*, Ed. P. Foner, New York, 1945, vol. 1, p. 412, Thomas Spence, *The Restorer of Society to Its Natural State*, 2nd Edn., London, 1807, p. 47.

21. John Bone, *The Reasoner*, London, 1808, pp. 229, 502; *Black Dwarf* 1, no. 14 (30 April 1817), 213, no. 46 (10 December 1817), 759; *Gorgon* 1, no. 10 (25 July 1818), 74, no. 12 (8 August 1818), 90–1; *Wooler's British Gazette* 3, no. 25 (24 June 1821), 3,

22. James Brodie, *Fair Prices For Ever! Live and Let Live, or, We are All Friends*, London, 1820, p. 3.

23. R. Owen, *Report of the Proceedings at the Several Public Meetings Held in Dublin*, Dublin, 1823, pp. 56–60.

24. *Ibid.*, pp. 158–60.

25. *Economist* 1, no. 7 (1 March 1821), 103–4, *Political Economist and Universal Philanthropist*, no. 2 (25 January 1823), 30, 41, 43–5.

26. John Gray, *A Lecture on Human Happiness*, London, 1825, p. 11. It is easy to misread Gray on this point, as he appears here to refer to all six occupations as productive.

27. *Ibid.*, pp. 12–16, 57–8.

28. *Ibid.*, pp. 18–20, 26.

29. *Carpenter's Monthly Political Magazine* (December 1831), 137, 142–7.

30. *Trades' Magazine and Mechanics' Weekly Gazette*, no. 49 (18 June 1826), 779–80, British Library Additional MS. 27834, f. 78.

31. David Ricardo, *The Principles of Political Economy and Taxation*, London, Dent, 1973, p. 186, see also p. 94. See also Ricardo's *Works*, Ed. P. Sraffa, Cambridge: University Press, 1973, vol. 6, pp. 292–5.

32. Lauderdale, *An Inquiry into the Nature and Origins of Public Wealth*, 2nd edn., London, 1819, p. viii.

33. John Stuart Mill, *Works*, Toronto: University Press, 1975, vol. 4, pp. 283–4.
34. James Mill, *Selected Economic Writings*, Ed. Donald Winch, London: 1966, pp. 322–5.
35. J. R. McCulloch, *The Principles of Political Economy*, 2nd edn., London, 1830, pp. 527–9. See also McCulloch's edition of the *Wealth of Nations*, Edinburgh, 1828, pp. lxxi, 95–7.
36. Mountifort Longfield, *Lectures on Political Economy*, Dublin, 1834, p. 22.
37. Nassau Senior, *Four Introductory Lectures on Political Economy*, London, 1852, p. 68.
38. G. Poulett Scrope, *Principles of Political Economy*, London, 1833, p. 43.
39. Thomas Chalmers, 'On Political Economy', p. 340.
40. J. Broadhurst, *Political Economy*, London, 1842, pp. 125–6.
41. *E.g.*, Egerton Brydges, *The Population and Riches of Nations*, London, 1819, pp. 1–2; T. R. Malthus, *Principles of Political Economy*, London, 1820, pp. 25–51; John Cazenove, *Outlines of Political Economy*, London, 1832, pp. 87–90.
42. J. S. Mill, 'On the Words Productive and Unproductive', pp. 283–4.
43. James Bernard, *The Theory of the Constitution*, London, 1834, pp. 435ff. On Bernard see my 'A Utopian Tory Revolutionary at Cambridge: the Political Ideas and Schemes of James B. Bernard, 1834–39', *Historical Journal* 25 (1982), 583–603. On the resolution of some of these problems in radicalism prior to the Owenite phase see my 'The Effects of Property on Godwin's Theory of Justice', *Journal of the History of Philosophy* 22 (1984), 81–101.
44. See the discussion of Harold Perkin on this point in 'Land Reform and Class Conflict in Victorian Britain', in J. Butt and J. F. Clarke (eds.) *The Victorians and Social Protest*, Newton Abbot: David and Charles, 1973, pp. 182–4.

PART II

THE SCIENTIFIC APPROPRIATION OF MAJOR PUBLICS

MEDIA SENSATIONALISATION AND SCIENCE

The Case of the Criminal Chromosome

JEREMY GREEN

University of Lancaster

1. Introduction

This paper takes as its subject an episode in the history of human genetics — the discovery of the so-called 'XYY syndrome' and the response this discovery elicited in the popular media. The purpose of this paper is not simply to chronicle this episode, but rather to use it as a means of studying one of the corporate myths of the scientific community, and the workings of this myth in the reconstruction of scientific history. The myth under discussion might be stated, succinctly, thus: *Popularisation equals Pollution*. That is, in the process of transforming and re-packaging scientific knowledge so that it can be understood by non-specialists, the content of the knowledge becomes degraded, so that it is distorted and less true. A subsidiary but important element of the myth, and one which lends it a moral dimension, is the attribution of responsibility for the polluting process to external forces and extra-scientific agencies. Popularisation, in these terms, is something *done to* Science, and the distortion and degradation of the scientific content which it entails derives from either the ignorance of the popularisers, or their irresponsibility. In calling this belief, or set of beliefs, a myth, I do not mean to suggest that they have no basis in fact. Rather, I use myth here to mean a powerful ideological representation of reality. As such, the 'Popularisation equals Pollution' myth can be seen as a component of a greater corporate ideology of scientists (1).

Turning now to the operation of the myth that shall concern us here, it is widely held among scientists who participated in research on the XYY chromosome abnormality, or who were on the periphery of this research, that proper scientific work on XYY was ruined because of 'media sensationalisation'.

Terry Shinn and Richard Whitley (eds.), Expository Science: Forms and Functions of Popularisation. Sociology of the Sciences, Volume IX, 1985, 139–161.
© *1985 by D. Reidel Publishing Company.*

According to this view, a false account of the significance of the chromosome abnormality, which over-emphasised the criminological aspects, and a false image of the typical XYY man, grew up because of the appropriation by journalists of scientific knowledge. The journalists, it is believed, observed the process of *formation* of knowledge, and either through ignorance – 'getting the wrong end of the stick' (2) or through self-interest, misrepresented that process. Thus, this false image was not the fault of the scientists. As early as 1969, Kessler and Moos argued that the suggestion 'That XYYs are uncontrollably aggressive psychopaths appears to be nothing more than a myth promoted by the mass media' (3); and more recently, Patricia Jacobs, who may be justly credited with initiating the interest of the scientific community in the phenotype of XYY has written: "In common with many other individuals working in this area, I was quite unprepared for, and unable to adequately deal with, the media's sensationalist attitudes and blatant disregard for the facts" (4).

Similarly, during the 1974–76 controversy over an XYY screening project at Harvard Medical School, defenders of the project repeatedly asserted that the unfortunate 'criminological associations' with which XYY had been invested were the product of 'media sensationalism' (5).

In all, journalists are accused of *sensationalising* the XYY findings, of making them seem more newsworthy and exciting, and thus of giving birth to a *popular* myth, that of the bogeyman XYY male.

In the discussion that follows, I shall call this the 'sensationalisation model' of the history of XYY. Such a model has, of course, a respectable ancestry in the work of sociologists of mass communications (6), and of deviancy (7), who have described the ways in which the imperatives of the news industry, through selective presentation and unwritten but crucial interpretative 'frames', transform the events reported in the media. If this model is applicable to the development of knowledge about XYY, then we should expect to find the following:

(1) That there is flow of information, over time, from specialist journals, perhaps via intermediate publications, to popular publications; in the terms of Fleck's 'concentric rings', a flow outwards.

(2) That the *quality* of this information, in terms of the accuracy and truth of the representations of scientific knowledge therein, should be degraded in this flow, so that the further down the popularisation sequence

we look, the more distortion and factual errors we should expect to find. (3) That in this process of degradation, and through the operation of *journalistic* imperatives, the false image of the XYY man is created.

In this paper, I wish to argue, firstly that the 'sensationalisation model' is not an accurate historical account but an ideological one, and secondly, that there is abundant evidence to suggest an alternative model of the popularisation of XYY, and of the creation of the XYY bogeyman, which suggests a unity rather than an opposition, between scientific activity and popularisation.

2. The Discovery of the XYY Man

The first case of a man with an extra Y chromosome in each of his cells was reported by a group of physicians in Buffalo, New York (8). The man had been discovered fortuitously during an investigation into his fertility problems, and the investigators did not attribute any clinical significance to his clinical abnormality. Indeed, the *absence* of 'mental and physical stigmata' was taken to be evidence that the patient was an XYY male. Over the next four years, several more XYY patients were found, but there seemed to be no specific XYY phenotype. However, in 1965, Patricia Jacobs and her co-workers at the MRC cytogenetics laboratory in Edinburgh, working on a programme of research in population cytogenetics, discovered that there was a significant statistical excess of XYY males among the inmates of the state hospital at Carstairs, a maximum security institution for abnormal offenders (9). Nine of the men in the sample proved to by XYY, 3.5% of the surveyed population; while Jacobs *et al.*'s estimate of the normal population prevalence of 1 in 1,300 males was of necessity only a 'guesstimate', this was undoubtedly a very significant over-representation.

Jacob's findings, published in *Nature* on 25th December 1965, attracted considerable scientific interest, and formed the subject of several letters and editorials in the medical journals (10, 11). The report also provided the impetus for a series of similar studies of the chromosomal status of offender populations, and since Jacobs had implied in her discussion that 'an extra XYY chromosome predisposes its carriers to unusually aggressive behaviour', the report also led to in-depth psychological and psychiatric examinations of the identified XYY men. By early 1967, accounts of the developing knowledge about XYY had begun to appear in the intermediate publications which attempt to straddle the gap between medical and scientific journals proper and the popular press; articles on XYY were published in *Science News* (12), in *World Medicine* (13), in *Crime and Detection* (14) – shortly to become the more upmarket *The Criminologist* – and in *Science Digest* (15). In June a brief report appeared in the London *Times* (16).

In April 1968, there was a dramatic change in popular awareness of the XYY abnormality. On 21st of that month, a front-page headline in the *New York Times* proclaimed "Genetic Abnormality is Linked to Crime" (17). The article itself described the bizarre circumstances surrounding the trial of David Hugon, a stable boy (and former employee of the Aga Khan) charged with the murder of a Parisian prostitute. After fleeing to the countryside, Hugon gave himself up and confessed to the murder; while awaiting trial, he attempted suicide, and as a result, the court ordered a comprehensive medical and psychiatric examination. It was this examination, which included a chromosome typing, which revealed that Hugon was XYY. According to the *Times*, the court's reaction to this disclosure was to appoint a panel of experts – comprised of Dr. Leon Derobert, a professor of legal medicine; Dr. Jean Lafon, a psychiatrist and Dr. Jerome Lejeune, a geneticist – to advise it of the scientific and legal significance of the XYY chromosome abnormality.

The opening of the trial inspired a burst of coverage on XYY, and provided the opportunity for the *Times* to interview leading scientists for their opinions on the subject. On the following day, 22nd April, there was a further sensational revelation in the *New York Times*: according to another front-page article, the mass-murderer, Richard Speck, awaiting sentence of death, was to make an appeal against this sentence on the grounds that he too was XYY, and therefore not criminally responsible (18). The *Times* quoted Speck's lawyer, Gerald Getty, then Public Defender of Cook County, as having said:

I am aware that an analysis was made, and that it showed that he (Speck) is XYY . . . . We had a mutual agreement that it would not be disclosed since we're in the infancy of an appeal . . . . We're not going to work it in at this point, but if it so develops at a later time, we may be able to make it part of the record (19).

In fact, despite that fact that Speck was described in the article as typical of the "XYY pattern", Speck was *not* an XYY male. The error had arisen through a curious set of unlikely contingencies. Richard Lyons, the reporter who had written the preceding day's Hugon article, had 'got to wondering' whether Speck *might* also be an XYY male, and had begun telephoning laboratories in the Chicago area (where Speck was being held) in order to find out if anyone had examined Speck's chromosomes. When he had called the laboratory at the Michael Reese Hospital, a Dr Hideo Sato, newly arrived in the USA, and with a less than complete command of English, had taken the call, and misunderstanding Lyon's question, had given the reporter to understand that Speck was indeed an XYY male.

Lyons' mistake was not apparent until late in September of 1968, when Speck's lawyer finally declared that his client had been, after all, an XY male (20). In the meantime, however, the Speck story was repeated widely in the press, and provided an opportunity to discuss the possible implications of the new discovery. Thus, an editorial in the *New York Times* claimed that "The New Genetics shows signs of reviving the old argument as to whether it is nature or nurture that creates a criminal" (21), and asked, "Should such persons (XYY males) be held responsible for their crimes, or treated as victims of conditions for which they are not responsible, on a par with the criminally insane?" (22).

Articles in *Time* and *Newsweek* entitled 'Chromosomes and Crime' and 'Born Bad?' explored the same themes (23, 24), the latter asking, "Can a man be born a criminal? Can his genetic endowment predispose him to bizarre sexual acts and violent attacks on other people?" (25).

From then on, there was to be an almost continuous stream of XYY material in the news. In October, the Hugon trial ended (with a verdict of guilty), and in the same month two further 'XYY' trials opened. One of these, held in Melbourne, Australia, occasioned the following comment in *The Australian*:

Male prisoners who stand in the box in Australian courts in future with a record of criminal aggression now have a one in four chance of getting off, provided they are over six feet tall . . . .
It now comes down to how unlucky a man happens to have been in the biological dice game that went on at the moment of his conception as to whether he will be a normal chromosome holder of the XY ticket, or whether an extra Y chromosome will make him over six feet tall in height and give him an alibi for irrational and aggressive behaviour. It begins to look to the biologists that while the man is in the dock it is the chromosome that is the criminal" (26).

The other, the trial of Sean Farley, for what the *New York Times* termed a 'rape-slaying' (27), prompted a nine page report on the state of knowledge about XYY in the *New York Times* Sunday Magazine (28), which once again wondered what the implications of the 'new biology' were for legal theory and for concepts of human nature, such as 'free will' and 'morality'.

By the early 1970s, there had been at least two 'thriller' films in which the main character is a violent criminal driven by a chromosome abnormality (29), a series of crime novels with an XYY hero (who constantly wrestles with his inner compulsion to commit crimes), and as a spin-off from the novels, a TV series called "The XYY Man" (30). Moreover, a definite picture had emerged of what XYY meant. It was clearly linked to crime, aggression and violence, and XYY males were certainly predisposed, if not inevitably fated, to be aggressive criminals. The excessive aggressiveness of the XYY male, it was suggested, might derive from his 'double maleness'; just as men, with one Y chromosome, were more aggressive than women, who had no Y chromosome, so XYY males, with an extra Y, could be expected to have more of male traits − like aggression. The upshot of all this was said to be that the prevailing intellectual consensus that crime was the product of *social* influences, might be in need of revision, and that theories of 'bad seed' might be revived (31); and, it was suggested, revision of the judicial process might also be required.

3. The Myth about XYY Males prior to Popularisation

There is little doubt that much of this 'folk-knowledge' about XYY males was wrong, that it was full of distortions of what was really known about XYY men, and also contained plain factual errors. For example, the weight of research evidence suggested that XYY men were *not* particularly violent or aggressive; they were likely to be institutionalised for repeated crimes against property rather than against persons, and that these were often of a petty kind. In the institutions, they were *less* violent than other offenders (32). As a group, they were criminologically insignificant, since even if *all* XYY males were criminals, they could not account for more than a tiny proportion of the crimes committed; and in any case, it had not been shown that all XYY males were criminal. Rather, from the meagre population data which had been obtained, it seemed that the institutionalised XYYs constituted a small minority of the XYY population. Therefore, the suggestion that the XYY was a 'criminal chromosome' complement was based on a logical error. The evidence had shown that there was an association between XYY and institutionalisation that was highly significant, statistically; it had not shown that XYY had a high level of *predictive* significance. Finally, the 'double-male' hypothesis had little, if any, demonstrated validity. XYY males with their extra 'male' chromosomes, were not the only chromosomally abnormal group that were over-represented in institutions; XXY males, with an extra 'female' chromosome were also over-represented. In fact, the Carstairs study of Jacobs *et al.* had followed on from a programme of investigations into the prevalence of these chromatin-positive (i.e., with an extra X chromosome) males in institutions (33).

But if the popular image of the XYY male was false, as it was, it is not apparent that this was the fault of 'media sensationalisation'. It seems to me that there are three good reasons for rejecting this claim. Firstly, let us consider the significance of the 'XYY trials'. It is undoubtedly true that the press coverage of these trials was instrumental in drawing public attention to the questions apparently posed by XYY, and that without them, the image of the uncontrollably violent XYY man would not have been transmitted to the public. On logical grounds alone, however, it is easy to see that this image, the 'myth of the XYY man' must have predated both the press coverage and the trials. If not, why was Daniel Hugon subjected to a chromosome test? In 1966, the preparation of this text was lengthy and complicated. There is no reason to suppose that this procedure was part of a routine medical examination, however comprehensive, or that it became relevant because of Hugon's suicide attempt. It seems likely, therefore, that Hugon's chromosomes were tested because someone – perhaps the prison medical officer charged with the examination – had heard about the latest findings on XYY and had a 'hunch' that Hugon fitted the picture. Unfortunately, this is, and must remain, speculative, as the details surrounding the decision to karyotype Hugon have been lost.

Fortunately, however, there is corroborative evidence of a kind. In 1966, before they became aware that XYY might become an issue in the Hugon trial, a group of researchers at Vanderbilt University in Tennessee had asked permission of Gerald Getty to perform a similar test on Richard Speck (34). Amidst the denunciations of Richard Lyons, for irresponsibly spreading the false story that Speck was an XYY male, it is often forgotten that several groups of scientists seemed to have shared Lyons' hunch. One such scientist, the biochemist Mary Telfer, told Lyons that she 'was personally interested in the (Speck) case' because 'if I had to pick anyone who fit the XYY pattern, I would have chosen Mr Speck'; and she was later to claim that she had been able to diagnose Speck as an XYY from descriptions of him in the newspapers (35). The group at Vanderbilt, headed by Eric Engel, had decided that a more empirical procedure was required and obtained a sample of Speck's blood. While the fact that Speck, contrary to their expectations, was an XY male is of some note, so too are the assumptions that they had made which suggested to them that a karyotyping might be valuable.

In his own account of the circumstances surrounding the Speck episode, Engel wrote that

It seems probable that a number of human cytogeneticists wondered at the time of the Chicago carnage whether the notorious suspect did not naturally fall into the YY class of 'supermales' described only months earlier in the British Publications (36).

Engel has more recently commented,

There was at that time (mid-1966) a strong feeling among the cytogeneticists that many an XYY man was bound to be tall, mean and stupid (37).

In other words, the false image of the XYY man was already current among cytogeneticists two years before the Hugon and Speck cases made it public 'knowledge'. The media have given wider circulation to this image, but it was not created by them.

4. The Adequacy of the Sensationalisation Model; Scientists versus Journalists?

The sensationalisation model of the formation of false knowledge about XYY also assumes, implicitly if not explicitly, that popularisation and consequent distortions, occurred at the hands of journalists rather than scientists. On close inspection of the material of popularisation, however, this distinction is hard to maintain. Much of the *work* of communication in the newspaper and magazine articles is done through quotations from scientists. Sometimes these quotations are drawn from reports; thus readers of *New York Times* could note that Professor Jerome Lejeune had told the court in the Hugon trial that

Everything about Hugon's life history . . . indicated that he was doomed to be a sick man from the moment of birth and that this hereditary affliction prevented him from exercising normal responsibility (38).

At other times, the quotations came directly from interviews. Of particular importance here is the use, by scientists, of newspaper interviews as an opportunity to present their more creative, and less empirical interpretations and speculations. Thus, Curt Stern, Professor of Genetics at the University of California, told the *New York Times* that

It could be that it is the interaction of double Y aggressiveness and social environment which can get people more easily into trouble . . . . It is also tempting to speculate that the female sex owes its gentleness to the absence of a Y chromosome and the normal male, his moderate aggressiveness, to the single Y . . . (39).

Dr Kurt Hirschorn, Chief of the Division of Medical Genetics at New York's Mount Sinai Hospital, was also tempted to speculate in the columns of the *New York Times:*

What if the genes for aggression and tallness do exist in the Y? They would have had survival value for the caveman, and there might have been an evolutionary selection for them. But civilised man has been breeding against aggressive genes – aggressive people have been killed in wars, put away in jail, and they don't pass on these genes. The average man has just the single Y. Now, today, we find a man who gets a double dose of Ys; it's understandable that they might well be too much for him to handle – (40)

It would be possible to quote other examples of this sort of speculation. Of course, Stern and Hirschorn made it clear that they *were* speculating, and strictly speaking, did not claim scientific authority for their pronouncements. On the other hand, it seems reasonable to assume, as it must have seemed reasonable to the newspaper readers to assume, that two eminent scientists would not have introduced into a discussion ideas that they believed to be wrong, misleading or irrelevant. Moreover, seen in the context of the articles in which they are situated, these quotations take on a further meaning. Here, as elsewhere, the newspaper deals with a subject that is both complex and uncertain, and perhaps also politically sensitive, by reference to a norm of 'balance'. Often this attempt to maintain balance has an awkward formal air; the *New York Times* editorial of April 23rd 1968, writes that "*Some* scientists now believe that one particular kind of error may predispose *some* men towards criminality" (41), and continues "There is no ground for hasty conclusions. Certainly chromosomes are not the whole story in these cases" (42).

Similarly, *Time* magazine points out that "The theory that a genetic abnormality may predispose a man to antisocial behaviour, including crimes of violence, is deceptively and attractively simple, but will be difficult to prove" (43).

Formally, the media has, by asking the questions which they have chosen about XYY, set the agenda, or constructed a 'frame', in which the discussion can now take place. Within this frame, however, the contribution of scientists such as Stern and Hirschorn assume a special significance. By introducing the themes of 'caveman genetic heritage' and 'double male aggression', themes not present in the original research finding, they link the discussion of the XYY to a tradition of biomedical knowledge about human nature. This tradition, the roots of which have been explored by Durant (44), represents human aggression as the left-overs of our animal heritage; as Durant has shown, it has found expression both within scientific research, as in the notion of 'reptilian rage' (45) and in popular culture – perhaps best expressed in Robert Louis Stevenson's *The Strange Case of Dr. Jekyll and Mr. Hyde*. In their 'speculative' comments Stern, and more obviously Hirschorn, broadly hint that the XYY findings should be seen in the context of this perspective. Indeed, Hirschorn's discussion of the role of history in weeding out 'aggressive genes' is very close to classical Social Darwinism.

Other scientists also played their parts. Alun Griffiths, a psychiatrist employed by the prison service, told viewers of the BBC's *Panorama* that the XYY discovery was 'without hesitation the most important single fact found in the history of criminology' (46), adding that the possession of an extra chromosome was 'of almost volcanic significance'.

5. Scientists as Participants in the Popularisation Process: Intermediate Publications

In addition, the articles which appeared in 'intermediate publications', often written by scientists, were if anything rather more sensationalist than those in the 'popular' press. In *World Medicine*, Dr. Eliot Slater, Director of the Psychiatric Genetics Research Unit at the Maudsley Hospital in London (and Editor-in-Chief of the *British Journal of Psychiatry*) wrote:

It is possible that here might be some biological basis for the remarkable fact, which has puzzled criminologist for decades, that the male is many times more prone to delinquent behaviour than the female. If two Y chromosomes put their possessor in serious danger of antisocial behaviour, perhaps a single one can contribute some of the risk (47).

Slater also described the XYY males as having 'an aggressive tendency' and 'more than a normal tendency to violence' (48). In *Think* magazine, Mary Telfer, a biochemist at the Elwyn Institute in Pennsylvania, wrote a piece entitled 'Are some Criminals Born That Way?' Telfer asked 'Why do some men commit crimes of violence? For some the urge to violence may be inborn – may be traced to something called the Y chromosome'. She went on to describe the XYY male as

. . . The 'supermale'. He is also unusually tall, and somewhat retarded, but appears to be highly, perhaps too highly, sexually motivated . . . . It seems quite possible that in the XYY male, exemplified by Speck, biologists are describing in genetic terms a certain type of defective criminal who has long been explicitly recognised by the forensic psychiatrist (49).

Even environmentalists, like the liberal anthropologist Ashley Montagu were not immune. In a *Psychology Today* article, 'Chromosomes and Crime', he summarised the import of the XYY findings.

Some individuals . . . seem to be driven to their aggressive behaviour as if possessed by a demon. The demon, it would seem, lies in the peculiar nature of the double Y chromosome complement . . . . The Y chromosome, so to speak, seems to possess an elevated aggressiveness potential, whereas the X chromosome seems to possess a high gentleness component. It seems probable that the ordinary quantum of aggressiveness of a normal XY male is derived from his Y chromosome, and that the addition of another Y chromosome presents a double dose of those potencies (50).

Montagu also refers to "the high frequency with which individuals with XYY chromosomes commit crimes of violence" (51).

It is worth noting here that Montagu, together with Max Levitan, published a text book on human genetics within two years of the appearance of this article (52), and that Mary Telfer, shortly before her *Think* piece, had published on XYY in *Science* (53). Slater's position, as a director of psychiatric genetics in what is arguably the most notable of Britain's psychiatric hospitals, has already been mentioned. Thus the identification of rationality with Science, and sensational comment with Media, begins to appear less tenable.

The XYY myth, then, did not simply emerge from the press coverage of the trials; nor did it originate in ignorant distortion. Rather the myth was in being before the trials, and indeed was a precondition for them. While the trials may have occasioned the appearance of the myth in specifically popular publications, part of the work of popularisation, even in these fora, was done by scientists working in genetics. The false image of the XYY male, the notion of the 'supermale' and of the chronically violent XYY men, were endorsed by scientific comment as much as by journalist and editorial comment.

6. The Criminalisation of a Chromosome Abnormality

Patricia Jacobs' *Nature* report of the Carstairs study bore the title 'Aggressive Behaviour, Mental Subnormality and the XYY male' (54). According to Jacobs, an unlikely variation in the distribution of the chromatic-positive males in the institutionalised population (there were more of the rare XXYY males than could be expected from known population frequencies)

... led us to wonder whether an extra Y chromosome predisposes its carriers to unusually aggressive behaviour. We decided that if this were the case, then we might expect an increased frequency of XYY males among those of a violent nature (55).

Jacobs has since regretted the use of the words 'aggressive behaviour' in the title, which suggests an awareness that they were inappropriate (56).

It seems unlikely, however, that Jacobs was unaware of the implication this gave to her research findings, or that she would have resisted a criminological interpretation. The director of the Edinburgh unit in which she worked, W. M. Court Brown, presented the new discoveries to the Royal College of Physicians in a paper entitled 'Genetics and Crime' (57), which began by situating genetic studies of criminality in a tradition within criminology. Court Brown chose as forerunners the Italian School of Criminology, the *Scuola Positiva* of Lombroso and Ferri, which had developed the theory of criminal atavism and suggested that criminals could be recognised by physical 'marks of degeneration'. While refraining from an endorsement of these specific views, Court Brown wrote that "The work of the Italian School raised the question of how much criminal behaviour might be due to a man's inheritance and how much it owes to his environment" (58). He also noted that, currently,

... while we may pay lip service to the possible influence of genetic factors, any suggestion of biological determinism runs counter to the large body of opinion that believes a man, unless he is clearly a moron ... to be able freely to choose his own line of action (59).

Against this large body of opinion, Court Brown set the evidence from the cytogenetic studies conducted at Edinburgh. He was in similarly combative mood before the Leeds meeting of the British Association for the Advancement of Science, in the same year; here he noted that ". . . the influence of many psychiatrists and criminologists has resulted in too narrow a conception of the nature of the well-springs of behaviour with too predominant an accent on environmentalism" (60).

Similar hints were also present in the way in which Price and Whatmore, who conducted psychological and psychiatric tests on the Carstairs XYY men, presented their findings. Price and Whatmore's study, published in a preliminary form in *Nature* in February of 1967 (61), and in more detail in the *British Medical Journal* (62) in the following month, led to much of the first generation of comment on XYY — Slater's *World Medicine* article, for example. Both reports contain a crucial ambiguity as to the *causal* role of the extra Y chromosome. Price and Whatmore rule out other causes of the men's criminality: "There is no predisposing family environment and their criminal activities often start at an age before they are seriously influenced by factors from outside the home" (63). They suggest that "There is no reason to believe these patients would have indulged in crime had it not been for their abnormal personalities" (64).

As to the origins of these abnormal personalities, they believed that 'the extra Y chromosome has *resulted* in a severely disordered personality, and that this disorder has led these men into conflict with the law' (65), (my emphasis).

Later, they write again that the men 'suffered from a severe disorder of personality ... which it is suggested is *due* to the extra Y chromosome' (66), (my emphasis). On the other hand, Price and Whatmore also add the caution that "It is as well to remember, however, that the men we have described may represent a selected group of XYY males, and that others found in the ordinary population ... may show different features" (67).

The point is a good one, but it seems to be in conflict with the chain of causality to which the authors attribute the criminal behaviour of the Carstairs

XYY men. In them, the extra Y was of itself *sufficient* explanation of their behaviour, a clear indication of what the possession of such an extra chromosome meant. The interpretations placed on this ambiguity by Slater, and others, is one way of resolving it, and neither Price and Whatmore, nor Court Brown, took issue with it at the time.

It is perhaps helpful to think of the early history of the presentation of, and the reception of, the XYY data, as one in which the criminological associations of XYY are progressively enriched. Thus, a 1966 leading article in *Lancet* greeted the discovery of 'a fairly specific mental disorder associated with a highly specific lesion' and introduced the term 'The XYY Syndrome' (68). Some months later, a letter to *Lancet* wondered ". . . whether our psychiatrist colleagues could tell us what the chances are of restoring a YY psychopathic individual to full social insight and responsibility . . ." (69).

Early in the following year, an editorial in the *British Medical Journal* headed 'Criminal Behaviour and the Y Chromosome', claimed that "Perhaps these findings may provide a clue to the genetics of at least some forms of aberrant human behaviour" (70).

7. Biology and Crime; The Social Context of Popularisation

By the time the XYY trials began, in 1968, the investment of XYY with criminological significance was well under way. In 1968, interest in XYY, at least as measured by the *Cumulated Index Medicus*, admittedly a crude measure, was taking off. In 1966, there were two articles on XYY listed; in 1967, three, and in 1968, twenty-three. Citations of Jacobs' 1965 paper also leapt from fourteen in 1967 to twenty-six in 1968 and thirty-eight in the following year. It is no coincidence that interest in XYY reaches a peak shortly after public interest in Crime also reaches its peak. In 1968, the regular Gallup Poll question, 'What is the most serious problem facing the country today?' found that most Americans regarded crime to be this problem; and a Harris Poll, in the summer of the same year (the fifth summer in a row of race riots in the USA), found that 81% of those polled believed that Law and Order had already broken down.

The return of Crime as a political issue, and its rapid rise up the political agenda, was reflected in the structure of scientific research. As Durant has noted, scientific interest in aggression, as measured by reference in *Biological*

Abstracts, 'annually jumped by an order of magnitude in a single decade (1965–74) (71), after a long period of quiescence; and Crabtree and Moyer, in a bibliographic review of the field, express the relationship between the political and the scientific agendas neatly: "Along with the explosion of violence, there has been an explosion of literature on the problem of violence" (72).

Thus during the late 1960s and 1970s, there was a renewed and sustained attempt by some biomedical scientists to demonstrate that their expertise could contribute to the solution of the 'nation's gravest problem'. Crucial to this programme was the reconceptualisation of the problem of order into terms which would allow it to be researched upon by the techniques and methodologies of the biomedical sciences. Thus, researchers involved were keen to develop and promulgate a notion of social disorder as caused by deficient individuals. Having identified these individuals, the problem was then to find out what was wrong with them.

Some of the new-found advocates of biological explanations of social disorder were either direct survivors of, or influenced by, earlier attempts at biological contribution to the solution of social problems. Others were more recent 'converts', who saw in the political conjuncture of the time an emerging pattern of opportunity. The upsurge of interest in crime, the apparant failure of programmes based on *social* intervention (73), and the new technological possibilities which were incorporated into proposals for the substitution of *medical* intervention, taken together seemed to hold out the prospect of access to the citadels of social policy-making.

The alarm generated by this project, heightened by the historically specific (but for all that, very real) association between biological explanation and far-right political movements, prevented the 'enterpreneurs' of the biological project in criminology from realising the full potential of their support. To some extent denied the cultural resources of medicine as a humane institution, these entrepreneurs were nevertheless able to draw on other sources of justification. The residues of the previous attempt to biologise criminology still lingered on; as late as the 1920s and 1930s, there was a strong Lombrosian tradition in US criminology (74). Also, popular beliefs about the origins of violence, and popular understanding of the nature of criminality, heavily influenced by the idea of the 'beast within' was well prepared for a biological explanation of crime. Indeed, the relationship between popular and scientific theories of criminal behaviour, historically, has been a reciprocal one, with popular conceptions entering into scientific methodology and then being 'recycled' as scientific facts, to emerge anew in popular knowledge of the criminal. The progress of the term 'psychopath' may be seen as one example of this process; and Lombroso's respect for Italian folk-knowledge about the physiognomy of criminals is another (75).

This feedback process seems to have operated within the short history of XYY. According to Jacobs, some researchers and scientists first learned of the XYY findings via accounts in the popular press (76). In addition, the progress of the 'double male' metaphor into the scientific literature seems to owe something to this mechanism. The double-maleness explanation of the XYY male's elevated levels of aggression was never used by any members of the original Edinburgh research group (nor, indeed, did they refer to a 'syndrome'); and as discussed above, XXY males, with an extra 'female' chromosome, were also over-represented in institutions. Nevertheless, 'double male' and 'supermale' both entered into scientific discourse about XYY males. Furthermore, as several researchers have somewhat ruefully point out, XXY research has attracted much less interest, both from scientists and the general public.

8. The State of Cytogenetics; The Professional and Disciplinary Context of Popularisation

The assimilation of the XYY data to this context thus begins to appear somewhat more explicable; but crucial to this development was the situation of Cytogenetics as a discipline, and of the Edinburgh workers as a research group.

In 1965, human medical cytogenetics had reached something of a crossroads. The discovery of XYY in 1961 had had something of the character of a final piece in a puzzle; the XYY chromosome abnormality was already, on theoretical grounds, believed to be viable, but until Sandberg *et al.*'s 1961 case, no example had been found. Thus the "place" for XYY had in a sense been prepared before its appearance. The early 1960s had been a heroic period, and new technical developments provided cytogenetics research with new tools almost faster than they could be used. It seemed almost incredible that Tijo and Levan had correctly established the human diploid chromosome number as recently as 1956 (77). By 1969, the link between Down's syndrome and trisomy-21 had been discovered, as had the association between inter-sexuality and sex-chromosome abnormalities. Jacobs was personally involved in the finding that Klinefelter's syndrome was related to the XXY chromosome complement, and to the discovery of an XXX 'superfemale'. (Seen in this context Jacobs' assumption that there must be some phenotypic mani-festation of the XYY genotype becomes more explicable. Jacobs *et al.* were accustomed to seeing a close causal link between chromosomal abnormalities and phenotype abnormalities. All the other sex chromosome abnormalities were closely related to abnormal physical and behavioural development). With the Carstairs study, Jacobs *et al.* believed that they had made the most important discovery yet (78).

But, for Jacobs, the technical and cognitive developments in cytogenetics, and the bountiful material provisions available in Edinburgh, with its glori-ously well-equipped laboratory, were not matched by the cultural status of cytogenetics as a scientific discipline. There was no specialised journal for the publication of findings; many of these were therefore published in the *Lancet*, a journal which 'doctors read with their breakfast on Friday morn-ings', according to Jacobs. Until April 1966, the Edinburgh Unit produced its own newsletter, *Human Chromosomes*, which it circulated to co-workers.

Much of the biomedical audience did not really understand what chromo-some were, and, to Jacobs' and Court Brown's considerable disappointment, neither medical nor psychiatric, nor behavioural science workers, seemed interested in the XYY discovery.

The decision to present the results to the Carstairs study in criminological terms must be seen in this light. Cytogenetics seemed to be a marginal sub-speciality within biomedical research. Steven Shapin has suggested that modes of scientific exposition, and in particular the extent to which the language of exposition takes on esoteric or exoteric form, may be causally related to the size and structure of the scientific community. Here, in the absence of a clearly defined or securely institutionalised audience, the Edin-burgh group were attempting to address a heterogeneous medical community. Thus, they were driven towards an expository strategy, and a particular kind of popularisation, which was especially susceptible to sensationalisation.

Thus, Court Brown's presentation of the new discoveries from cytogenetics to the Royal College of Physicians as being in the tradition of Lombroso may be interpreted as bearing two meanings. On the one hand, Court Brown may have been attempting to present a complicated and technical argument, which really necessitated an understanding of the methodology of population cyto-genetics, to an audience that was relatively unsophisticated in these matters. The Lombrosian allusions may therefore have served as a kind of shorthand, whereby Court Brown was able, by reference to a tradition that he believed his audience knew of, to introduce the kind of claim he was making. On the other hand, there may have been an additional message, which hinted broadly that these new discoveries would be of some significance in the professional struggle with environmentalist explanation; if Court Brown himself was hardly involved in this struggle, he may nevertheless have assessed that this kind of 'gloss' on the research findings would make them seem more interest-ing to scientific and medical audiences. Jacobs' allusions to 'Aggressive Behaviour' in her paper had already attracted some attention and this must have suggested a strategy for increasing interest in cytogenetic phenomena (79).

In Bourdieu's terms (80) Jacobs, Court Brown and Price had all made sub-stantial investments of symbolic capital in cytogenetics. Jacobs' investment, in terms of specialised training and the achievement of accreditation and status, is most obvious, but Court Brown, as an epidemiologist presiding over a unit increasingly involved in the development of cytogenetic techniques, and Price, as a psychiatrist attached to that unit, with a developing expertise in the clinical assessment of chromosomally abnormal patients, also had a substantial stake in the continued expansion of the field. The XYY discovery, presented as a key contribution to the study of behaviour, and perhaps even to the understanding of the sources of all criminal behaviour (a suggestion which Court Brown made to the Royal College of Physicians) offered the possibility of moving from an investment strategy of risk-free profits from innovations within accepted limits, to one of more hazardous investment, with the potential for higher profits (81).

The hazards should not be overstated; the kind of claim that Court Brown, Jacobs and Price made was not unfamiliar, or, in a British context, particularly provocative; and, as we have seen, the American market was ripe for 'products' of this nature. The ready acceptance of the posited 'behavioural syndrome' associated with XYY, first by cytogeneticists and then by other groups of biomedical researchers who had turned their attentions to the study of crime, is indicative of this. These others had made their own symbolic investments, and the emerging XYY data offered the opportunity for them to raise the value of their own capital.

Concerns reflected in, and transmitted through the popular media had created the conditions in which the association between XYY and crime could become meaningful; and, this association *was* increasingly represented as being important. From the first months of XYY's career, the possibility that it might have some bearing on the course of a criminal trial had been raised (82); when this possibility was realised in 1968, in the Hugon trial, and raised speculatively in the Speck trial, it then made world news in the terms already set for it in the scientific literature. The journalists did have an interest in a new scientific discovery which was involved in a murder trial, and which had previously been presented as a key finding in the search for the causes of crime; and, as the imperatives of news production dictated, they did have an interest in presenting it as exciting. In this, however, their interests were not so very different from those of the scientist-entrepreneurs who together (although not in concert) worked the XYY data up from knowledge about population cytogenetics into criminological knowledge.

If these two interests were not always entirely complimentary, they did not become opposed until the changing fortunes of the attempts at the medicalisation of deviance (83) began to suggest that crime was no longer a profitable area to invest in; at this point Medical Geneticists, and cytogeneticists, including some who had previously worked on XYY-and-Crime projects, became keen to divest XYY of its criminological associations (84).

9. Conclusion

As we have seen, the content of what came to be scientific knowledge about XYY *was* decisively shaped by the context and conditions of its exposition. This did not occur, however, in the rather narrow fashion which the XYY researchers themselves have (retrospectively) suggested. The 'false image' of' the XYY male, the XYY 'myth', was not created by the ignorant degradation of scientific knowledge; the posited link between XYY and criminality did not arise out of sensational media coverage of the Hugon and Speck trials. Rather, it predated them; this link had been discussed within the cytogenetics community before the trials, and indeed made it possible for the question of chromosomal status to enter into the courtroom. The strategy of exposition to which the XYY researchers, and members of their audience, turned, was at least as significant in the creation of the 'XYY myth' as was the subsequent role of the media.

It seems then, that in their retrospective accounts of the XYY episode, scientific commentators have misrepresented the process of exposition. They have translated it into terms perhaps more suited to a morality play, with a contrast between 'good' science, with purely cognitive interests, and 'bad' media, with corrupt commercial interests. Science is portrayed as rationality in pursuit of truth, while Media is sensation, which leads to error and false-hood. Such an account, in itself something of a modern myth, has a functional aspect. It is not accidental that the 'sensationalisation model', and the idea of a media-created myth was most fully developed during the controversy around the Harvard Medical School screening study. By the mid-1970s, the link between XYY and criminality, which had originally promised to facilitate the expansion of research in this area, had become a positive hindrance, and now posed a threat to the continuation of research. Perhaps then, a recon-struction of the history of the link with criminality, so that the scientific community was seen as having rejected this link from the first, offered a partial way out of this dilemma.

This has some general implications for a theory of scientific exposition and for a consideration of the tales scientists tell about science-media relations. Science, as Bourdieu points out, portrays itself as a " 'kingdom of ends' knowing no other laws than that of the perfect competition of ideas..." (85). In the terms of the Mertonian model, it characterises itself as a community guided by the civilised cultural norms of disinterestedness, scepticism and universalism. As Barnes and Dolby have suggested (86), and as the Harvard case bears out, this self-image can serve as a resource in situations where scientific expertise or autonomy was questioned. Perhaps equally important, however, it can serve as a means whereby scientists may partake of a sense of collective solidarity and identity in the face of specialisation and disciplinary fragmentation. Thus, tales about the media might, by way of providing a contrast, reinforce that sense of identity. By stressing the ways in which the media *fails* to understand scientific knowledge, the special status of that knowledge, and of its producers, is reasserted; and the boundaries which separate scientists from one another seem more trivial than those which separate them from non-scientists.

References

1. S. B. Barnes and R. G. A. Dolby, 'The Scientific Ethos: A Deviant Viewpoint', *European Journal of Sociology* 4 (1970), 3–25.
2. D. R. Pitcher (Psychiatrist), personal communication.
3. S. Kessler and R. H. Moos, 'XYY Chromosome: Premature Conclusions', *Science* 165 (1969),
4. P. A. Jacobs, 'The William Allen Memorial Award Address: Human Population Cytogenetics: The First Twenty-Five Years', *American Journal of Human Genetics* 34 (1982), 689–698.
5. See, for example, B. Davis, 'XYY – The Dangers of Regulating Research by Adverse Publicity', *Harvard Magazine* (October 1976), pp. 26–30; see also J. Green, *The Social Construction of the XYY Syndrome*, unpub. Ph.D. thesis, University of Manchester, 1983.
6. S. Cohen and J. Young (eds.), *The Manufacture of News, Social Problems, Deviance and the Mass Media*, London: Constable, 1981.
7. S. Cohen, *Folk Devils and Moral Panics: The Creation of the Mods and Rockers*, London: MacGibbon and Kee, 1972.
8. A. A. Sandberg, G. F. Koepf, T. Ishihara, and T. S. Hauschka, 'An XYY Human Male', *Lancet* 11 (1961), 488–9.
9. P. A. Jacobs, M. Brunton, M. M. Melville, R. P. Brittan, and W. F. McClement, 'Aggressive Behaviour, Mental Subnormality and the XYY Male', *Nature* 208 (1965), 1351–2.
10. Editorial, 'The XYY Syndrome', *Lancet* 1 (1966), 583.
11. Editorial, 'Criminal Behaviour and the Y Chromosome', *British Medical Journal* 1 (1967), 64–5.
12. Anon, 'Crime Chromosome', *Science News* (18th March, 1967), p. 258.
13. E. Slater, 'Genetics, of Criminals', *World Medicine* (21st March, 1967), pp. 44–5.
14. ' "John Bourne", "Crime and the Psychopath" ', *Crime and Detection* (May 1967), pp. 67–71.
15. J. A. Maxtone-Graham, 'Chromosomes and Crime', *Science Digest* (December 1967), pp. 38–40.
16. Anon, 'Hidden Perils for Some Tall Men', *Times* (28th July 1967).
17. R. Lyons, 'Genetic Abnormality is Linked to Crime', *New York Times* (21st April 1968).
18. R. Lyons, 'Ultimate Speck Appeal may cite Genetic Defect', *New York Times* (22nd April 1968).
19. *Ibid.*
20. Ernest Hook, personal communication, and R. Lyons, personal communication. Speck was revealed to be a 46, XY male in the *Chicago Tribune* on 24th September, 1968.
21. Editorial, 'Nature or Nurture?', *New York Times* (23rd April 1968).
22. *Ibid.*
23. Anon, 'Chromosomes and Crime', *Time* (3rd May, 1968), pp. 45–6.
24. Anon, 'Born Bad?' *Newsweek* (6th May, 1968).
25. *Ibid.*
26. Anon, 'The A-B-C of the X-Y Factor', *The Australian* (11 October 1968).

27. Anon, 'Murder Suspect Pleads Imbalance of Chromosomes', *New York Times* (18th October 1968).
28. R. W. Stock, 'The XYY and the Criminal', *New York Times Magazine* (20th October 1968).
29. 'Twisted Nerve', a National General Pictures Release, produced by George W. George and Frank Granat; and 'Cat O'Nine Tails', an Italian production, shown on US TV on 29th July 1977 (information from Ernest Hook).
30. Kenneth Royce, *The Concrete Boot* and *The Miniatures Frame* (both) St. Albans, Granada, 1977. (By 1982, *The Concrete Boot* had sold 21,000 and *The Miniatures Frame* 19,000 copies in paperback editions.)
31. New York Times, *op. cit.*, 1968, note 21.
32. W. H. Price and P. B. Whatmore, 'Behaviour Disorders and Pattern of Crime among XYY Males Identified at a Maximum Security Hospital', *British Medical Journal* 1 (1967), 533–6.
33. W. M. Court Brown, 'The Study of Human Sex Chromosome Abnormalities with Particular Reference to Intelligence and Behaviour', *The Advancement of Science* 24 (1968), 390–397.
34. E. Engel, 'The Making of an XYY', *American Journal of Mental Deficiency* 77 (1972), 123–7.
35. M. A. Telfer, 'Are Some Criminals Born That Way?', *Think* (Nov–Dec 1968).
36. Engel, *op. cit.*, 1972, note 34.
37. Engel, personal communication.
38. New York Times, *op. cit.*, 1968, note 27.
39. Lyons, *op. cit.*, 1968, note 17.
40. Stock, *op. cit.*, 1968, note 28.
41. New York Times, *op. cit.*, note 21.
42. *Ibid*.
43. Time, *op. cit.*, 1968, note 23.
44. J. Durant, 'The Beast in Man. An Historical Perspective on the Biology of Human Aggression', in P. F. Brain and D. Benton (eds.) *The Biology of Aggression*, The Hague, Alphen aan den Rijn, 1981, pp. 17–46.
45. A. Montagu, 'Reptilian Rage', *The Sciences* (March 1983), pp. 57–9.
46. Panorama – transmitted by the BBC on 29th April 1968.
47. Slater, *op. cit.*, 1967, note 13.
48. *Ibid*.
49. Telfer, *op. cit.*, 1968, note 35.
50. A. Montagu, 'Chromosomes and Crime', *Psychology Today* (October 1968), pp. 43–7.
51. *Ibid*.
52. M. Levitan and A. Montagu, *Textbook of Human Genetics*, New York: Oxford University Press, 1971.
53. M. A. Telfer, D. Baker, G. R. Clark, and C. E. Richardson, 'Incidence of Gross Chromosomal Abnormalities among Tall Criminal American Males', *Science* 159 (1968), 249.
54. Jacobs, *op. cit.*, 1965, note 9.
55. *Ibid*.
56. Jacobs, *op. cit.*, 1982, note 4.

57. W. M. Court Brown, 'Genetics and Crime', *Journal of the Royal College of Physicians* 1 (1967), 311–17.
58. *Ibid.*
59. *Ibid.*
60. Court Brown, *op. cit.*, 1968, note 33.
61. W. H. Price and P. B. Whatmore, 'Criminal Behaviour and the XYY Male', *Nature* 213 (1967), 815.
62. Price and Whatmore, *op. cit.*, 1967, note 32.
63. *Ibid.*
64. *Ibid.*
65. *Ibid.*
66. *Ibid.*
67. *Ibid.*
68. Lancet, *op. cit.*, 1966, note 10.
69. W. Wallace Park, 'The XYY Syndrome', *Lancet* 11 (1966), 1468.
70. British Medical Journal, *op. cit.* (1967), note 11.
71. Durant, *op. cit.*, 1981, note 45.
72. J. M. Crabtree and K. E. Moyer, *Bibliography of Aggressive Behaviour: A Reader's Guide to the Research Literature*, New York: Alan Liss, 1977.
73. J. Harwood, 'Heredity, Environment and the Legitimation of Social Policy', in B. Barnes and S. Shapin (eds.) *Natural Order: Historical Studies of Scientific Culture*, Beverley Hills: Sage, 1979, pp. 231–252.
74. A. R. Lindesmith and Y. Levin, 'The Lombrosian Myth in Criminology', *American Journal of Sociology* 42 (1937), 653–71.
75. M. E. Wolfgang, 'Cesare Lombroso', in H. Mannheim (ed.) *Pioneers in Criminology*, London: Stevens, 1960, pp. 168–227.
76. Jacobs, *op. cit.*, 1982, note 4.
77. M. J. Kotler, 'From 48 to 46: Cytological Technique, Preconception and the Counting of Human Chromosomes', *Bulletin for the History of Medicine* 48 (1974), 465–502.
78. Jacobs, personal communication.
79. Jacobs, *op. cit.*, 1982, note 4, and Jacobs, personal communication.
80. P. Bourdieu, 'The Specificity of the Scientific Field and the Social Conditions of the Progress of Reason', *Social Science Information* 14 (1975), 19–47.
81. *Ibid.*
82. See, for example, Wallace Park, *op. cit.*, 1966, note 71.
83. A serious treatment of these issues is impossible given the limitations of space; but see, as an example of the perception of this process by a veteran campaigner for the medicalisation of deviance, C. R. Jeffrey, 'Criminology as an Interdisciplinary Behavioural Science', *Criminology* 16 (1978), 149–169.
84. For a fuller discussion of this, see Green, *op. cit.*, 1983, note 5.
85. Bourdieu, *op. cit.*, 1975, note 90.
86. Barnes and Dolby, *op. cit.*, 1970, note 1.

SPEAKING OUT ABOUT COMPETITION

An Essay on 'The Double Helix' as Popularisation

EDWARD YOXEN

University of Manchester

Introduction

Popularisation is didactic, in two senses, one obvious, the other more subtle and oblique. On one level it is about the translation of complex and esoteric ideas into the terms of everyday life. On another, it is concerned with the diffusion of images of science which suggest how people might operate as scientists. This paper deals with the latter aspect of popularisation. I shall show that popularisation tends to produce accounts of the activity of science which are highly schematic and incomplete. I shall also argue that under the pressure of structural and cultural change in biology new issues and concerns can be brought into popular discourse, which transform the nature and tenor of writing for the lay public. These claims will be illustrated by reference to James Watson's *The Double Helix*, first published in 1968 and still in print. This book, I shall suggest, was written essentially to popularise a new style of research, to signal its appearance and to propagandise its technical superiority over the classical forms of biological enquiry. It was designed to appeal to student readers, in the hope that they might join the new discipline. Finally, it will be shown that an important effect of this publication has been to make competitive, individualistic, arrogant behaviour by scientists publically admissible and correspondingly to present the work on the double helix as a race.

The research, about which Watson came to write so iconoclastically, was done in the early 1950s. It led to the production of two classic papers, in which a model of the structure of DNA was described and its implications for genetics discussed. The theoretical significance of the double helix has been rehearsed and celebrated to a truly remarkable extent. In no other area

163

Terry Shinn and Richard Whitley (eds.), Expository Science: Forms and Functions of Popularisation. Sociology of the Sciences, Volume IX, 1985, 163–181.
© 1985 *by D. Reidel Publishing Company.*

of contemporary science have the 21st and 30th anniversaries of the publication of a classic paper been the occasion of such adulation. Usually discoveries have to wait for 50 years, for example the splitting of the atom, which was celebrated in 1982, or discoverers 100 years after their death, for example, Darwin's centenary was held in 1983 and Mendel's in 1984. But in the case of the double helix a mere 21 years elapsed, both of the principal scientists were still alive and active in science and took part in the festivities. In 1974 a BBC film was made, which brought Watson together with his erstwhile collaborator, Francis Crick, and *The Times* carried a short piece about molecular biology coming of age (1). The journal *Nature* also produced a special supplement on the double helix, to which Crick and others, but not Watson, contributed brief essays (2). On the cover was a cartoon of the two men sliding helter skelter down a helix, two *enfants terribles* 21 years on. In 1983 *Nature* again took the lead in organising the celebratory rites, with two conferences '30 years of DNA', one in Cambridge, England and the other in Boston, Massachusetts (3).

These two occasions merely represent peaks of interest in a twenty year history of special concern, throughout which the centrality of this work to molecular biology has been constantly emphasised. In effect its significance has been continually restated and re-emphasised as part of a mythology of heroic achievement (4). It is obviously important to ask why this should be so. There are several possible reasons for this particular prominence, but none of them are very satisfying.

Firstly, one might argue that the fact that this work occurred in 1953, at a moment when the field of molecular biology was not crowded, makes it ideally suited as a seminal achievement. Much research *can* be shown to be related to this early and relatively isolated achievement. Such a reconstruction would be true conceptually but not historically, in that several research traditions flowed right past the work on the double helix. To describe the prominence of this discovery in this way, as an act of invention that in itself inaugurated a whole research programme, is not only historically inexact but also begs the question of why molecular biologists should choose to construct the history of the discipline by giving this achievement such attention. Secondly, it could be argued that the elegance and tangibility of the molecular model, compared with say the more recondite notion that bacteria have genes, makes this model much more easily translatable into popular discourse and imagery. It has a real graphic power. Yet even this iconic representation is problematic, as the concepts of sequence hypothesis, genetic coding and semi-conservative replication are every bit as abstruse as the finding that occasionally bacteria reproduce sexually. Thirdly, one might suggest that the appearance of an extraordinary book about the double helix from one of the men involved was the decisive influence in ensuring its lasting popular appeal. This too seems plausible, except that, as I shall show in this paper, Watson's and Crick's achievement was already being popularised as science of historic importance before Watson wrote his book. Indeed one reason why he wrote *The Double Helix* was as a reaction against that. By the mid-1960s Watson knew that his work was of lasting technical importance, but unusually he sought to redefine its meaning, by writing about it in his own way. Indeed it is easier to analyse Watson's motivation in so doing than it is to explain the underlying interest in DNA against which he was reacting.

The Double Helix must rank as one of the more remarkable attempts at popularising the act of scientific investigation ever written, even though the exposition of complex ideas and simple terms is not an obvious concern. For example the mastery of helical diffraction theory by Watson and Crick was crucial to their success, but Watson does virtually nothing to explain what it is. The book sets out instead to counter a myth of simplicity and innocence in science and tacitly to argue for a different image and an ethic for science. All kinds of literary and psychological devices are drawn upon to defend a new realism about competition, aggression, and self-confidence. This, Watson seems to be saying, is how science has to be done, if the fundamental questions in biology are to be laid bare and answered. Its function was to display a canonical example of a new scientific style, with ruthless predation on other fields and other's work, minimal courtesy to supporting colleagues and peers, continual defiance of troublesome data and a positive contempt for traditional intellectual concerns. Written in the mid-1960s when biological research was beginning to take on some of the characteristics of Big Science, it suggests that new ways of working are now the norm, even though in the early 1950s, the period to which *The Double Helix* is limited, the threat to survival came not from ambitious competitors but from a myopic older generation still to be outrun.

The Double Helix From 1953 to 'The Molecular Biology of the Gene'

James Watson was born in Chicago in 1928 (5). He was something of a child prodigy, entering University of Chicago to study zoology at a very early age. He was awarded his Ph.D. at Indiana University in 1950, under the supervision of Salvador Luria, thus being influenced by the so-called phage group. After a period abroad, in Copenhagen and Cambridge on a post-doctoral fellowship, he returned to the United States to work at the California Institute of Technology. In 1956 he moved to Harvard, where he was professor of molecular biology until 1976. Just before *The Double Helix* appeared he also accepted the Directorship of the Cold Spring Harbor Laboratory, where the phage group summer schools had been held, and this institution has, through his efforts in getting grants support for cancer research, increased significantly in size. This post he still holds.

Watson arrived in Cambridge in the autumn of 1951. In the Cavendish Laboratory he met Francis Crick, then a research student. He was however an older man and clearly had some influence, intellectually and socially, upon young Watson. They collaborated over an 18 month period, drawing on the published and unpublished work of a number of other people in the field. This led in April and May of 1953 to the publication of two important papers in *Nature* on the molecular structure of DNA, its implications for an understanding of the mechanism of genetic replication and the basis of hereditary specificity (6).

The initial building of their second, successful model of the molecular structure of DNA was carried out by Watson and Crick at the end of February 1953. It took the form of two helical, phosphate-sugar chains linked together by the hydrogen bonds between complementary bases. The subsequent publication and informal communication of their success to their colleagues and competitors is described in *The Double Helix*. It is covered more fully in Robert Olby's monograph *The Path to The Double Helix* and in Horace Judson's more recent *The Eighth Day of Creation* (7). Both these books, impressive though they are in the kind of scholarly detail they supply, have helped to confirm the central status of the work on DNA, with narratives that either lead up to 1953 or away from it.

Watson's departure for Paris in May 1953, with which *The Double Helix* closes on a revealingly pathetic note, marks the end of one phase of the reception of the DNA structure model. By the end of May 1953, two papers, along with confirmatory work from groups at King's College, London had been published in the leading British scientific journal. The model had been reviewed and approved by those in Britain best able to evaluate its plausibility and an international network of scientific contacts had been alerted to its existence. All this had occurred without serious dissent, although the organic chemists in Cambridge had sarcastically dubbed it in 'W/C model'.

But more than a month passed before any press report of the work appeared. This makes an interesting contrast with the much more rapid reporting of highly publicised achievements of roughly comparable technical importance in the late 1960s, such as the synthesis of viral DNA on a natural template and the isolation of a bacterial gene. These have been discussed elsewhere (8). An example from the 1980s makes an even starker contrast. In 1980 scientists from Geneva announced at a press conference at the Waldorf Hotel in New York that they had succeeded in cloning in bacteria the genes for human interferon, a result of sensational scientific and commercial importance. This was described to the world's press before any article had been accepted for publication in a refereed journal and the scientists concerned were later criticised for this reason (9).

The primary reason for this seeming reticence was the norms of professional conduct in the 1950s which powerfully inhibited publicity-seeking. Similarly the expectations of support were such that scientists felt no pressing need to dramatise their work for a popular audience, at least not immediately. The same is true of their sponsors, the Medical Research Council (MRC) in Crick's case and the National Foundation for Infantile Paralysis in Watson's. Thus the institutional and professional stimuli to such extravagant acts of popularisation were scarcely present in that milieu at that time, nor was an idiom such as 'the secret of life' available to scientists like Watson and Crick as a professionally acceptable device for exciting scientific interest had they wanted to use it. By the 1960s the taboo on allusions to the nature of life had weakened (10).

Also, the links between scientific institutions and journalism were not as developed in the 1950s as they are today. Science journalists were fewer in number, periodicals like *Nature* and *Science* had many fewer pages for the presentation of scientific news and were evidently much less disposed to comment editorially on the significance of scientific discoveries. Magazines like *New Scientist*, able to report rapidly on new events in science, and indeed basing their commercial existence on this ability, had yet to come into existence. One of its precursors, *Discovery*, reported the work, but in the form of an unspectacular article by Crick, in January 1954 (11).

Nevertheless, after a time their work was reported in the newspapers. What I take to be the first notice appeared in the *News Chronicle* on May 12th 1953 (12). The stimulus behind the publicity was a talk in London by Laurence Bragg, head of the Cavendish Laboratory (13). The science editor of the *News Chronicle*, Ritchie Calder, published a front page single-column article, 'Why You Are You: Nearer The Secret Of Life' which reported Watson's and Crick's work, but made no mention of their names, nor those of the King's College group, which had provided corroborative data. The article amounts to a bare minimum for presenting a breakthrough in the chemistry of heredity on the front page of a national daily newspaper. On June 13th 1953 the *New York Times* carried a story of Watson's and Crick's work on an inside page (14). The double helix then eventually found its way into the national press in Britain and America. The reporting was unsensational, and said nothing of the way in which the work had been done.

When the *New York Times* printed its report, Watson was back in America to work at the California Institute of Technology. That summer he attended the Cold Spring Harbor Symposium which was dominated by the group in which Watson had been trained in microbial genetics. Max Delbrück arranged that copies of the initial three papers on DNA structure should be distributed to all those attending and a talk by Watson was added to the programme.

In 1953 Francis Crick prepared two talks for the European Service of the BBC, but when the question of a broadcast on the Home Service came up, Watson vetoed the idea, because 'people he knew might hear it' (15). Even with Bragg's mediation this decision was unchanged and it led to bad feeling. However in 1955 Crick prepared four programmes for the Overseas Service and in 1957 a talk entitled 'Research into nucleic acids' (16). Watson's concern seems to have been that the model might still be shown to be wrong, even though its validity was not in serious question at this time. What had to be grasped generally was its actual relevance to biological research. Crick seems not to have shared Watson's anxieties about explanatory failure and it may be that Crick's greater professional insecurity in the early 1950s led him to think much more about popularisation of a non-controversial kind, only to find such impulses vetoed by Watson.

Gradually the double helix received support from other work, including that on semi-conservative replication by Meselson and Stahl in 1957 and by Kornberg's studies of DNA polymerase at that time. Maurice Wilkins' more exact crystallographic studies of DNA led to minor improvements in the double helical model. Crick's judgement was that by the late 1950s scepticism about the problems of the replication of a double helix was declining. Winstanley's study of the diffusion of Watson's and Crick's work at research, undergraduate, school and popular levels reveals that all the seven textbooks published in 1955–1956 mentioned their work. By 1961 all undergraduate texts that could be located referred to their papers; by 1965 100% of school texts mentioned their work, whereas in the popular literature, more references appeared earlier, although it was again 1965 before they appeared in all texts (17).

By the end of the 1950s not only could one read about DNA in university textbooks, there was much more institutional support for research in molecular biology than there had been ten years earlier. In Cambridge the Medical Research Council opened a lavishly endowed Laboratory of Molecular Biology, where Crick worked, and a group of scientists based there founded the *Journal of Molecular Biology*. Then in October 1962 Watson, Crick and Wilkins were awarded and Nobel prize for work on DNA. In December, when the prizes were actually presented, both the *Sunday Times* and *The Observer* carried long articles on the prize winners (18). The impression one gains from all the reports written by outsiders is that on the basis of freely available evidence Watson and Crick suddenly decided to build a structural model, and the puzzle was consequently soon solved in the early part of 1953. Most reports gave almost no attention to the actual details of what they did. Their work was truncated to the minimal form of an 'achievement', filled only with the content, 'the structure of DNA'.

Even John Kendrew, as someone much closer to them than most commentators, produced a very simple account of what happened.

Jim Watson was a young American, aged only 24 at the time (1953) who had come to work with me at our laboratory in Cambridge on protein structure. It was my loss, but a great good fortune for biology, that Jim really did not take to the protein field, – as he was the first to admit, it was too much like hard work for him – and instead of continuing in it he began to talk to Francis Crick, who was already in our laboratory, about the importance of solving the structure of DNA. They looked at the new X-ray photographs, they wondered about Chargaff's base-pairing rules, they tried out all sorts of models, and the upshot was that in only a few weeks, after one or two false starts they actually solved the whole thing. I would find it very hard to explain just how they did solve it – indeed I think they would too. It is a good example of one of those intuitive jumps which happens in science from time to time. You may call it genius, you may call it inspiration, or what you will (19).

Watson also assisted in his time with the propagation of the conventional, truncated account of the work on the double helix, as for example in his undergraduate textbook, first published in 1965, *The Molecular Biology of the Gene* (20). Thus far, it can be seen, the conventionalised accounts of their work on DNA placed little emphasis on its experiential, as opposed to its cognitive and conceptual aspects. What Watson did in *The Double Helix* was to attempt to bring into the limelight, for purposes about which we can only speculate but which certainly derived from the changing structure and ethos of biology, the actual experience of doing Nobel-prizewinning science at the age of 24 in the Cavendish Laboratory in 1953. In so doing he created an intense controversy about the propriety of his remarks about his colleagues and about his assault on what many scientists took to be the public image of the dedicated scientific worker, whose competitive individualism is held to be regulated by a professional moral code relating to intellectual property rights, priority of discovery, the distribution of scientific results, the operation of a reward system and the social basis of mutual respect.

The Gambit of 'The Double Helix': Arrowsmith Revisited

The Double Helix is to a considerable extent about working with Francis Crick, and any fully adequate account of Watson's motives in writing the book would have to take into consideration how Watson saw his early relationship with him in retrospect and how he thought their respective contributions had come to be judged. Although Watson has sought and enjoyed more institutional and managerial power than Crick and is widely respected as a reviewer of scientific trends and as the director of a major research centre, his reputation as a scientist of continuing originality is not as great as Crick's. This was already the case by the mid 1960s. The book is also about the experience of an American in Europe for the first time. Indeed it is about an exceedingly young man, who already had a Ph.D. at the age of twenty two, with a passion for research but with few social graces, attempting to cope with the culture of the English academic elite. Continually Watson affects the pose of someone for whom research was an occasional pastime, like tennis or the cinema, whilst simultaneously revealing that in fact he cared very much about success. Behind the attempt to emulate the English is a strong commitment to the American way, which involved driving ahead on a very competitive basis. After all, the success with DNA was based on a silent decision to ignore the gentleman's agreement with Bragg to leave the problem alone. Certainly by and large the European reviewers were far less impressed by the tone and message of the book than were those trained in and working in American institutions. For the Europeans Watson's style of research and the way in which he presented himself was just a little too outrageous to be acceptable.

By the mid-**60s,** with the establishment of a secure conceptual framework for molecular **biology** and the solution of some of its fundamental problems, some of the impetus and direction of molecular biology was lost. Some molecular biologists turned their attention to new areas of research, like tumour virology, as in Watson's case, or developmental biology or neuro-chemistry; some turned to the history of the subject. This movement is reflected in the Festschrift for one of the founders of the phage group, Max Delbrück, *Phage and the Origins of Molecular Biology*, of which Watson was a co-editor, which appeared in 1966. The contingent factor of Delbrück's retirement was a stimulus for Watson to turn back to his earlier scientific experience. As one critic has remarked of the contributions to this volume the re-living of shared experience is particularly intense and esoteric (21). Watson's contribution, 'Growing Up in the Phage Group' is very similar to *The Double Helix* in its insensitive tone and self-revealing style.

Watson's first version of his account was completed in January 1966, based on letters that he had sent to his parents, and was called *Lucky Jim*. It was shown to Wilkins and Crick, who both pronounced themselves violently against publication, as well as to friends of Watson's in Cambridge, Massachu-setts, some of whom are said to have taken the same line, some of whom did not. This opposition from Wilkins and Crick deepened as time went on, despite emendations to the text by Watson and the controversy eventually reached the newspapers, through an article in *The Harvard Crimson* (24).

The manuscript was offered to Harvard University Press where Watson's editor was Thomas Wilson. AFter the President of Harvard, Nathan Pusey, ordered the press to discontinue publication in June 1967, the book was transferred to the New York publishing firm, Atheneum, for whom Wilson was then working. At this stage it is said that Wilkins and Crick threatened to bring suit against the publishers. Chapters were offered to *Look, Life* and the *Saturday Evening Post* magazines, whose editors failed however to see the inherent excitement of the book. The *Atlantic Monthly* took a different attitude and excerpts were published there (23). In November 1967 the media attention given to the biochemist Arthur Kornberg in the press persuaded the managers at Atheneum that the demand for the book would be considerable and their initial print order was increased. *The Double Helix* finally appeared, with a quite remarkably forgiving preface by Sir Laurence Bragg that must have served to legitimate some of its comments, in February 1968 (24).

Such a complex book would be remarkably difficult to summarise, and I shall assume in what follows that this need not be done. Suffice it to say that it is Watson's account of his work with Crick on the problem of the molecular structure of DNA from the autumn of 1951 to June 1953, although the book actually covers a slightly longer period in Europe. It is markedly unpleasant to Crick from the notorious opening sentences, 'I have never seen Francis Crick in a modest mood. Perhaps in other company he is that way, but I have never had reason so to judge him. It has nothing to do with his present fame.' It is particularly vicious about Rosalind Franklin, a crystallographer then working at King's College, London. It is about Watson's and Crick's behaviour as scientists vis-à-vis several other research groups, in pursuit of the goal of DNA structure, and concomitant social interactions in Cambridge and elsewhere.

It is also a book which makes a number of statements about the priority and originality of their work, and its relation to that of others, particularly Franklin and Wilkins, and more generally about the support, advice and material assistance that Watson received. This aspect of the book has produced historical work in its own right, which I shall not discuss. In this respect it is a remarkably ungrateful book.

Finally it should be underlined that, to an almost unparalleled extent, it is about the experience of doing research, and not to any great degree about scientific ideas, as creations with a significance of their own. It is therefore intensely personalised. For this reason it is significant that it covers basically the Cambridge period alone and is not Watson's complete scientific auto-biography. It is about the experience of doing research outside America on a fundamental problem in molecular biology and succeeding. The book is conceived out of the psychological legacy of that experience.

Let us now consider how Watson's iconoclastic message was perceived in the press. What follows here can only be a comment on a small sample of the very interesting and varied reviews from 1968, of which 40 are listed in the *Book Review Digest* for that year and of these I have looked at 20. The total number is certainly higher. Also, we are not concerned here with the references and allusions to *The Double Helix* in journalistic, scientific, historical and sociological articles since then, of which there have been many. Whilst its publication in 1968 was a *succès de scandale*, the book has remained in print since them, with repeated printings of the paperback edition from 1970. In 1981 Gunther Stent produced a critical edition of *The Double Helix*, in which the original edition and a selection of reviews were reprinted. Not every scientific autobiography gets that treatment in the author's lifetime.

In 1968 there were fears that it would fracture existing productive working relationships in science and lead to the formation of factions and that it would damage the public image of science. But the balance of scientific opinion, even from the severest critics, was that the existence of such a candid and realistic account was a welcome development. It is also significant that much more attention and thought was given to the manner and style of the book than to its contents, initially at least.

The *New York Times* in mid-February 1968 had carried a series of reports on the controversy at Harvard concerning its publication, which in America eventually took place on 26th February, whilst the British edition appeared in May. On Monday 19th February it was favourably reviewed in that news-paper and received this generous comment: 'This is all drama of a very high order. But the book's real service is to show at last and quite movingly how science is done.' (15) On February 25th the book was reviewed in the *New York Times Book Review* by Robert Merton, who gave it his informed ap-proval as being a realistic account of research in modern science (26).

The reviewer in *Newsweek* on 26th February chose to reproduce an exaggerated version of Watson's account of his career, and made a comment that indicates the hold that Watson's sexist portrayal of Rosalind Franklin was to have.

By hook or by crook, he managed to stay on and became friends with a renegade physicist whose career was apparently at a dead end, the fabulous, stentorian Francis Crick.
Garrulous, womanizer extraordinary, Crick talked louder and faster than anyone else ... while Miss Franklin was a superb experimentalist and a mousy feminist who bristled at male interference with her work (27).

The following month it was reviewed by Jacob Bronowski in *The Nation*, with a characteristically urbane and ironic approach, but in a basically approving way.

James Watson and Francis Crick both enjoy (and I use the verb literally) the reputation of *enfants terribles* among their fellows in biology. Francis Crick likes the stress to be on the word *terrible*, of course, as any Englishman does. But James Watson is a child of America, the culture indifferently of the spoiled child and the child wonder and he has never baulked at the simple art of playing the *enfant* (28).

Bronowski concludes, '. . . this book expresses the open adventure of science; the sense of the future, the high spirits and the rivalry and the guesses right and wrong, the surge of imagination and the test of fact.' In view of Bronowski's reputation as an interpreter of science this seems a remarkably inaccurate and myopic comment on *The Double Helix*.

The *New York Review of Books* chose Sir Peter Medawar as the reviewer, and he produced a piece that is surprisingly justificatory and approving, although he made a few patrician asides. He is careful to mention, however, the structure of earlier results on which the final achievement was based, such as Frederick Griffith's discovery of bacterial transformation. But then having made this point he slowly begins to undermine it by laying out an explanation of Watson's lack of courtesy. 'Scientific understanding is the integral of the curve of learning; science therefore in a sense comprehends its history itself. No Fred, no Jim; that is obvious, at least to scientists and being obvious it is understandable that it should be left unsaid.' (29)

In Erwin Chargaff the editors of *Science* chose as their reviewer someone who is actually mentioned slightingly in *The Doyble Helix*. His work had been of considerable importance to Watson and Crick, and he had already published very acerbic criticism of molecular biology for having usurped the domain of biochemistry, the discipline in which Chargaff had been trained. The review begins in a characteristically sardonic tone.

Unfortunately, I hear it very often said of a scientist, "He's got charisma". What is meant by "charisma" is not easy to say. It seems to refer to some sort of ambrosial body odor: an emanation that can be recognised most easily by the fact that charismatic individuals expect to be paid at least two-ninths more than the rest . . . . But what does one do it two men share one charisma?

This would certainly seem to be the case with the two who popularised base-pairing in DNA and conceived the celebrated structural model that has become the emblem of a new science, molecular biology . . . . The book as a whole testifies, however, to a regrettable degree of strand separation which one would not have thought possible between heavenly twins; for what is Castor without Pollux (30).

Chargaff continues in this vein, with comments on the proximity to the material of gossip columns, 'a sort of molecular Cholly Knickerbocker' and the propriety of publishing such a work in one's own lifetime. It is difficult to know how much allowance to make for Chargaff's wounded pride, for the exaggerations of his particular adjustment to American culture and post-war science and for his delight in performing as a satirist.

Chargaff's review, although it does take up specific issues in the book, such as Watson's unpleasant portrayal of Rosalind Franklin, '. . . the merciless persiflage concerning "Rosy" (not redeemed by a cloying epilogue)', is much more a disquisition of the nature of the contemporary enterprise of research. Using the book as a symbol, Chargaff reacted against Watson's tacit sociological message, that research has developed beyond the stage of elaborate courtesies and a certain studied amateurishness. It has become a far more intense, competitive and predatory enterprise, and, Watson is saying, new recruits to the profession should know that.

The Double Helix was launched at the English market in May 1968, although *New Scientist* had printed a highly approving two-page editorial review on 22nd February on the quality and significance of the book, which is described as 'one of the most valuable and fascinating scientific essays of the centtury' (31). The editor of *Nature* published a similar piece on 18th May 1968, on the phenomenon of Watson's book, beginning with the marked reluctance of any distinguished molecular biologist to act as a reviewer. It gives the impression of considerable tensions building up behind the scenes and the politically revealing question taken up by the article is whether science will suffer.

Are Watson's indiscretions damaging or helpful? And will the book begin a tradition in which there will be a kind of Pepys in every laboratory? As always, the worst fears are unlikely to be realised. Different people will no doubt find different faults in the book, but in the long run, its influence will be beneficial. It can do no harm, for example, to have a frank public discussion of the spur of competitiveness in the pursuit of research. Everybody knows that competition exists and this it is often fierce and sometimes less than open (32).

The review that appeared in *Nature* the following week was thoughtful, and mildly sarcastic.

In this account the desire to reach the treasure before the rival prince (in the case Linus Pauling) seems to have acted on the two researchers with an energising power lying somewhere between those of religion and pharmaceuticals. It is this apparent revelation made all the more radiant by the casualness of its exposure which will perhaps be taken by some scientific readers as testing the limits of frankness far more than some of the tedious and rather imperceptive observations about Cambridge life . . . (33).

Each of these reviews, in *Nature, New Scientist* and *Science* may reasonably be taken as having been read by large numbers of scientists on both sides of the Atlantic. The same would be true of the extended review in *Scientific American* by the distinguished French molecular biologist André Lwoff in July 1968. Here the concern is less with the public image of science and less with the historical novelty of such candour, although these issues are considered, but rather with Watson's behaviour in writing the book, which Lwoff considers rather paternalistically.

On re-examining the book one finds that Jim's objectivity is applied to persons he likes, admires, or respects as it is to crystals or base-pairings. Very few are spared. May God preserve us from such friends. . . . He seems completely unaware of the injuries he inflicts, completely unaware of the harm he can do his friends, to the friends of his friends, to say nothing of those he dislikes. His portrait of Rosalind Franklin is cruel. His remarks concerning the way she dresses and her lack of charm are quite unacceptable. . . . It should be added that Jim's attitude towards "Rosy" as he calls her is far from being unequivocal (34).

The Double Helix then was widely seen as an attack on established notions about how scientists behave; and reactions to the book were essentially shaped by how strongly reviewers felt it necessary to uphold such traditional beliefs, or alternatively to lay them aside in a spirit of candour. This iconoclastic message was combined with an image of molecular biology as exciting, intellectually innovative and self-assured. It made the practice of science in this form attractive to students reading the book. Yet Watson's iconoclasm, generated by the contingencies of his own personality, experience and success, wrought its effects at a time when the social image of science and its portrayal in the media was becoming an important political issue. One would therefore expect to see some attempt made to legitimate or neutralise Watson's message. I believe we can see Medawar's and Bronowski's reviews in this light.

The period of the immediate impact of *The Double Helix* may be concluded somewhat arbitrarily with the *New York Times* magazine article on August 18th 1968, "Says Nobelist James (Double Helix) Watson, 'To Hell with Being Discovered When Youre Dead' " (35), which is made up of much of the biographical and anecdotal information about *The Double Helix* that has been discussed here. The book appears there as a symbolic by-product of the continuing frenzied, driving advance of molecular biology. In particular it is made clear that Watson saw his book as an updated version of Sinclair Lewis' famous novel, *Arrowsmith*, about the dedication of a medical researcher, a book which Watson had read in the 1930s and by which he had been greatly moved.

The production of *The Double Helix* was a gambit, a spectacular move in a game with his peers, concerning the popular image of science. It was inspired partly by the complexities of his relationship with Francis Crick and other scientific mentors, partly by his irritation at the conventional stroke of genius explanations of Nobel prize winning work and partly by his sense that the culture of research was changing. Watson knew that his book was iconoclastic and that it would be controversial but quite simply he followed his instinct for a kind of brutal realism born of a desire for truth-to-experience. In much of his writing the theme of impatience with what is thought of retrospectively as stupidity, either by himself or by others, recurs over and over again. The message of *The Double Helix* could be summed up as, This is what it felt like, it is useless to pretend otherwise, and we won because we were less silly than everyone else. His observations on the moratorium on recombinant DNA research have the same tone and his conclusion — that the signatories of the Berg letter, of which he was one, had made the initial mistake in writing the letter but got first to the right conclusion that regulation was totally unnecessary — was homologous (36). In a sense then Watson's impulses are very subversive in a characteristically American way, since received wisdom can always be attacked. His is a sort of laboratory director's populism, that justifies the articulation of what he believes many others feel but are reluctant to say. *The Double Helix* was the most spectacular instance of this, with Watson speaking for his scientific colleagues, past the guardians of conventional notions of the scientific ethos, directly to the common reader. Molecular biology is *the* way to do research, Watson implies, but it is idle to pretend that is is not very competitive. No wonder then that the early 1950s are also presented as a Golden Age, when people had time to play tennis, go to the cinema and try somehow to make contact with members of the opposite sex.

Interest in *The Double Helix* continues and more recent comments by Watson have only served to underline the theme of competition. Horace Judson elicited this comment from him:

I remarked that some former colleagues say *The Double Helix* exaggerates the competitiveness of science. Watson's manner changed. He bit the words out sharply. "I probably understated it. It is the *dominant motive* (original emphasis) in science. It starts at the beginning; if you publish first, you become a professor first; your future depends on some indication that you can do something by yourself. It's that simple. Competitiveness is very, very dominant. The chief emotion in the field. The second is you have to prove to yourself that you can do it – that's the same thing. You've got to keep doing it; you can't just – once." (37)

There in the bewildering maze of Judson's disquisition on molecular biology is Watson's statement. *The Double Helix* was a tract on competition in science and the constant need to confront it. It was an exemplary tale about how one young American coped with the complexities of English character and culture, by trusting his sense that there was a race in progress and by co-operating with another maverick who shared that view. Watson's most recent comments continue the theme. Although his remarks on the thirtieth anniversary contain fulsome acknowledgement to former patrons and friends and some praise for Rosalind Franklin, whose closeness to the Cricks in what were to be her last months is mentioned, the tone is much the same.

Linus Pauling didn't deserve to get the structure. He really didn't read the literature. And he didn't talk to anyone either. He'd forgotten his own paper with Delbrück which said that a gene should replicate by complementarity. He seems to consider that he should have got the structure because he was so bright, but really he didn't deserve it. . . . But I have no guilt feelings. Both Francis and I were products of a tradition that wanted to solve the problem, right through (38).

Thus the pride of a man, who clearly believes he sees to the heart of the game of science and who has successfully confronted the challenge of having to compete and who equipped himself to win.

Conclusion

In this paper I have tried to address two basic questions, how did *The Double Helix* come to be written and what does the book have to tell us about the sociology of scientific popularisation. As to the first issue, the answer is a combination of individual, psychological and social factors. James Watson set out to challenge the received account because he felt that one more consistent with contemporary scientific mores should be produced. Speaking from a high-level plateau of scientific achievement, he set out didactically to create a new image of scientific dedication in an age of highly competitive endeavour, when one's own lapses could lose one the race. It was his way of telling people how to take science seriously and how to conduct oneself within a set of norms that took competition as a basic fact of life. As to the second issue, clearly I have presented *The Double Helix* as a rather special kind of book. Certainly, it could have emerged from many areas of science today. But by going beyond the limits of conventional popularisation and virtually ignoring the usual task of simplified exposition, it reveals the conventions more clearly. Atypically, it sought to display a style of research and the psychological effects of adopting it. It made clear what much popularisation passes over in silence, that the experience of doing important science now is coloured by the constant external threat of pre-emption and the internal threat of passing myopically over a significant clue.

Notes and References

1. The programme was *The Race for the Double Helix*, in the Horizon series, broadcast on Monday 8 July 1974: see also D. Paterson, 'The Race for the Double Helix – Providence and Personalities', *The Listener* **92** (July 22, 1974), 41–43; P. Vaughan, J. D. Watson, and F. H. C. Crick, 'The Double Helix Re-Visited', *The Listener* **88** (December 14, 1972), 819–21; J. Maddox, 'When only the Uncertainties are Certain', *The Times* (April 25, 1974), 7.
2. F. H. C. Crick, 'The Double Helix: A Personal View', *Nature* **248** (April 26, 1974), 766–9; L. Pauling, 'The Molecular Basis of Biological Specificity', *ibid.*, pp. 769–771; E. Chargaff, 'Building a Tower of Babble', *ibid.*, pp. 776–9; R. C. Olby, 'DNA before Watson-Crick', *ibid.*, pp. 782–5.
3. J. Maddox, 'Thirty Years of DNA', *Nature* **302** (April 14, 1983), 557–8; 'Thirty years of DNA', *Nature* **302** (April 21, 1983), 651–4; P. Newmark, 'Thirty Years of DNA', *Nature* **305** (September 29, 1983), 383–4.

4. E. J. Yoxen, *The Social Impact of Molecular Biology* (Unpub. Ph.D. thesis, Cambridge University, 1978); P. Abir-Am, 'Essay Review: How Scientists View Their Heroes: Some Remarks on the Mechanism of Myth Construction', *Journal of the History of Biology* 15 (1982), 281–315.

5. See J. D. Watson (Biographical notes), *Les Prix Nobel en 1962* (Stockholm: Imprimerie Royale, 1963), pp. 71–73; J. D. Watson, 'Growing up in the Phage Group' in J. Cairns *et al.*, (eds.) *Phage and the Origin of Molecular Biology* (New York: Cold Spring Harbor Laboratory, 1966), pp. 239–245; L. Edson, 'Says Nobelist James (Double Helix) Watson, "To Hell With Being Discovered When You're Dead" '; *New York Times* magazine (August 16, 1968), pp. 26–27, 31–46.

6. J. D. Watson and F. H. C. Crick, 'Molecular Structure of Nucleic Acids: A Structure for Deoxyribose Nucleic Acid', *Nature* 171 (April 25, 1953), 737–8: *idem*, 'Genetical Implications of the Structure of Deoxyribose Nucleic Acid', *Nature* 171 (May 30, 1953), 964–67.

7. R. C. Olby, *The Path to the Double Helix* (London: Macmillan, 1974); H. F. Judson, *The Eighth Day of Creation: Makers of the Revolution in Biology*, New York: Simon and Schuster, 1979.

8. Yoxen, *op. cit.* (note 4 above).

9. S. Andreopoulos, 'Gene Cloning by Press Conference', *New England Journal of Medicine* 302 (March 27, 1980), 743–6.

10. E. J. Yoxen, 'The Meanings of Life', *Trends in Biochemical Sciences* 3 (February 1978), N29–30.

11. F. H. C. Crick, 'The Structure and Function of DNA', *Discovery* 15 (January 1954), 12–17; Crick followed this with an article in *Scientific American* in March 1954. This was the source of the erroneous diagram of DNA, which remained in the textbooks for about fifteen years.

12. R. Calder, 'Why You Are You: Nearer the Secret of Life', *News Chronicle* (May 15, 1953), p. 1.

13. See Yoxen, *op. cit.* (note 4 above).

14. Anon, 'Clue to Chemistry of Heredity Found', *New York Times* (June 13, 1953), p. 17.

15. Crick, *op. cit.* (see note 2 above).

16. This information was obtained for me from the Programme Index of the BBC by Michael Totton, to whom I am grateful.

17. M. Winstanley, 'Assimilation into the Literature of a Critical Advance in Molecular Biology', *Social Studies of Science* 6 (1976), 545–9.

18. Pendennis, 'The Crown Jewel from a Ramshackle Hut', *Observer* (December 9, 1962), p. 10; T. Margerison, 'The Architects of Life', *Sunday Times* Colour Supplement (December 19, 1962), pp. 19–21.

19. J. C. Kendrew, *The Thread of Life; An Introduction to Molecular Biology*, London: G. Bell, 1966. This was based on a BBC television series of the same name.

20. J. D. Watson, *The Molecular Biology of the Gene*, Menlo Park, California: W. A. Benjamin, 1965; revised editions, 1970, 1976.

21. R. C. Lewontin, Review of Cairns *et al.*, *Journal of the History of Biology* 1 (1968), 155–161.

22. Anon, 'Watson's DNA Book Called Inaccurate', *New York Times* (February 17, 1968), p. 27; W. Sullivan, 'The Competition Can Get Personal', *New York Times* Part 4 (February 18, 1968), p. 8.

23. J. D. Watson, 'The Double Helix; The Discovery of the Structure of DNA', *Atlantic Monthly* **221** (January 1968), 77–79; (February 1968), 91–117.

24. In his review in *The Times*, Bragg mentioned that he was asked by someone named in the book to withdraw his preface; 'How a Secret of Life was Discovered', *The Times* (May 16, 1968), p. 13.

25. E. Fremont-Smith, 'How Science is Done', *New York Times* (February 19, 1968), p. 37.

26. R. Merton, 'Making it Scientifically', *New York Times Book Review* (February 18, 1968), p. 8. The title is an allusion to the book by Norman Podhoretz, *Making It*, New York: Random House, 1968, on the alleged guilt of American intellectuals about their wish to succeed.

27. R. A. Sokolov, 'The DNA Story', *Newsweek* (February 26, 1968), pp. 54–5.

28. J. Bronowski, 'Honest Jim and the Tinker Toy Model', *The Nation* **206** (March 18, 1968), 381–2.

29. P. B. Medawar, 'Lucky Jim', *New York Review of Books* **10** (March 28, 1968) 3–5.

30. E. Chargaff, 'A Quick Climb up Mount Olympus', *Science* **159** (March 29, 1968), 1448–9.

31. Anon, 'The Double Helix', *New Scientist* **37** (February 22, 1968), 397–8.

32. J. Maddox, 'Science Intended to be Read as Literature', *Nature* **218** (May 18, 1968), 630–1.

33. J. Hollander, 'Honest Jim and the Double Helix', *Nature* **218** (May 25, 1968), 791–2.

34. A. Lwoff, 'Truth, Truth, What is Truth (About How the Structure of DNA was discovered)?', *Scientific American* **219** (July 1968), 133–8.

35. Edson, *op. cit.* (note 5 above).

36. J. D. Watson and J. Tooze (eds.), *The DNA Story: A Documentary History of Gene Cloning*, San Francisco: Freeman, 1981; for a review see E. J. Yoxen, 'Historical Manipulation', *Radical Science* **14** (1984), 150–5.

37. Judson, *op. cit.*, 194–5 (see note 7 above).

38. See 'Thirty Years of DNA', *Nature* **302** (April 21, 1983), 653–4.

POPULARIZATION AND SCIENTIFIC CONTROVERSY

The Case of the Theory of Relativity in France

MICHEL BIEZUNSKI

1 Boulevard du Temple, Paris 75003

The Best Moment to Study Popularization

The novelty of a scientific revolution is marked by the absence of consensus among the scientific community. A new perspective is not accepted immediately: there is the time of debate. It can last from several months to several decades. The question of the exposition of the theory during that period is not a trivial one. When there is no consensus, the usual scheme of popularization cannot be applied: it is no longer a neutral means of transmission of knowledge: popularization becomes a part of the struggle to make the new ideas accepted. In most cases this process is limited to scientific circles. Nevertheless, it sometimes happens that the debates also take place among the public at large. In such a context, what is at stake in popularization is revealed with more evidence. This has been the case with Einstein's theory of relativity.

Popularization is usually considered as a positive means of transmitting knowledge from those knowing something to those knowing less. The subsequent problem is then: how can one express in simple form scientific ideas or results in order to be understood by the greatest possible audience?

Perhaps this scheme of "translatability" works in a "normal" situation where scientists have made a "good" discovery and want to communicate it to the widest possible public. But it does not work if the discovery is not considered to be a good one by the majority of the scientific community. Yet the activity of popularization subsists and may encompass something else.

When I started to work on the reception of the theory of relativity in France, I thought the study of the texts of popularization could explain the many errors and misunderstandings concerning Einstein's theories and find the origin of the so-called paradoxes. But I discovered something very

Terry Shinn and Richard Whitley (eds.), Expository Science: Forms and Functions of Popularisation. Sociology of the Sciences, Volume IX, 1985, 183–194.

different. The definition of popularization as a simple transmission of knowledge from scientists to the lay public had to be altered.

The Theory of Relativity: A Unique Case

Nowadays the special theory of relativity is considered a part of "physics orthodoxy" and is seen as a basic theory by a majority of physicists. It is viewed as a classic work and integrated with general knowledge. But this has not always been true. It took a long time — almost half a century — for the theory, often considered as "hazardous metaphysical speculations", to become recognized by the majority of working physicists.

Simultaneously, for laymen, the theory of relativity was covered by a mythical veil: because of its fantastic consequences, it seemed very unlikely. "One must be a genius to understand Einstein", went the legend. This reputation originated in fact within the scientific community itself. In spite of the support of the major physicists of the twenties, the majority of their colleagues considered it too removed from their previous knowledge to become motivated enough to spend time studying it. The issue of incomprehensibility was a key, and was used as an argument against the theories. Attention has to be paid to this point, considered not as a fact, but as a problematic question in itself. It has to deal with popularization, as well as with the reception of the theory among the scientific community.

The corpus I used is centered on Einstein's visit to Paris. It lasted two weeks, from March 28 to April 10, 1922. Einstein came for scientific exchanges, because Langevin — his main follower in France — worried about the gap between the development of modern physics and the delay taken in the introduction of these new ideas in France.

Science Becomes Fashionable

Einstein's visit made a sensation. Relativity was in fashion. The newspapers were filled with photographs, anecdotes, cartoons, controversial opinions and popularization articles on Einstein and the theories of relativity. His visit was seen, by some newspapers, as a matter of political scandal, because the boycott of German science was still on (it lasted from the end of the First World War until 1926).

The questions raised by Einstein's theories created great excitement. By their very content, the issues of time and the finitude of the universe were caught up in "up to date" preoccupations; these were also found in literature and art. This situation has to be related to the post-war atmosphere. It was considered a necessity to have a cultural "breath of fresh air" after all the suffering caused by the war.

People felt excited by the fact that agreement had not been reached within the scientific community. This did not happen very frequently and was an event in itself. Science, still influenced during that period by the scientistic doctrine, was expected to produce certainties. The experimental method, in the form propounded by Claude Bernard, appeared as a "dogma" that was to overthrow religious ones. This reason explains why statements in the press saying that physicists themselves were unable to understand modern physics could have appeared as something puzzling in the public's eyes. For example, a physicist, who remained anonymous, said in an interview with a journalist (1):

I would certainly have understood Einstein (. . .) if Einstein had expressed himself in the international language of scientists, i.e., by means of a blackboard and a piece of chalk. But Einstein didn't want to use any formulas, because, by expressing himself in a foreign language, he wanted to be understood by journalists, the 'gens du monde' (fashionable society) and '*polytechniciens*'. Thus, he came among his own but they didn't recognize him.

This statement can be interpreted in two ways. At first sight, it can be seen as a rejection of Einstein and his ideas for the reason that he didn't behave the way he should have. On another level, this represents an example of a physicist betraying in a mass-circulation newspaper his own ignorance of contemporary physics. This second point is the most amazing, albeit involuntary.

Order was troubled in that "everybody" (2) wanted to know what Einstein's theories were about. But there was a problem: a scientific controversy was going on among the community, and not every scientist was willing to face the challenge of the public: the credibility of science was at stake. The public could see not only that there was no scientific agreement, but also that the arguments used by scientists to fight ideas were not always noble and intelligent. Scientists themselves were considered to be subject to political or cultural contingencies. Scientific truth was questioned, as well as scientific practice.

Scientific Disagreements

Scientists' reactions towards relativity were very diverse, and can be placed on a continuum between full agreement and full disagreement. One can nevertheless distinguish four general characteristic attitudes:

— The first was that of enthusiastic, and often active, support. That was the case, for example of Paul Langevin. But as a physicist, he remained an exception along with Jean Becquerel and a few others. The main followers of the theory of relativity were mostly mathematicians or mathematical physicists, Elie Cartan and Emile Borel for example. Langevin's lectures at the Collège de France, however, were followed by only a handful of scientists, the majority remaining outside of his influence.

— Neutrality represented the second type of attitude, consisting in weighing arguments for and against the new ideas. Such was the position of Paul Painlevé, a prominent mathematician very influential because of his major political role. He had been Prime Minister during the First World War and was to become Prime Minister again in 1924. The opinion he expressed in one of the most widely-read newspapers, *Le Petit Parisien* (in the April 1, 1922 issue) can be summarized as follows: Einstein's theories represent a major challenge for scientists. They have to be seriously taken into account, and with all the attention they merit. But one has to be careful and not adopt them too quickly.

— The third attitude was that of active ignorance. Some scientists were simply not interested. They did not see why they had to change their methods, their way of thinking. They were trained in the classical tradition which appeared to them as a solid construction. Although this attitude might have been the major one, no professional trace remains, due to the fact that they had nothing specific to say . . . except in the newspapers of course. The atmosphere of the time can be reconstituted from the newspapers' material.

— The 4th attitude was that of hostility. E. Guillaume, for example, came specially from Switzerland to Paris to exchange arguments with Einstein. He refused to admit that the absolute time of classical mechanics should be abandoned, and proposed to consider a relative speed of light instead. Other opponents didn't present such sophisticated arguments. Henri Bouasse, a distinguished physics professor, defended "laboratory physics" against "metaphysical speculation" (3). Einstein's theory was considered to be an hallucination by C. Cornelissen, who wrote a very violent pamphlet with anti-Semitic accents (4).

Even the experimental records, supposedly capable of settling the quarrel, were interpreted in quite different ways (5). It was not possible to try to make people believe in the possibility of any "objective" point of view in such a troubled period.

Attitudes Towards Popularization Reflect the Same Disagreements

The four above-mentioned attitudes had an effect on how people conceived the possibility of popularization of the theory of relativity.

Popularization articles were written by scientists committed to Einstein's theories. During Einstein's visit, Langevin gave a public lecture for students that was attended by more than 1,000. His long paper won enthusiastic support from the audience. The text, published one month later (6), remains a very good example of popularization (which could even still be used now, especially concerning the special theory).

Painlevé's attitude towards popularization reflected, on another level, the ambiguities he expressed about the scientific value of the theory. He wrote in *Le Petit Parisien* (7):

It would be unjust to consider with contempt the passionate interest raised, in all milieus, by the theory of relativity; even when it appears in a somewhat turbulent form, it responds to the most noble instinct of humanity, its anguish in face of the unknown.

But Painlevé's favorable opinion to large diffusion of new ideas was tempered by this statement

When doctrine is as difficult to penetrate as Einstein's, those who adopt it by enthusiasm risk being less attracted by the profound truth it contains than by the errors of interpretation that it could produce. It is like a wine that is too strong, and which befuddles those brains insufficiently trained by severe discipline.

Painlevé's attitude toward popularization was therefore rather ambiguous. On the one hand, he understood that people could be interested by Einstein's theories. On the other hand, he warned them against possible abuses, in a paternalistic and reassuring manner, that suited a great scientist and former Prime Minister. The quoted sentences constituted the introduction to an article in which Painlevé described the broad outlines of the life and works of Albert Einstein. A few days later, a journalist replied to him in *Le Figaro* (8):

I read with great interest a remarkable article by M. Painlevé. It seemed to me that the prominent mathematician wanted to make us feel that laymen have to abandon hope of being initiated to the sublime hypotheses of the master.

I thus conclude that these theories have not yet been able to be applied to any tangible phenomenon, that they float far above us in the irreality of abstractions and that later only our nephews will see them applied to concrete uses.

I also understood that there is no longer any ether, which will certainly suppress the etheromaniacs. I did not understand anything else. This is not enough to be invited for dinner.

This reply to Painlevé is interesting because it gives an idea of the impact produced by such an article. The ambiguity of Painlevé's attitude towards the theory influenced his attitude towards popularization. This statement may seem obvious, but texts expressing this possibility of popularizing so clearly are rather infrequent.

The attitude of the opponents of the theory also found an echo in what they say about popularization. Bouasse, for example, considered the theory to be incomprehensible for physicists. This prevented any possibility of popularization for a larger public (9): "In the end we, the laboratory physicists, will have the last word: we accept the theories that are comfortable for us. We refuse those we cannot understand and, for that reason, are useless."

But the most interesting phenomenon was the side-effect produced by the indifference ("active ignorance") of the majority of physicists towards new science. It makes popularizers face a delicate situation: they were not able to fulfill their task, because they did not find the sources. It was most embarrassing for them because of the multiple signs of public interest. Many journalists thus described what they saw happening before their eyes, and tried to find explanations of that situation.

Consider the following example (10):

I do not want to obtain an advantage from it. But I didn't understand anything about Einstein's theories. I must admit that I did not listen to him; I have only read articles of competent people who, perhaps, did not understand much more of them.

Some popularizers found they had to explain what they usually meant by popularization. For example one can read, in an article published in *L'Ere nouvelle* (11):

It is somewhat presumptuous – and ridiculous – to pretend, as an unfortunate journalist, to possess and explain Einstein's system.

Nonetheless, the average public, which also is not familiar with transcendental mathematics, likes to find in a newspaper an indication, a note, a hint, something superficial but precise, which helps them to not seem too poorly informed when these problems are discussed in their presence.

This "confession" is particularly interesting because it reveals the conception of popularization of a popularizer. What was important for him was not for the public to be informed, but to seem informed in order to talk. This implied that the public accepted the renunciation of access of scientific knowledge, considered almost sacred, or at least the private property of the élite.

The interest of the majority of scientists was the same. Because they did not see any profit in studying these strange ideas, it was important for them, in order to keep their special positions as scientists, to maintain the gap relative to the laymen's level of knowledge. For that reason, popularization was not a means of gaining knowledge (one does not become a scientist by just reading popularization articles in the daily press – or even in the scientific popularization press). On the contrary, popularizers perceived their role as preserving a certain kind of order troubled in a period of scientific revolution.

This can be illustrated by the following two examples:

I declare being totally unable to get a personal idea of the value of Einstein's theories. The kind of questions he is dealing with are infinitely beyond my skills and don't interest me. But it is undeniable that very elevated minds are concerned with them (12).

We believe in science and we contemptuously maintain that outside of it there is no metaphysics, no philosophy. We do not always understand it, but we know that we could do so and this is enough. (. . .) Einstein speaks and we accept not knowing what he is speaking about, as long as Mr. Langevin and Mr. Borel assure us that it is true (13).

This order is not exactly social order, because the different categories cannot be distinguished simply by their social class in an economic scheme. It can be rather called a "socio-epistemological order", in that it differentiates categories according to the kind of relationship they have with knowledge.

Thus, the main preoccupation for popularization is not to make new ideas known, but to use any possible means to maintain this order.

Science as an Explicative Process

Maintaining the order of the hierarchy to the access of knowledge is valuable for the social standing of scientists, but can be a brake on the advancement of science.

This means that attitudes towards popularization have direct consequences for attitudes towards science. The lack of interest shown by some scientists spares them the effort of questioning their theoretical bases and prevents any kinds of popularization. Thus, the consequence of this situation is an attempt to "retain" knowledge. This is the opposite of the vision of science as being motivated by the will to knowledge. The philosopher Emile Meyerson (14) opposes "science for knowledge" to "science for action" and related the second term to the positivist interpretation of science, where searching for laws describing phenomena leads to a utilitarian point of view. In his major book *De l'Explication des Sciences* (15), he states that explanation is located in the very heart of scientific activity. Explanation constitutes the source of rationality. Science is then acted upon first of all by curiosity, the desire of knowing.

And, from this point of view, this is exactly the same motivation that leads anybody to read popularization articles. The public of popularization is composed of people who want to know more about nature. Within that perspective, there is a similarity between science and popularization.

But there is something else which constitutes the distinction. It is the question: what does the desire of knowing become? When a scientist discovers a new phenomenon or when he formulates a new explanatory theory, he is fully conscious, at that moment, of the immensity of the things he does not know. That's true, of course, even if he is not discovering anything! It is like the construction of the polders in the Netherlands: the sea recedes, but is still there; one can see it and the Netherlands would not be the Netherlands without the sea. Scientists can support the existence of the "ocean" of the unknown, because they live from it.

The Two Barriers

In the struggle for popularizing the theory of relativity, there are not only two "opposite camps": scientists and the lay public. These categories are not distinguishable by the quantity of knowledge they possess – a plumber also possesses a part of knowledge – but by the way they cope with their desire of knowing.

From this point of view, it appears that there are not two categories, but three: scientists, the ignorant and a third category which is referred to in French as "les gens du monde", or "fashionable society", and which represented an influential group in France in the early 1920's. This category is satisfied with the awareness of not knowing. It can be characterized by its art of using language: these people talk and write a lot. Journalists and popularizers are included in this category: it is not their job to know everything. But they must be able to talk about any subject.

Thus the question here is no longer that of knowing, but of making others think one knows. The "gens du monde" felt comfortable in sharing with others a common position of not knowing. In an article, probably written by the essayist Julien Benda (16), one can read:

It seems in such a case that the mutual activity of being up to date, and the encouragement we give each other are like a revenge for the force abdication from our knowledge. We have less remorse in admitting this when we feel that we share it with a great number of people; we will even come to experience a strange feeling of satisfaction from contemplating crowds united with us, in the adoration of an idol incomprehensible to all of us.

There is thus a secondary advantage to the non-accessibility to knowledge.

Scientists were fully conscious of this fact, especially those who did not want to consider the theory of relativity. This explains why one finds in the press so many statements qualifying every man or woman interested by Einstein's theories as "snobbish". This opinion was sufficient to reject the desire expressed by the "gens du monde" for knowing what was going on in the area of physics.

Finally, the credibility of science was at stake. It is not the fact that theories necessarily follow one another which disorients people, but rather the high visibility of the differences dividing the scientific community. Scientism was the target, in the sense of being the affirmation of the infallibility of science, of being the possession of a truth able to destroy religious truths. The fact that epistemological questions were publicly discussed weakened the force of the dogma. In this manner, Einstein's theory introduced a critical dimension into the very heart of physics.

The "result" of the struggle was the following. Attempts were made, on the one hand, to keep the order established at a socio-epistemological level. On the other hand, accepting the revolutionary ideas expressed in physics was a necessary condition for the development of science in France. It is difficult to precisely establish the winner. Scientism was actually on the decline as an ideology, but science was to become recognized as a fully professional activity. France was absent from the new challenge of the mid-1920s and 1930s, quantum physics. Perhaps this could be related to the choices made concerning Einstein's theories – considered as revolutionary physics – among the majority of the scientific community in France. Popularization was a crucial point at the very heart of the debate.

Notes and References

1. J'aurais sans doute compris Einstein, me dit ce physicien, si Einstein s'était exprimé dans le langage international des savants, c'est-à-dire par le truchement d'un tableau noir et d'un morceau de craie. Mais Einstein n'a pas voulu employer de formules, car il a voulu, s'exprimant dans une langue qui n'est pas la sienne, se faire entendre des journalistes, des gens du monde et des polytechniciens . . . . Ainsi, il est venu parmi les siens, et les siens ne l'ont pas reconnu." G. de la Fouchardière: 'Relativement', *L'Oeuvre* (2 avril 1922), p. 2.
2. By "everybody" I refer to the term frequently used in the newspapers to qualify the public interested by Einstein's theories. In fact, it represents only a certain category of people, "les gens du monde", whose characteristics will be developed later in the text.
3. H. Bouasse, *La question préalable contre la théorie d'Einstein*, Paris: Librairie A. Blanchard, 1923.
4. Christian Cornelissen: *Les Hallucinations des Einsteiniens ou les Erreurs de méthode chez les Physiciens Mathématiciens*, Paris: Librairie A. Blanchard, 1923.
5. The discussion held during the April 3, 1922 session of the Académie des Sciences was over an experiment by Pérot on the gravitational redshift of solar metals. Very different comments were made on the value of confirmation of this experiment.
6. Paul Langevin: 'L'aspect général de la théorie de la relativité', *Bulletin scientifique des Étudiants de Paris*, no. 2 (avril–mai 1922), 2–22.
7. "Il serait d'ailleurs injuste de traiter avec dédain l'intérêt passionné qu'excite, dans tous les milieux, la théorie de la *relativité*, même quand il se manifeste sous une forme un peu turbulente, il répond au plus noble instinct de l'humanité, à son tourment de l'inconnu. Mais quand une doctrine est aussi difficile à pénétrer que celle d'Einstein, ceux qui l'adoptent d'enthousiasme risquent d'être moins attirés par les vérités profondes qu'elle recèle que par les erreurs d'interprétation auxquelles elle prête. Elle est comme un vin trop fort, qui grise les cerveaux que n'a pas entraînés suffisamment une sévère discipline." Paul Painlevé, 'Einstein', *Le Petit Parisien* (1er avril 1922).

8. "J'ai lu avec attention un remarquable article de M. Painlevé. Il m'a semblé que l'éminent mathématicien se proposait de nous y faire sentir que le vulgaire doit renoncer à l'espoir d'être initié aux sublimes hypothèses du maître.

   J'en conclus que ces théories n'ont pu encore être appliquées à aucun phénomène tangible, qu'elles planent bien au-dessus de nous dans l'irréalité des abstractions et que plus tard seulement nos neveux les verront appliquer à des usages concrets.

   "J'ai compris aussi qu'il n'y avait plus d'éther, ce qui supprimera sans doute les éthéromanes. Je n'ai pas compris autre chose. C'est insuffisant pour être invité à dîner." Janot, 'Notes d'un Parisien', *Le Figaro* (6 avril 1922), p. 1.

9. "*En définitive nous, les physiciens de laboratoire, aurons le denier mot*: nous acceptons les théories qui nous sont commodes; nous refusons celles que nous ne pouvons comprendre et qui par cela même nous sont inutiles." H. Bouasse, *La question préalable contre la théorie d'Einstein, op. cit.*

10. "Ce n'est pas pour me vanter: mais je n'ai rien compris aux théories d'Einstein. Il faut dire que je n'ai point entendu Einstein et que j'ai seulement lu les articles des gens compétents qui, sans doute, n'y avaient pas compris advantage." V. Snell, 'Oiseaux de nuit', *La Lanterne* (4 avril 1922).

11. "Il y a quelque outrecuidance − et quelque ridicule − de la part d'un malheureux journaliste, à prétendre posséder et expliquer le système d'Einstein.

    "Pourtant, le moyen public qui, lui non plus, n'est guère familier avec les mathématiques transcendantales, aime bien à trouver dans un journal une indication, une note, une fiche, quelque chose de superficiel, certes, mais de précis tout de même, qui l'aide à ne pas avoir l'air trop mal informé quand on agite devant lui ces problèmes vertigineux." Milliardet, 'Pour comprendre Einstein − Qu'est-ce que le temps? Qu'est-ce que l'espace?', *L'Ere nouvelle* (30 mars 1922), p. 1.

12. "Je déclare être complètement hors d'état de me faire une idée personnelle sur la valeur des théories d'Einstein. Le genre de problèmes où il s'évertue est infiniment au-dessus de ma compétence et ne m'intéresse pas. Mais il ne saurait être contesté que de très hauts esprits s'y évertuent." André Lichtenberger, 'Einstein à Paris', *La Victoire* (28 mars 1922).

13. "Nous croyons en la science et nous professons dédaigneusement qu'il n'y a ni métaphysique, ni philosophie en dehors d'elle. Nous ne la comprenons pas toujours mais nous savons que nous la pourrions comprendre et cela suffit. (. . .) Einstein parle et nous supportons de ne pas savoir ce qu'il dit pourvu que MM. Langevin et Borel nous assurent que c'est vrai." Gonzague Truc, 'La Religion de la Science', *La Grande Revue* **26** no. 4 (avril 1922), pp. 315−317.

14. Emile Meyerson, Lublin, 1859 − Paris, 1933 played a major role in the debate over Einstein's theory of relativity. His book, *La déduction relativiste*, Paris: Payot, 1925, provoked reactions: Einstein was very favorable (see A. Einstein: 'A propos de la déduction relativiste de M. Emile Meyerson', *Revue philosophique*, 1928, CV, 161−166) whereas Bachelard wrote a book aimed at refuting his arguments (see G. Bachelard, *La Valeur inductive de la théorie de la relativité*, Paris: Vrin, 1928.

15. Emile Meyerson, *De l'explication dans les Sciences*, Paris: Payot, 1921.

16. This article entitled "Snobisme nouveau" was published in *Le Temps* (April 7, 1922), p. 1. It is signed J. B. The reasons that lead me to think that it is Julien Benda is that he published in *Le Gaulois* (October 28, 1921), an article entitled 'Einstein et les salons', which is about the same kind of subject and in the same

style as the article quoted. "Il semble que dans un cas semblable, l'entraînement mutuel à se mettre au ton du jour, l'encouragement que l'on se donne les uns aux autres soient comme une revanche sur l'abdication forcée de notre ignorance. Nous avons moins de remords à avouer celle-ci lorsque nous la sentons partagée par un grand nombre de personnes; nous finirons même par goûter une étrange satisfaction à contempler des foules entières qui s'unissent avec nous, dans l'adoration d'une idole incompréhensible pour tous."

THE CATHEDRAL OF FRENCH SCIENCE

The Early Years of the 'Palais de la Découverte'

JACQUELINE EIDELMAN

Sociologie de l'Éducation, CNRS, Paris

> It will be very pleasing and, at the same time, a great work of education and propaganda.
>
> J. PERRIN, 1935
> (on the future *Palais de la Découverte*)

> One rainy day about noon, a man, his wife and their two children enter the Palais de la Découverte. It's raining and the Palais seems a cozy place to have a quiet lunch. He has his provisions in a shopping bag. Having arrived at the rotunda, he looks around for a long time, goes out, and says to the attendant in the clock-room: "look after my food; one does not eat in a cathedral".
>
> A. LEVEILLE, 1937
> (an anecdote related during a lecture).

The *Palais de la Découverte* was conceived by a group of innovative scientists concerned with the organization of research in France between the two World Wars. It was inaugurated on May 24, 1937, in the context of the *Exposition Internationale des Arts et des Techniques dans la Vie Moderne* (referred to as the Universal Exhibition of 1937), which was held in Paris from May until November of that year. The *Palais* was more the main-spring of an effort to legitimate the power of French science than a vehicle for the diffusion of scientific culture or for a "sharing of knowledge". A modernistic phantasmagoria based on a popular representation of laboratory work and anchored to the dominant epistemological bias of the French scientific community,

195

Terry Shinn and Richard Whitley (eds.), Expository Science: Forms and Functions of Popularisation. Sociology of the Sciences, Volume IX, 1985, 195–207.
© 1985 *by D. Reidel Publishing Company.*

the spectacle of discovery to which J. Perrin invited the *Palais*'s visitors was
to assure the museum's success, attesting thereby to the existence of a consensus with respect to the scientific enterprise.

Here we seek to shed some light on the genesis of this science museum for
which the Universal Exhibition of 1937 provided the original backdrop and
ideological references, suggesting that science then was still a part of humanist
culture.

I. The Strategy of the Science Museum

The goal of the group of scientists (led by J. Perrin and P. Langevin) that
guided the promotion of French science was to get the state to undertake the
development of research, together with the institutional reforms necessary
to that end; in the words of Perrin, they wanted "to have science appointed
to the councils of government" (1). One has to distinguish two periods in
this "crusade" directed at the political class. The first, 1901–1935, is characterized by a gradual increase of state participation in the financing of research
(and a decrease in patronage) as well as the creation of a network of institutions, the initial stages in the organization of research. The second period,
from June, 1936, is characterized by the unification of this institutional network under the aegis of a central body (the *Centre National de la Recherche
Scientifique*) and by the creation of a suitable budget (very much greater than
the government subsidies before the advent of the *Front Populaire*) (1b). In
the transition period between these two eras, at a time when the effects of
the crisis of 1929 were making themselves felt in France, the prospect of a
Universal Exhibition in Paris furnished Perrin with an opportunity to address
himself directly to public opinion.

Thus public opinion, both "acclamatory" and "enlightened" (2), will be
required as the source of legitimacy of scientists' undertakings. Therefore
these scientists anchor their own strategy of legitimation simultaneously in
two antagonistic ideas of democracy (Rousseau's and Encyclopédistes'), or, to
transpose into the 1930's context, of socialism (either "mystical" or "scholarly" (2)), in which the pedagogical mission plays the part of the conciliator.

The political will behind the science museum's creation expressed itself
in a demonstration of the legitimacy of French science. Seeking both to
avoid criticism and garner public approval, the organizers of the *Palais de la
Découverte* presented a picture of science as incontrovertible knowledge. At
one with the majority view in the French scientific community and with a

popular notion of discovery, the keystone of their pedagogical strategy was to be the production of an epistemological bias that gave pre-eminence to experiment over theory in deciding what was to count as a discovery (3). One of the by-products of this strategy was to be the legitimation by the consensus of scientific opinion of the spectacular science exhibition.

II. "The Palais de la Découverte will be one of the Exhibition's Highlights" (4)

In 1934, E. Labbé became commissioner general of the Exhibition, taking over, thereby, the 14 groups that had been finalized by the consultative commission. From October to December, 1934, these groups were further organized into commissions. At the heart of the *Commission de Synthèse et de Coopération Intellectuelle* (main-spring of the *Groupe de l'Expression de la Pensée*), the future *Palais de la Découverte* took its place (5). Two major considerations seem to have justified such placement:

(1) The Exhibition was held in connection with the celebration of the tricentenary of Descartes' *Discourse on Method*. At the time of the commission's first meeting, presided over by H. de Jouvenel (succeeded, after his death in 1935, by Paul Valéry), Labbé expressed his conviction that "the *Exposition* will brilliantly manifest our fidelity to the Cartesian genius. It is necessary that this be a Cartesian *Exposition*, that it mark a new triumph of method over prejudice, idleness, and scepticism." (6) It was also at this meeting that the idea of a science exhibition, a *Palais des Eléments*, as a possible element in this manifestation was first advanced (7). Serious attention was given to the suggestion; and among the subcommissions then constituted, one was formed to pursue this possibility. These subcommissions included:
   − the *Commission Descartes*, chaired by P. Valéry,
   − the *Commission des Sciences et Palais des Eléments*, chaired by J. Perrin,
   − the *Commission de l'Ensemble des Idées*, chaired by F. Simiand,
   − the *Commission de la Coopération Intellectuelle Internationale*, chaired by C. Bouglé,
   − and the *Commission des Rapports des Techniques et des Arts*, chaired by P. Rivet.
   Thus, let us note that the majority of participants in the future *Groupe de la Pensée* belonged to a network whose coordinates were the *École Normale Supérieure* at the time of the Dreyfus Affair (F.

Simiand, C. Bouglé, J. Perrin), the *Institut de Coopération Intellectuelle* (Mme. L. Weiss), and the *Comité de Vigilance des Intellectuels Antifascistes* (P. Rivet, P. Langevin) (8).

In answering "the Cartesian preoccupations with its certain and progressive deductions, the *Palais de la Découverte* will be, in itself, the symbol of a manifestation which, devoted to Technique and to the Arts, must be, above all, governed by logic and method" (9). Indeed, the *Palais* bears an inscription from the *Discourse on Method* (Part VI) as a frontispiece:

> A practical philosophy by which, knowing the force and the actions of fire, water, air, the stars, the heavens and all other bodies that surround us, we would be able to employ them in the same way for all uses to which they are suited and to make ourselves the masters and possessors of nature.

(2) The second reason justifying the attachment of the *Palais de la Découverte* to this commission was that it was there that the debate on the role of Thought in the *Exposition* and the desirability of celebrating it by constructing a Palace — possibly even a City — of the Mind (echos of which filled the press from 1935 to 1936) was carried on. In an article which triggered a polemic, G. Duhamel had argued: "The 1937 *Exposition* ... must reserve a place of honour for intelligence or, more accurately, for the Mind, (*l'Esprit*) the first principle of all our civilization's undertakings .... It is the Mind that one must honour; it is to it that we must raise a shrine, and not to one or another of its applications." (10) Perrin, whose plan was to exhibit pure science in contrast with its applications — putting back-to-back science and technology, research and invention — shared this "politics of the Mind" promoted both by Duhamel (who, however critical he might be of the moneyed bourgeoisie, never stopped praising the "other bourgeoisie" of scientists, writers, and articles (11)) and Valéry (who "frequented" Perrin's laboratory and represented for both the older and younger members of the Perrin-Langevin group "a sort of ideal of the philosophic spirit applied to science" (12)).

As a frontispiece to the *Palais de la Découverte*, opposite the quotation from Descartes, is inscribed this sentence of Perrin's:

> The *Palais de la Découverte* has been organized in order to make it clear that we have not achieved anything truly original in the past, nor can we hope to achieve

anything truly original in the future, anything which has changed or can change the destiny which seems imposed on men, except through scientific research and discovery.

However, one might just as easily have found there another of his remarks, the philosophical correlate of the above: "In giving itself over to the noble play of Science, the Mind justifies itself and Man is contented." (13)

III. Palais de la Découverte: Paradigm of a Modern Science Museum or a Museum *ad hoc*?

The first meeting of the *Sous-commission des Sciences et du Palais des Éléments* took place in December, 1934. Straight away, Perrin was anxious to register his desire "to see a project realized which is not destined uniquely for the *Exposition*, but which is rather conceived in such a way that at the closing of the *Exposition* there will remain a useful edifice for science and the organization of research." (14) A discussion followed concerning a name for the edifice, the scientists in the group finding *"Palais des Éléments"* – and the project that it represented – unsuitable (15).

Several names were proposed including *Palais de la Science* and *Palais de la Recherche*, but the majority of the commission opted for *Palais de la Découverte*. Two study groups were formed, one for the physical and chemical sciences and another for the natural sciences. At the two following meetings in January of 1935, the study groups were enlarged to include other disciplines (in particular, astronomy was added to the first), and it was decided that the museum would consist of six distinct sections (physics, chemistry, mathematics, astronomy, biology, and medicine), the programs for which were already nearly ready. With the exception of André Leveillé, author of the *Palais des éléments* project who was soon to become the Palais' Secretary General, all other members (such as C. Bouglé, sociologist, or M. Leroy, referred to as a "man of letters") quit the commission, which now consisted only of scientists.

Thus, only a few weeks were necessary to establish the broad outlines of an undertaking which would be brought to term in less than two and a half years. The facts that its initiators were well-known educators (16) and science popularizers and that they were participating on the *Encyclopédie Française* (which appeared between 1935 and 1939) explain this promptness and resolution, but diminish the scope of Perrin's claim that "this scientific exhibition (will be) of an entirely new sort" (17). A study of the educational and propaganda objectives assigned to the future museum by Perrin in 1934 will help us to understand why, in the event, his claim fell short of the mark.

a. *Objectives, Strategy and Pedagogical Supports*

While the propaganda objective was made largely explicit and recalled on every occasion that Perrin addressed either the private sphere of Exhibition organizers ("The *Palais de la Découverte* must make the public understand that for the future as for the past, scientific research and discovery are the indispensable conditions of all human progress" (18)) or the public sphere of potential visitors ("And you will then ask yourselves if it is not worthwhile for society to make the feeble effort necessary in order to multiply the number of researchers" (19)), his use of the notion of "education" was ambiguous and merits our particular attention. Are we to understand it in its ideological implications (scientific progress is synonymous with material, social and moral progress) or as a genuinely didactic concern to remedy the deficiencies of the school system? (20) Here, according to whether he addressed the private or the public sphere, his approach differed appreciably:

Private Sphere	*Public Sphere*
1935: ... and it is necessary to understand that the progress of civilization is not just material, but that it will also assure the progressive emancipation of men and, thanks to increased leisure, the possibility of opening up for everyone the joys of art and thought. (21)	*1937*: Finally, putting our hopes in this people which in every country brings to science the hommage of a confused, touching faith, we have wanted to promote among the adolescents who crowd before our experiments the opening up of vocations which will renew the miracle of the worker/bookbinder Faraday, who became his country's most prestigious physicist. (23)
1936: ... On the other hand, one can hope that in this people, with its immense, untapped reserves, there will be among those young visitors who have not been favored with an education − a privilege until now reserved for the very few − some minds particularly apt for research and to whom their vocation will be revealed. (22)	

Thus, two options coexisted, giving the project its "socialist" colouring.

However, by situating the propaganda campaign and the desire to create vocations on the same plane, it would seem that it was more a mystical than a scholarly socialism that had inspired Perrin. Betting more on the "miracle" than on pedagogy, his action was rooted in the populist perspective of the *Universités Populaires* and not in the *"Normalienne"* perspective of the *École Socialiste* (24).

In its first "milling", the *Palais de la Découverte* was defined as "a modern museum of science, one in the style of the Luxembourg museum compared with which the *Conservatoire National des Arts et Métiers* would be a Louvre, that is, a museum of the past" (25). In practical terms this was supposed to mean that the exhibitions were to be temporary with the accent on current science and not on conservation. As a correlate, the visitor's experience was to be of a "laboratory in activity" (26). The constituent elements of the museum were to be set out according to the principal of organization in the *Encyclopédie Française*, "of which it will be a living illustration" (27). The pedagogical method was to be "modern". The realization and explanation of experiments by demonstrators, on the one hand, or with the aid of audio-visual materials, on the other, was to actively involve the visitor (evoking the methods inaugurated a few years earlier by C. Freinet (28)).

Saint-Lague's project for the mathematics section was an excellent illustration of these principles in practice (29). Because "the particular beauty of mathematical discovery by reason of its abstract character rarely presents a spectacular aspect," it was essential to use as many "modern" techniques as possible to make this part of the exhibition attractive. Classical style (graphics, explanatory panels, murals, diagrams, etc.) was to be abandoned wherever possible; where this was impossible, the methods of publicity posters – including recourse to light in order to produce relief and deformation effects – were to be widely employed on the grounds that "everything that moves inevitably attracts the eye". For the rest, the visitor was to be made to participate, if necessary "taking him by the throat in order to pose questions and beseech him to take part". As a principle of museum animation, one will try to "create for the visitor a personal interest, attract him to a particular area (thereby creating further activity, for people will come in order to find out what it is others are looking at), and so fully arouse his attention that, upon returning home, he'll declare himself to be very pleased" (30).

At the time of the project's realization, the reiteration, the insistance, the emphasis given to certain principles was to result in a departure from the original idea. We will mention three examples. To begin with, the museum's emphasis underwent major transformation. The plan to present the most recent advances in science was abandoned for one which would present only the most recent advances in French science. Placed in the context of the "fundamental discoveries" that had marked the scientific development of previous centuries, French science took on greater relief and adornment: "While this exhibition is clearly French, it is also obviously international in the hommage it has rendered to researchers. A place has been made for them regardless of their origin – Galileo, Newton, Euler, Volta, Oersted, Faraday, Crookes, Mendel, Maxwell, Mendeleev, Hertz, Blakeslee . . . ." (31) Thus, in the physics section the references were international until the end of the 19th century (the portrait gallery ended with Lorentz), but for the 20th century they were almost exclusively French. A brief mention was, indeed, given to Einstein's work in the form of an experimental demonstration designed by Francis Perrin that was intended to show the equivalence of gravitational and acceleration fields (Principle of General Relativity) (32). But there was no reference at all to work of the Copenhagen School, nor to German and Italian physicists – a fact which the political context of the 1920's and the 30's does not suffice to explain. At the same time, the few French physicists whose work had been rewarded with a Nobel Prize (P. and M. Curie, Becquerel, J. Perrin, L. de Broglie, F. Joliot) were spotlighted, reinforcing thereby the hagiographic image of the French scientific community (33).

In the second place, Perrin's orders "to draw up a list of realizable experiments offering an educational and spectacular interest" (34) in the event became a collection of more than 200 experimental arrangements where, most often, the spectacular features overrode the educational. The acme of this tendency was attained with the Van de Graaff Electrostatic Generator constructed by F. Joliot and M. Lazard. In Perrin's words: "Here we have the largest electrostatic machine that has ever been built: at the summit of two 12-meter pylons are two spheres 3 meters in diameter between which a potential difference of 5 million volts causes a gigantic spark to leap." The visitor coming into the *Palais de la Découverte* through the main entrance would have before his eyes, henceforth, the most impressive of all the experimental arrangements in the museum.

Finally, the pedagogical method for which the experimental apparatus provided the didactic support was to rest more on rehearsal than on explanation: "The experiments will be performed in a spectacular manner by demonstrators (35), films, and recordings" (36). In keeping with the same principle, panels and a brochure were to take the place of a delivered talk when the visitor was invited to manipulate the apparatus himself.

A skillfully organized press campaign (37) was employed to convince the public, even before the opening of the *Palais de la Découverte*, that an innovation in museums was at hand compared with which foreign science museums would seem anachronisms.

b. *The Grip of Physics or "The Sovereign and Pacifying Experiment"* (38)

"Physics, the conquering science, to which, perhaps, the most striking advances of our civilization are due, lends itself particularly well to the spectacular comprehension of discovery." (39) The laconic character of this "statement of purpose", the sole justification given for the physics section's project, is itself a sign that physics did not have to explain itself, that, instead, it laid down the law. The entire museum was under its sway, as is evidenced, for example, by the fact that while 23 rooms were devoted to physics, only three were given to mathematics. And though the museum was essentially the exhibition of a series of paradigms (the details of which we won't go into here), methodologically the one which was particularly intrusive everywhere was the definition of discovery as bringing new phenomena to light.

E. Crawford (40) has shown, in her study of Nobel Prize awards in physics between 1901 and 1915, that a theory was considered to be a discovery only if there were experiments confirming its value. The large majority of French physicists subscribed to this "experimentalists" model. Its origins are to be found in the Comtian tradition which defined physics as a science of facts, of phenomena, upon which a theoretical edifice is erected. In T. S. Kuhn's view (41), the cleavage between mathematical and experimental physics was responsible for the decline of French physics from the middle of the 19th century, a decline at once distinct from, and more profound than, the general decline of French science and symbolized by Poincaré's failure to discover the theory of relativity before Einstein (42). This cleavage, even if it tends to be reabsorbed — in Perrin's words, "the two must be intertwined in order to lend one another mutual support" — barely left room for the institution of a theoretical physics (43).

The predominance of a phenomenological physics at the expense of a

synthetic physics enables us to understand how, in the French case, it was
uniquely experiment that determined what was a discovery and what was not.
It is this conception of experiment as the administrator of proof that, in the
Palais de la Découverte, was set up as the selection principle for what was
worthy of exhibition. Such being the case, it becomes perfectly comprehen-
sible that discoveries proceeding from conjectures and refutations (44) or
those aiming at the construction of a unitary theory would find no place in
the exhibition.

This grip of physics and its major paradigm on all of the *Palais de la
Découverte* explains the discrepancies between the development and the
implementation of the project; but more than that it is at the heart of a representation of science whose salient features are: an indestructible attachment
to the Comtian model of the hierarchization and subdivision of disciplines;
a vision of the history of science as the cumulative succession of discoveries;
a definition of scientific method based on hypothesis and verification, and
a hagiographic vision of the scientific community where consensus overrides
debate.

Bringing into play an epistemological bias making experiment primary and
theory secondary (and, consequently, privileging results over argumentation)
removed neither the lag between the production of science and its diffusion
in the public sphere, nor the gap between scientific and ordinary language —
drawbacks of most science museums that the *Palais de la Découverte* sought
to overcome. In so doing, it presented the image of "an imposing edifice of
frozen and triumphant science" (45), suitable for garnering consensus and
approval perhaps, but hardly conducive to inciting debate.

IV. Epilogue: From "Modern Museum of Living Science" to the "Louvre of Science"

"More than 2,000,000 visitors have filed before the experiments, respectfully,
as one does before a church, and full of stirring enthusiasm." So J. Perrin
expressed himself in his 1938 appeal (46) for the maintainance of the *Palais
de la Découverte* as a permanent institution. The installation in June, 1936,
of L. Blum as Prime Minister (*President du Conseil*) and the repeated successes
of the Langevin-Perrin group had eliminated the necessity of focusing on
the initial goal of the enterprise, though Perrin still mentioned it by way of
reminder: "We wanted to make the masses and the governing classes under-

stand that it is of the first importance for the public well-being to encourage research". The educational objective – of lesser importance in the beginning, serving mostly to legitimate the undertaking – now came to the fore, undergoing as it did so a metamorphosis. From the didactic register of propaganda, one moved to the cultural register, making it seem as if it had been there all along, underlying the project: "We wanted to spread the taste for scientific culture among the public," Perrin recalled, "and, at the same time, those qualities of precision, critical integrity, and free judgement – useful and valuable to every man regardless of his career – that such culture develops." At the same time Perrin sought to make its modalities more precise and clarify the exigencies of its diffusion: "And we have to believe that our popularization has not lowered the level of science, since not only the ill-instructed crowd, but even scientists and researchers . . . have expressed their admiration for this work of their French colleagues." The image of the *Palais* as a finished work, as a "Louvre of Science", intrudes at this point. When, in the last paragraphs of the appeal, Perrin has recourse to the idea of a "Popular University plunging its roots in the people of Paris" – a powerful formula with an idealist resonance that corresponds to the mythological image of J. Perrin – it is obviously only a patch. (47)

Notes and References

1. Perrin, J., From a speech delivered in his capacity as a Minister for the *Front Populaire* in Strasbourg, 1937.
1b. See for example, R. Gilpin, *La Science et l'Etat*, Paris: Gallimard, 1970 and Sp. Weart, "J. Perrin and the reorganization of Science" in *Physics Today*, June 1979.
2. J. Habermas, *L'Espace public*, Paris: Payot, 1978.
2b. Ch. Andler, *Vie de L. Herr*, Paris: Maspéro, 1977.
3. See Crawford, E., 'Definitions of Scientific Discovery as Reflected in Nobel Prize Decisions, 1901–1915', communication to the Société Francaise de Sociologie, Paris, October 15–16, 1981.
4. Labbé (ed.), Commissioner of the Exposition Internationale des Arts et des Techniques (1937), 1936.
5. Archives of A. Leveille, Archives du Palais de la Découverte, Paris. The *Groupe de l'Expression de la Pensée*, the final form of the *Commission de Synthèse et Coopération Intellectuelle*, consisted of 7 classes: 1. Scientific Discovery, 2. Literary Events, 3. Museums and Exhibitions, 4. Theatrical Events, 5. Musical and Choreographic Events, 6. Film Events, 7. Congresses and Lectures.
6. Minutes for the meeting of November 9, 1934, Archives de l'Exposition 1937, Archives Nationales, Paris, série F12.

7. In his 'Note concernant la section de Coopération Intellectuelle', Paris: 1933, A. Leveille sketched the broad outlines of a project for exhibiting the sciences; he elaborated his idea for a *Palais des Éléments* in a text appended to the minutes of the meeting for November 9, 1934.

8. This network also partially intersected other commissions such as the Commission de l'Enseignement, headed by H. Ducos, which attempted to annexe itself to the Palais de la Découverte during its developmental phase. Let us note that H. Ducos was reporter for the budget de l'Éducation Nationale in 1933. He then proposed an increase in funds for scientific research.

9. Labbé, Ed., 'Introduction', *Rapport sur l'Exposition de 1937*, 1940.

10. Duhamel, G. in *Les Nouvelles littéraires*, April 6, 1935; see also Rougemont, D. de. in *Esprit* (October 1, 1935), who offers a chronology of the debate.

11. Duhamel, G. in *Marianne*, quoted by Levy, C., 'L'image de la puissance française dans *Marianne*', *Relations Internationales*, No. 33, 1983.

12. Memoires of P. Auger who evokes the atmosphere in Perrin's laboratory in *Fonctions de l'Esprit, 13 savants redécouvrent P. Valéry*, Paris: Hermann, 1983.

13. Quoted in Ranc, A. *J. Perrin, un grand savant au service du socialisme*, Paris: Ed. de la Liberté, 1945.

14. Minutes of the meeting for December 6, 1934, Archives Nationales and Archives du Palais de la Découverte.

15. A. Leveille's project was "to present the elements to the general public in a manner which appeals directly to the eye"; elements here meant the sea, the earth, fire and air.

16. We are thinking especially of J. Perrin's *Les Atomes* and of the courses he gave, particularly at the *École Normale de Jeunes Filles de Sèvres*.

17. Minutes of the meeting for December 6, 1934.

18. 'Préambule au project de Palais de la Découverte', written in December, 1935, and reappearing in the 'Rapport d'activité' presented to the Commissioner General in 1936.

19. From a talk given by J. Perrin on Radio Paris, 1937.

20. For the reforms in physics teaching in the interwar period, see D. Pestre, 'Physique et physiciens en France dans les anées de l'entre-deux guerres (1918–1940)", doctoral thesis, *École des Hautes Études en Sciences Sociales*, Paris, 1982.

21. 'Préambule au projet de Palais de la Découverte', 1935.

22. J. Perrin, 1936.

23. From a speech delivered at the inaugural reception at the *Palais* by Jean Perrin, July, 1937.

24. See Andler, Ch., *Vie de L. Herr*, Paris: Maspero, 1977.

25. Minutes of the meetings for December 6, 1934 and January 10, 1935.

26. *Idem.*

27. *Idem.*

28. For the biography of C. Freinet, see E. Freinet, *Naissance d'une pédagogie Populaire*, Paris: Maspero, 1968.

29. Sainte-Lague, 'Projet pour la section de mathématiques', Archives du Palais de la Découverte, Paris.

30. *Idem.*

31. J. Perrin, 1937.

32. Although J. Perrin and P. Langevin were chiefly responsible for the introduction of the new physical theories into France at the beginning of the 20th century, they devoted a very small place to them on the 1937 Exposition. The first retrospective of 20th century physics at the *Palais de la Découverte* was held in 1952. (Archives du Palais de la Découverte.)

33. Henceforth, Perrin regularly invoked Joliot as the symbol of the recovery of French science and the first "results" of the new organization of research.

34. Minutes of the meeting for January 10, 1935.

35. There were a total of 75 demonstrators for the Exposition: 21 in physics, 33 in chemistry, 14 in biology, 2 in astronomy, 2 in mathematics, and 3 in medicine.

36. J. Perrin, 1936.

37. Notably by A. Leveille. From 1935 through May, 1937, no fewer than 70 articles appeared; from May through November, 1937, there were another hundred or so.

38. A. Ranc on J. Perrin's work on the structure of the atom, *op. cit.*, note 13.

39. 'Projet pour la physique', 1935.

40. Crawford, E., *op. cit.*, note 2.

41. Kuhn, T. S., 'Mathématiques et expérimentation', *Les Annales*, No. 5 (1978).

42. Broglie, L. de, *Savants et découvertes*, Paris: Albin-Michel, 1951.

43. See Biezunski, M., 'La diffusion de la relativité en France', doctoral thesis, Université de Paris VII, 1981.

44. Popper, K., *Logique de la découverte scientifique*, Paris: Payot, 1972; on Einstein.

45. Prigogine, I. and Stengers, I., *La nouvelle alliance*, Paris: Gallimard, 1980.

46. Perrin, J., Appel de 1938, in Préface to the Catalogue of the Palais de la Découverte, 1938.

47. For which M.-J. Nye in her various studies seems to have opted.

SPREADING THE SPIRIT OF SCIENCE

*Social Determinants of the Popularization of Science
in Nineteenth-Century Germany*

KURT BAYERTZ

University of Bielefeld

I consider it to be the duty of scientists not only to occupy themselves with improvements and discoveries within the confines of their specialities, not only to devote themselves to the investigation of the particular, but to make available to society as a whole the important, general results of their particular studies, and to help disseminate scientific learning widely. The greatest triumph of the human spirit, the true understanding of the most general laws of nature, should not remain the possession of a privileged caste of the learned, but must become the common possession of all the educated (1).

The need for popularization of the natural sciences arose during the 18th century as a result, on the one hand, of increasing institutional and professional differentiation of the scientists from the wider society and, on the other, of the fact that literacy was no longer the privilege of a tiny caste of scholars. An extensive literature arose during the Enlightenment for the purpose of familiarizing the "educated classes" with the new results in the natural sciences. But it was neither in the 18th century nor in the present that popular science reached its heyday, but in the 19th century. This is due not so much to the amount of popular literature produced and read it that century, but to the significance of popularization for the self-image of the period. The natural sciences were considered to be the motive force of progress in all areas of social life; whoever wanted to be "up with the times" had to be familiar with their success and method of thought. As a result popularization

Terry Shinn and Richard Whitley (eds.), Expository Science: Forms and Functions of Popularisation. Sociology of the Sciences, Volume IX, 1985, 209–227.
© 1985 *by D. Reidel Publishing Company.*

became a fad that affected virtually all levels of society. Neither before nor after this "century of the sciences" can one find that efforts at popularization had a comparable cultural influence.

If one defines "popularization" as including all efforts at disseminating the results of research beyond the scientific community and the attempt to awaken the "spirit" of science in the public at large, we are dealing – in the 19th century – with an international phenomenon. The trend was characteristic not for a particular country, but for the times. Of course, these efforts assumed a particular form in each country depending upon the national system of science under consideration and the specific social conditions. A systematic comparison of different countries – which would not only show up certain parallels but significant differences – cannot be attempted within the limits of this paper. I will focus my attention, therefore, on Germany and concentrate on the questions: What interests were being pursued by the scientists who devoted so much of their time and energy, beyond their efforts in research and teaching, to the dissemination of the results of their work? What interests were being pursued by that small but industrious group of popularizers that took up the popularization of science as a profession and brought it to its pinnacle of social influence? We will be concerned, in effect, with the *social determinants* of the "epidemic of popularization" (2) that so infected the intellectual life of Germany in the 19th century.

I. Philosophy

One can hardly begin an investigation of the popular scientific literature of the 19th century in Germany other than with the figure of Alexander von Humboldt: he was not only the most famous scientist of his day, but he was the most significant and successful popularizer of the sciences in the first half of the 19th century. When, in the winter of 1827/28, Humboldt held a series of public lectures at the University of Berlin the lecture halls were not large enough for the crowds and he had to offer a second series for the general public, which was held in the largest lecture-hall of the time before an audience of more than 1400. An even greater success was the book *Kosmos* that emerged from this series of lectures, which was one of the most widely-read books of the century and was considered by his contemporaries and the succeeding generations as the quintessence of popular science (3).

Humboldt's conception in *Kosmos* has three main characteristics. *First*: Although Humboldt was an impassioned observer and collecter his goal went far beyond the presentation of individual empirical facts, or even of an ency- clopedic collection of theories and principles, he was interested in a synthesis of the whole spectrum of contemporary knowledge of nature, as it was to be found separately in the individual disciplines. *Second*: It was clear to Humboldt that the program of a synthesizing view of nature was at least as much a philosophical as a scientific program. His conception of this "reflec- tive observation" of nature goes beyond positive science not only philosophi- cally but also aesthetically. Humboldt expressly says that "the enjoyment of nature through a deeper insight into its inner essence" (4) was one of the main purposes of his *Kosmos*: we experience the successful synthesis of individual facts as a pleasure. With this we have arrived *finally* at the core of the type of natural theory represented by Humboldt, which also shows up the principal goal of his efforts at popularization. The unity of nature, which Humboldt attempted to reconstitute, is also seen as the foundation for regain- ing the unity of man and nature, which had been lost in the "narrow confines of civil life" (5).

There can be no question that Alexander von Humboldt was unique in his generation. Not only did his *Kosmos* exercise considerable influence histori- cally, but its basic philosophical conception evokes admiration even today. Nonetheless, as I will show, Humboldt's form of popular science was *not* representative of the 19th century. One can easily find certain aspects of *Kosmos* in authors of a later period; but the totality of the circumstances which characterizes the striving for popularization as such, undergoes a funda- mental transformation in the course of the 19th century. If one looks back upon Humboldt's theoretical efforts from the perspective of the end of the century and compares the dominant type of popular science to be found at that time with *Kosmos*, one could easily imagine that the latter did not belong to the 19th century at all, but that it at best had been written at its threshold. Basically, three things had changed in the course of the century, two of which I would like to analyze more closely in the body of this essay.

(1) Let us begin with the point that will not be the subject of the following pages: the goal of a synthesis of all the current knowledge of nature, already very ambitious in Humboldt's day, became completely unattainable in the following years due to the rapid progress of the natural sciences. Already in

1862 – only 4 years after the fourth volume of *Kosmos* had appeared –
Hermann von Helmholtz expressed doubt about the possibility "of one man's
being familiar with more than a small fraction of contemporary science" (6).
From the increasing *differentiation* and *specialization* of the sciences an ever
greater separation between science and its popularization necessarily resulted,
a separation that was diametrically opposed to Humboldt's conception.
Hence, popularization became an avocation of active scientists, which they
practised alongside their research; or else it became the main occupation of
writers who no longer engaged in research.

(2) Another difference lies in the fact that behind Humboldt's conception
of popular science there is a *philosophical idea*, whereas with the majority
of subsequent authors one finds social interests. Humboldt's point of departure was always an ideal of science that was represented by him as separate
from other considerations. Born into a wealthy family, and granted a generous
pension by the King of Prussia, Humboldt never had to earn his living by his
work in science. For all the other scientists who will be quoted here science
was a profession – and out of this different social condition arose a different
approach to the question of popularization.

(3) The philosophical idea Humboldt was following in his concept of
popularization was based, of course, on certain social conditions. His reference to "the narrow confines of civil life", implies these conditions. But
Humboldt never made them the explicit goal of his theory: it was not his
intention to exercise an influence on social conditions through *Kosmos*. But
this was precisely the growing motive for popularization in the second half
of the 19th century: instead of Humboldt's idea that the generalized knowledge of nature would "purify and pacify the spirit" (7), popular science was
now held to have an explicit *ideological* function. The program of scientific
enlightenment was radicalized politically.

II. Profession

In the first decades of the 19th century the intellectual climate in Germany
was dominated by philosophy and philology. The sciences at the universities
were either part of the department of philosophy or were divided up between
the departments of philosophy and medicine. Governments had little interest
in furthering the sciences – their main interest in the universities was as

training schools for civil servants. Outside the universities there were no institution which could have given sustained support to the sciences comparable to the influence of the *École Polytechnique* in France. Finally there was no established bourgeoisie which could have had both the interest and the financial means to further the sciences. Those who were interested in the progress of the sciences — above all the scientists themselves — were therefore forced to take matters into their own hands. Already in 1822 Lorenz Oken had founded the *Versammlungen deutscher Naturforscher und Ärzte*, which quickly developed into the central scientific forum in Germany. These congresses, which were held at a different location every year, facilitated the exchange of information and the discussion of scientific questions. But no less important were two of its social functions, which were closely related to each other: by becoming acquainted with each other, and through general discussion, the scientists, who were not concentrated in a national metropolis, developed a group consciousness and an awareness of common interests. Further, the congresses not only served the purpose of mutual understanding but of public presentation of the scientists' accomplishments, which was, of course, advertisement for the sciences. They were used as a means to exercise "a certain agitatorial influence" — as Rudolf Virchow called it — on the public:

For the most part our people always need a certain agitatorial influence to rise to the tasks set by science and medicine. The people must not be deprived of the agitatorial character the Naturforscherversammlung has always had. It cannot be replaced by any other authority, or made up for in any other way — a single person, a single society at a particular location, will never acquire a comparable authority. It is for this reason that I am requesting of you that you make efforts to find the means to make possible not merely the continuation of the conferences but also to make them into a truly effective body. In this manner they will become a support of national development (8).

The considerable echo that the congresses found in the press was not only the precondition for raising the public reputation of the sciences, but also an important means of bringing to the awareness of the responsible parties the necessity of an increased support for the sciences. In 1869 Hermann von Helmholtz — in his introductory address before the Congress of Natural Scientists in Innsbruck — drew attention to this connection between publicity and support for the sciences:

It is a great pleasure to see among us a large number of participants from the educated classes of our nation, as well as influential politicians. They all participate in our work and expect from us further progress and further victories over the forces of nature. It is they who must provide us with the resources for our work, and who are therefore justified in questioning us about the results of our labors (9).

The struggle for public recognition and support of sciences must be understood in connection with deep changes in the social groups from which scientists were recruited. In the 19th century, due to the increasing number of scientists that came from the middle and lower classes, science began to develop into a *profession* (10). This had had a profound influence on the conditions for scientific work. The gentleman-scientist Alexander von Humboldt was able to pursue his researches without financial worry, and even bore alone the immense costs of his 5-year research travels through South America including publication of the 36-volume evaluation of these travels, the costs of which alone totalled 226,000 Taler. There was hardly any other scientist in this fortunate position. Justus von Liebig, to take one example, was not only forced to live on an inadequate salary during his first years at the University of Gießen; even as a professor he continued to receive financial support from his father. Moreover he had to make do with extremely limited financial and material support for his research (11). Insofar as research experiments were undertaken at all in the science faculties, it was only rarely that the necessary equipment was paid for by the government: it was usually the professors who had to equip research and teaching laboratories out of their own pockets. Liebig, like other chemists of his day, was forced to conduct private laboratory courses – in particular for apothecary apprentices who wanted to further their knowledge of the theoretical foundations of pharmacy and applied chemistry – alongside his required instruction at the university (12). Liebig needed the fees charged for such private courses not only to cover his living expenses but for the enlargement and support of his laboratory. It is therefore not surprising that it was Liebig himself, representing the experimental natural sciences, who published, in 1840, *Über das Studium der Naturwissenschaften und über den Zustand der Chemie in Preußen* in which he attacked the state of the sciences in Prussia, and in particular the government's thoroughly inadequate support (13).

Against this background Liebig undertook to inform the German public, the high-point of his public activities being his famous *Chemische Briefe*, which he published in the years 1841–44 in 25 installments in the *Augsburger*

Allgemeine Zeitung. The sorry state of chemistry is no longer deplored in these letters; their goal was to give the "educated world" an exhaustive picture of chemistry as a science, to describe its history, its theoretical accomplishments, its problems and methods of work, and its social usefulness. These articles formed the basis for the most well-known work in popular chemistry, and one of the most widely disseminated works of popular science in the 19th century. In the introduction to the first book edition (by 1878 five more editions had followed), Liebig says that the letters

have the purpose of drawing the attention of the educated classes to the situation and importance of chemistry, as well as to the types of problems that concern the chemist, and the role this science has played in the progress of industry, mechanics, physics, agriculture and physiology (14).

It is clear that Liebig's purpose in popularizing chemistry was not only to make its results generally known; it was also intended to raise the reputation of the science in order to create the conditions for increased public support (15). Liebig was by no means alone here: other scientists found the strategic key to the further development of the sciences in public support. To this end Emil du Bois-Reymond called, in the revolutionary year 1848, for an extensive reform of the Prussian Academy of Sciences, one which would include opening the meetings of the academy to the general public. Du Bois-Reymond describes in a letter his reasons for making this suggestion:

I made it clear that in a constitutional state where the budget is approved by the chambers, a corporation is powerless unless it has the support of public opinion behind it; that moreover, the Academy stood so low in the opinion of the public that it could scarcely sink further; that by opening its meetings to the public it would have done itself the greatest service (16).

Nonetheless it would be wrong to conclude that there were only material interests behind the popularization efforts of many scientists in the 19th century. The professional and institutional interest that these scientists were pursuing did indeed include a more generous financial support, an increase in the number of positions, or a greater institutional independence, but it was not limited to these. To gain a position of respect in the cultural environment of the German *Bildungsbürgertum* it did not suffice to point to the economic usefulness of the sciences: they also had to satisfy "higher criteria". The social reputation of the scientists depended upon their activity's being intellectually cultivated and their being seen as men of culture. In a land in which "a luxuriant humanism opposes everywhere the progress of the sciences and of medicine" (17), the sciences were in intense competition with philosophy and the liberal arts and were forced to protest their "cultural value" (18). For many scientists popularization seemed the only possible means of overcoming existing (or suspected) prejudices against the sciences and of proving their value for cultural development. When Matthias J. Schleiden published a collection of 12 popular lectures entitled *Die Pflanze und ihr Leben* in 1848 he justified the publication by referring to a "professional vanity" that had brought him to convey to the reader a more "dignified image" of the botanist's work.

My main wish was to satisfy a professional vanity. Most laymen, even among the educated, are accustomed to seeing the botanist as a kind of shopkeeper dealing in barbaric Latin names, as someone who picks flowers, names them, dries them and wraps them in paper, and whose whole wisdom consists in identifying and classifying this artificial collection of hay. This idea of the botanist was, unfortunately, once true, but it pains me to see that now, when it no longer fits the majority of the profession it is still believed by many. In the lectures collected here I have tried to make clear to the layman the more important questions dealt with in botany, and to show how this science is intimately connected with almost all the most profound disciplines of philosophy and science. I've tried to depict how every fact, or larger group of facts, in botany as in every other field of human endeavor, is capable of inspiring the most serious and important questions and of leading man from what is given him through his senses to a surmised supersensible realm (19).

Schleiden's reference to the significance of botany for "the most serious and important questions" makes it clear that the only way the image of science could be improved would be to make credible its relevance for the general world-view of society. A number of scientists became convinced that popularization could not be limited to the communication of single facts or theorems since this would create the impression that the significance of the sciences for cultural progress lay only in its adding new facts to the already existing fund of knowledge. They emphasised that the goal of popularization was the communication of the particular *mode of thought* and of the *goals* of the sciences. The predominant literary education in Germany, Hermann von Helmholtz said, lacked methodical training in the art of observation and experimentation.

I am calling attention to these conditions here in order to make clear in what manner the sciences represent a new and essential element in the education of mankind, an element of indestructible significance for its future development. The true education of the individual – so also of the nations – will not be possible without combining the traditional literary-logical and the new scientific perspectives (20).

He does not forget to add that the general dissemination of the spirit of science will finally benefit science itself. The majority of the educated had never had contact with the scientific way of thinking – among them were to be found the political leaders of Germany who would have to take responsibility for necessary changes in the educational system of future generations. They could only be encouraged and pushed to this by *public opinion:*

It is not only the natural urge of every beneficent human being to convey to others what one has recognised as true. A powerful motivation for every lover of sciences to participate in such an effort lies in the realization that the development of the sciences themselves, and of their influence on the education of mankind – and, insofar as it is an essential aspect of this education, the health of the spiritual development of the people as well – depends upon the educated classes' insight into the nature and attainments of scientific research, at least as far as this can be obtained without an exacting study of the subjects themselves (21).

Ths intense involvement of many practising scientists in popularization can be explained at least in part as a result of their interest in obtaining recognition for the sciences as a social institution of fundamental importance. The dissemination of scientific knowledge and of a scientific mode of thought therefore was part of a professional strategy which aimed at an increase in the state's material support of science, at an improvement of the scientists' professional image and at a recognition of their cultural value.

III. Politics

In addition to the powerful motive for the popularization of science that resulted from the gradual development of professional interests a political motive was soon added. From the beginning the tendency to professionalize and institutionalize the sciences occurred in the context of efforts to make the backward feudal political conditions in Prussia and the other German states more modern and democratic. A connection between the two was felt as self-evident by a majority of at least the younger scientists. By this time, the proportion of members of the bourgeoisie had greatly increased, so that as a consequence of their social origins the majority of the new generation of scientists were receptive to the ideas of antifeudal reform. Thus, the current political conditions seemed to them an impediment to their professional ambitions. It was no coincidence that Du Bois-Reymond, in his speech in 1848 before the Prussian Academy of Sciences, drew an analogy between a constitutional state and science. Many scientists looked with favor upon the Revolution of 1848 and set great hopes in it, or even participated actively in it. Hopes for a positive influence of the revolution on science (such as had occurred with the French Revolution) and upon the long overdue political and social rejuvenation of Germany went hand in hand. Science was seen here not only as a potential benefactor of social change but also as an *agent* of that change. It was a catalyst in two ways: firstly, it led — in association with technology — to a revolution in the economic life of society, destroying the few remaining feudal social structures; secondly, science encouraged a type of thinking that refused to be impressed by any kind of authority. It furthered the secularization of the intellectual life of the nation, which was dominated by religion, and undermined the ideological foundations of the feudal states. This is illustrated in the inaugural lecture of Carl Vogt given on May 1, 1847, as Professor of zoology at the University of Gießen:

I believe then that the sciences are called upon to serve as a basis for spiritual progress in our time just as they have served for material progress. These two concepts of progress don't conflict with each other — not only goods but also ideas are transported by rail, and every commercial progress, every gain in industry and agriculture, is associated with spiritual progress, with the growth of the liberated spirit that the sciences embody. With the fall of material constraints spiritual bonds fall also (22).

Even if most of his colleagues would not have accepted the somewhat super- ficial revolutionary pathos at the end of the lecture — supporting instead more moderate reform ideas — the conviction Vogt expressed in the quoted passage was widely shared. This identification of scientific and social progress, which had gained general acceptance in the period before the Revolution of 1848, was not brought into question by the failure of the Revolution but became on the contrary more strongly emphasized. The bourgeoisie, which had emerged from the revolutionary events weakened and intimidated, hoped that the subversive, progressive power of the sciences would sooner or later bring about those goals that they had not been able to attain by revolution. The peculiar situation arose that science became at the same time a substitute for politics and a means of attaining political ends. Rudolf Virchow was probably the most important representative of this "strategy": he emphasized over and over again in his extensive activities as scientist and politician, that science not only did not recognize any existing authority, but that it was the highest authority for virtually all questions, and that even social institutions had to bow to it.

All seeking after the truth, especially after truth unrecognized up to then, is irreconcilable with the continued existence of certain dominant prejudices and doctrines and, as soon as practical matters are involved, with the continued existence of certain institutions. In this manner knowledge of the truth, or science, becomes destructive, the more so the greater the hindrances it faces; by overcoming these hindrances science is liberating, and the freer the society or state is, the more science is supported (23).

The widest possible dissemination not only of the results of scientific investigation, but above all of the specific method of thought of science came to seem to the bourgeoisie to be the key to the evolutionary transformation of Germany into a modern industrial and democratic state. It is not surprising, therefore, that the demand was made over and over again, throughout the 19th century for an improvement and extension of the science curriculum in the schools. Once again we find Virchow in the front lines here. The systematic dissemination of the scientific mode of thought and its firm establishment in the minds of the people was for him the decisive weapon in the struggle against religious orthodoxy, which he regarded not only as an antiquated world-view but also as an ideological support of the dominant political conditions. For him the importance of science instruction in the schools lay in the teaching of a coherent body of knowledge, whereas popularization could only convey unsystematic knowledge.

I'm of the opinion, therefore, that we must put all our efforts behind making the sciences a possession of all, not simply by means of the already extensive and successful popularization, but above all by means of *rational education*. Popular learning suffers from the basic flaw of remaining piecemeal: incongruent parts are grafted onto an already closed mind. . . . Our task must be to make certain that knowledge again becomes uniform and homogeneous, that it flow out of a common source (24).

The struggle led by Virchow and many of his colleagues for the reform of the school curriculum reached its ideological climax in the dispute that raged over the question of whether the Darwinian theory of evolution should be included in the school curriculum. Even though Virchow voted against

Darwinism in this dispute (25), he was still a representative of those who saw in the intensification of science instruction in the schools an essential element of the battle for a reform of the political and social conditions in Germany.

Although practicing scientists such as Virchow, Helmholtz and Du Bois-Reymond devoted a considerable amount of energy to the popularization of the sciences, they cannot be seen as the authors of the two most significant popularization movements which altered the intellectual life of Germany in the second half of the 19th century. In the 50's *scientific materialism* blew like a fresh wind into the reactionary intellectual climate of the post-revolutionary years. Its main representative was − together with Carl Vogt and Jacob Moleschott − the physician Ludwig Büchner who, in 1855, followed his active participation in the Revolution with the book *Kraft und Stoff* which made him overnight the leader of the whole materialistic movement. Although the book refers at most by implication to political questions, its intention was nonetheless political. Büchner himself stated this before the publication of the book:

> This kind of thing has strong appeal these days. The public is demoralized by the recent defeat of national and liberal aspirations and is turning its preference to the powerfully unfolding researches of natural science, in which it sees a new kind of opposition against the triumphant Reaction (26).

Kraft und Stoff was a tremendous success, being translated into 17 languages and going into its 21st German edition at the beginning of the 20th century. The significance of the work is not merely to be found in its large number of readers and editions; more importantly, it was the only attempt at a systematic presentation of the central convictions of the scientific materialists in a suitable popular form. The concept of popular science realized in *Kraft und Stoff* became the model for the mainstream of popular scientific literature in the second half of the century, still exercising its influence after the materialism debate of the 50's had been overshadowed by the conflict concerning Darwin's theories − which gave rise to the second wave of scientific popularization. Beginning slowly in the 60's, the latter grew rapidly, aligning itself with the political intentions of the materialists (whose main representatives immediately accepted the theory of evolution). The proponents of popular Darwinism were adherents − as were the materialists − of the "ideas of 1848" and considered the dissemination of the theory of evolution as a decisive contribution towards the realization of these ideas (27). Ernst Haeckel — the standard-bearer of German Darwinism — already from his first appearance as propagandizer of evolutionary ideas emphasized the political dimension of his interpretation of Darwin. Büchner's model for the popularization of science was developed further and perfected in the following years by such authors as Haeckel and Wilhelm Bölsche. Characteristic for this model are:

(1) Popularization is, to a certain extent, "emancipated" from the actual practice of science. In many cases popularization is no longer an avocation that practicing scientists engage in alongside their research, but has become an independent occupation. A considerable part of the popularizers were autodidacts in science and even those who had scientific training were usually no longer involved in research: science popularization was an activity they devoted themselves to alongside the profession by which they supported themselves, or it became their main occupation and source of income. Ernst Haeckel is an important exception, but popularization had a different meaning for him than for Liebig or Helmholtz. With Haeckel, on the one hand, it is difficult to draw a clear line between original research and popularization; on the other, he wrote as many popular as scientific works, so that one can no longer consider his efforts at popularization to be a secondary occupation.

(2) This "emancipation" is closely connected with significant differences in subject-matter between the popular literature of the second half of the 19th century and the popular works of the majority of scientists at the time. As a rule the latter were satisfied with making the results of scientific research available to the public in an easily understandable form, whereas a Haeckel or a Bölsche had "higher" aims. In *Kraft und Stoff* Büchner wrote a work that was more philosophical than scientific, in which the sciences were used to justify a comprehensive world-view. This explains why Büchner's materialism was attacked — despite all its anti-idealistic and anti-metaphysical invective — for regenerating the "German attraction to philosophy and metaphysics", this time in scientific garb (28). Popular Darwinism continued this trend: it sought a foundation for a world-view, the most thoroughgoing example of which is to be found in Haeckel's "monism". Haeckel criticized strongly the increasing tendency to positivism and the specialization of the sciences, and turned against the mere empirical collecting of facts. He argued that "the unshakeable edifice of the true, monistic science arises only through the most

intimate mutual influence and interpenetration of empiricism and philosophy." (29) The goal here is the re-establishment of a lost unity of worldview, which Haeckel wants to attain by re-philosophizing science. Bölsche has a similar conception: for him aestheticization is the means and popularization the locus for the rejoining of the dispersed knowledge of nature. He emphasizes that this goal can not be attained through research, but only through popularization. The goal of popularization

is to put back together what has been destroyed in the idea of science; to give a complete picture again, a picture suffused with the spirit that has been gained by a look deep into nature. It is a mistake to try to accomplish this restoration with the instruments of research. The only tools are the aesthetic and creative imagery of art. Therefore popular expositions of even the most abstruse and difficult scientific discoveries demand a certain plastic and dramatic style (30).

(3) Finally one must mention the political nature of this popular literature which is, in part implied and in part openly stated. The open atheism promulgated by the scientific materialists had to be understood as a political challenge in a land whose rulers invoked the "unity of Church and crown" – and it was intended to be understood in this way. The sciences seemed to embody a rationality that was completely at variance with the pre-scientific ideological foundations of the political system in Germany. Popularizing science was the means of freeing the people from the religious fetters that bound it to the existing feudal system, and also of filling it with the spirit of progress that the sciences in general, but Darwin's theory in particular, emanated. The increase in the influence of social Darwinism in the 80's does not alter the fact "that the bulk of popular Darwinism's influence was on the left half of the political, cultural and social spectrum" (31). This is also shown by the increasing reference to the sciences made by the worker's movement in the last third of the 19th century for legitimation of its political goals and justification of Socialist theory (32).

IV. Conclusion

We have become acquainted with three determinants of popular science in Germany in the 19th century: a popularization motivated (1) by a philosophical conception of science; (2) by professional interests; (3) by political ambitions involving social criticism. A major thesis of this essay is that the conception of popular science in the second half of the 19th century was controlled mainly by the second and especially the third determinants. This predominance showed itself not only in that these two had by far the largest readership and number of titles, but also with regard to cultural influence. The great efforts undertaken both by scientists and popularizers to disseminate the sciences, therefore, can be explained as an *expression of interests*.

In this paper I have focussed upon the popularizers. But the central role of social interests in the popularization of science in the 19th century is not to be found alone in their influence on the popularizers themselves. It's obvious that popular literature can only be successful insofar as it meets with a *response*. Certain inclinations of the public must correspond to the interests of the popularizers. In investigating these inclinations with regard to science popularization we find first that the public must have a sufficient school education, i.e., must be able to read and must have minimal previous knowledge, as well as sufficient funds to buy books and magazines: both conditions were fulfilled in Germany in the second half of the 19th century. But this only explains why a wide reception of popular science was possible, not the actual impulses behind this reception. One of these impulses certainly was that the sciences in the 19th century appeared to the public as something new and unknown. The attraction of the new – a motive not to be underestimated – was considerably magnified for many by the flair of the piquant, indeed of the forbidden, that was lent to the sciences by their conservative and clerical opponents. In this sense it cannot be doubted that the popularity of Darwinism in particular was, to a considerable degree, a matter of fashion, as Alfred Dove said in 1871 (33). But vogues don't fall from the sky, and even the often referred-to "spirit of the age" of the 19th century is grounded in social conditions.

This brings us back again to interests as an explanation for the response of the public to popular science. Since the Enlightenment there had been a widespread conviction in Germany that the sciences were a powerful force for social progress, not only freeing the spirit of man from prejudices, but also useful for his material well-being. As a result various social groups held that the fortunes of the nation, as well as their own social futures, were closely bound up with the sciences. They saw the raising of the backward German conditions in the economic, social and political sectors to the level of the progressive countries as their fundamental task. For the aspiring *Bourgeoisie* the sciences provided the theoretical foundation of industry and the motor of industrial progress (34). In keeping with this widespread conviction, the bourgeoisie found its strongest ally in the sciences and technology as it strove for an increase in economic influence and − on this foundation − for its political emancipation from the dominant feudal classes that still ruled in Germany. Closely allied with the industrial bourgeoisie was the increasing number of *technicians* and *engineers* whose social importance had increased: they were also interested in new developments in these areas which were so important to them. They found in science not only a support for their economic and social position, and a guarantee of the continued improvement of this position, but also the intellectual expression of the daily experience they gained in their industrial activities. The *workers* had an analogous interest; since their labour, in contrast to the traditionalist mode of labour of the artisan, was closely bound to the modern means of production they saw in science and technology a force for their liberation from the feudal guild obligations. Although their economic interests were contrary to those of the capitalists, they realized that they were bearers of industrialization in common with the capitalists (35). So the workers as a historically new class, developed their social identity essentially through their association with scientific and technological progress. The strong irrational defence reactions of certain sections of the "Bildungsbürgertum" couldn't prevent the continual increase in the numbers of those who believed that the decisive means for democratizing and modernizing all aspects of social life lay with science. Although the public's readiness to respond to the popularization of science is worthy of analysis of its own, it can be assumed that this readiness was founded on the same interests as underlay the efforts of the popularizers themselves, or upon similar ones.

My conclusion is that the far-reaching cultural influence of popular science in Germany during the 19th century was the two-fold result of a singular historical situation. On the one hand, the sciences became a social institution with a professional profile; on the other, society underwent a deep process of transformation. These two processes were not independent of each other: just as the scientists could safisfy their professional interests best in a "modern" industrial society, so industrial society needed the sciences in their modes of production and as a rationalist ideology. Historically this interdependence finds expression, among other ways, in the fact that the above-mentioned three determinants were not strictly independent from each other – just as the types of popular literature corresponding to them cannot be strictly distinguished from one another with regard to content or authors: despite all the contrasts there were points of agreement and transitions among them. As a whole the extensive efforts at popularization can be seen as one element of a "scientistic movement" of vast influence. Neither the secularization of intellectual life in the course of the 19th century, nor the rise of science to a powerful social institution (36) were the result of an automatic historical process. Both arose out of a long succession of political, social, philosophical and scientific conflicts, which were motivated by concrete interests and carried out by concrete persons. The popularization of the sciences was one of the most powerful weapons in these conflicts.

Notes and References

1. Ernst Haeckel, *Natürliche Schöpfungsgeschichte. Gemeinverständliche wissenschaft-liche Vorträge über die Entwicklungslehre*, 9th edition, Berlin: Georg Reimer, 1898, p. 3f.
2. Friedrich Fabri, *Briefe gegen den Materialismus.* 2nd enlarged edition. Gotha: Gustav Schloeßmann 1864, p. 127.
3. Alexander von Humboldt, *Kosmos. Entwurf einer physischen Weltbeschreibung*, Stuttgart: J. G. Cotta, 1945–58. – Susan Faye Cannon characterizes Humboldt's general perspective in his scientific work apart from *Kosmos*, and his influence in the early 19th century, in *Science in Culture: The Early Victorian Period*, New York: Dawson and Science History Publications, 1978, p. 105.
4. *Ibid.*, p. 18.
5. *Ibid.*, p. 34.
6. Hermann von Helmholtz, 'Über des Verhältnis der Naturwissenschaften zur Gesamtheit der Wissenschaft", in *Vorträge und Reden*, Volume 1, 5th edition, Braunschweig: Friedrich Vieweg, 1903, p. 159.
7. Humboldt, *op. cit.*, 1845, note 3, p. 23.
8. Rudolf Virchow, 'Rede auf der 62. Versammlung deutscher Naturforscher und Ärzte' am 18. September 1889 in Heidelberg, in Karl Sudhoff, *Rudolf Virchow und die Deutschen Naturforscherversammlungen*, Leipzig: Akademische Verlagsgesell-schaft, 1922, p. 273f. The British Association for the Advancement of Science, established in 1831, played a similar role in Great Britain. Presentation of the re-sults of scientific research to the general public – and of public appearances of the scientists – played a significant role, whereby dramatic effects were not frowned upon in the attempt to make science vivid. Jack Morell and Arnold Thackray, *Gentlemen of Science. Early Years of the British Association for the Advancement of Science*, Oxford: Clarendon Press, 1981, p. 161.

9. Hermann von Helmholtz, 'Über das Ziel und die Fortschritte der Naturwissenschaft', *op. cit.*, 1903, note 6, p. 373.

10. Cf. Everett Mendelsohn, 'The Emergence of Science as a Profession in Nineteenth-Century Europe', in Karl Hill (ed.) *The Management of Scientists*, Boston: Beacon Press, 1964, pp. 3–48.

11. Cf. Bernard Henry Gustin, *The Emergence of the German Chemical Profession 1790–1867*, Diss. University of Chicago, 1975, pp. 92ff.

12. *Ibid.*, p. 100.

13. Justus von Liebig, 'Über das Studium der Naturwissenschaften und über den Zustand der Chemie in Preussen', in *Reden und Abhandlungen*, (new printing), Wiesbaden: Martin Sändig, 1965, p. 27f.

14. Justus von Liebig, *Chemische Briefe*, 6th edition, Leipzig and Heidelberg: C. F. Winter'sche Verlagsbuchhandlung, 1878, p. VII.

15. Cf. The following quote from a letter Liebig wrote to Wöhler: ". . . My aim is to influence the public and the governments. Let heaven bring us success and liberate us. Up to now chemistry has been in a peculiar situation with regard to the other subjects – we're looked upon as intruders, as it were; but this has to be changed – chemistry has to stand alongside or above the others." Quoted from Borscheid, *Naturwissenschaft, Staat und Industrie in Baden (1848–1914)*, 1976, note 21, p. 31.

16. Emil Du Bois-Reymond, *Jugendbriefe an Eduard Hallmann*, Berlin, 1918, p. 131. My attention was brought to Du Bois-Reymond's statement by a work of Timothy Lenoir: *Social Interests and the Organic Physics of 1847*, unpub. M. Sc. 1983. The English translations of the quotes from Du Bois-Reymond and Ludwig come from this manuscript.

17. Justus von Liebig, *op. cit.*, 1965, note 13, p. 34.

18. In the 19th century in Germany it was widely held that the sciences belonged to the domain of "Zivilisation", not to the higher realm of "Kultur". For the meaning of these concepts cf. Fritz K. Ringer, *The Decline of the German Mandarins. The German Academic Community, 1890–1933*, Cambridge, Mass.: Harvard University Press, 1969, pp. 86–90.

19. Matthias J. Schleiden, *Die Pflanze und ihr Leben*. Populäre Vorträge, Leipzig: Wilhelm Engelmann, 1848, p. 1f.

20. Hermann von Helmholtz, 'Über das Streben nach Popularisierung der Wissenschaft', *op. cit.*, 1903, note 12, volume 2, p. 425.

21. *Ibid.*, p. 426.

22. Carl Vogt, *Über den heutigen Stand der beschreibenden Naturwissenschaften*, Gießen: J. Ricker, 1849, p. 21f.

23. Rudolf Virchow, 'Über die Fortschritte in der Entwicklung der Humanitäts-Anstalten', *op. cit.*, note 8, p. 11f.

24. Rudolf Virchow, 'Über die Aufgaben der Naturwissenschaften im Neuen nationalen Leben Deutschlands', *op. cit.*, note 8, p. 111.

25. I have analyzed the background of Virchow's position in my essay 'Darwinism and Scientific Freedom. Political Aspects of the Reception of Darwinism in Germany', 1863–1878', in *Scientia* 117 (1983).

26. This is quoted here from the English translation in cf. Frederick Gregory, *Scientific Materialism in Nineteenth-Century Germany*. Dordrecht/Boston: D. Reidel, 1977, p. 105.

27. Cf. A. Kelly, *The Descent of Darwin. The Popularization of Darwinism in Germany, 1860–1914*, Chapel Hill: The University of North Carolina Press, 1981.

28. Theobald Ziegler, *Die geistigen und sozialen Strömungen des Neunzehnten Jahrhunderts*, Berlin: Georg Bondi, 1899, p. 328.

29. Ernst Haeckel, *op. cit.*, 1898, note 1, Volume 2, p. 782. (Emphasized in the original.)

30. Wilhelm Bölsche, 'Zur Erinnerung an Carus Sterne'. Quoted here from: A. Kelly, *op. cit.*, 1981, note 27, p. 52.

31. A. Kelly, *op. cit.*, 1981, note 27, p. 8.

32. Cf. Kurt Bayertz, 'Naturwissenschaft und Sozialismus. Tendenzen der Naturwissenschafts-Rezeption in der deutschen Arbeiterbewegung des 19. Jahrhunderts', in *Social Studies of Science* **13** (1983), 355–393.

33. Alfred Dove, 'Was macht Darwin populär?' in Günter Altner (ed.) *Der Darwinismus. Die Geschichte einer Theorie*, Darmstadt: Wissenschaftliche Buchgesellschaft, 1981, p. 447.

34. In 1883 the scientist and entrepreneur Werner von Siemens states: "Scientific research will always build the foundation for technical progress; a nation's industry will never come to occupy a leading position internationally, and be able to maintain it, if it is not a leader in science. Research is the most effective way of promoting its industry". Quoted from Peter Lundgreen, 'Wissenschaft und Wirtschaft. Methodische Ansätze und empirische Ergebnisse (unter besonderer Berücksichtigung Deutschlands im 19. Jahrhundert)', in *Technikgeschichte* **44** (1977), 310. Lundgreen's review of current research makes clear what difficulties stand in the way of an attempt at a solid historical reconstruction at the *actual* connection between science and economic development. Contradicting the optimism expressed in the passage quoted from Werner von Siemens, recent empirical research makes "questionable the assumption of a one-sided scientific-technical determinism". *Ibid.*, p. 313.

35. Cf. Kurt Bayertz, *op. cit.*, note 32, pp. 381ff.

36. Cf. in contrast: "Science in Germany grew up as a part of a philosophical-educational enterprise and without the support of a powerful scientistic movement". J. Ben-David, *The Scientist's Role in Society. A Comparative Study*, Englewood Cliffs: Prentice-Hall, 1971, p. 126.

METRO-GOLDWYN-MAYER MEETS THE ATOM BOMB

NATHAN REINGOLD

Smithsonian Institution

Late in 1945 Metro-Goldwyn-Mayer (MGM), the premier Hollywood motion picture studio, decided to produce a film, on the building of the Atom Bomb. The result, *The Beginning or the End*, was released in the spring of 1947. To depict living, well-known individuals, MGM had to get their permission, resulting in written and oral interchanges. What follows is based largely on materials in the correspondence of J. Robert Oppenheimer, director of the Los Alamos Laboratory during World War II; Vannevar Bush, head of the Office of Scientific Research and Development (OSRD), which administered the wartime research and development effort including the atom bomb program in its early crucial stages; Leslie R. Groves, a general in the Army Corps of Engineers who headed the Manhattan Project which took over from Bush; and Albert Einstein, whose letter to President Roosevelt in 1939 started the effort (1). The correspondence makes possible a comparison of the original screenplay with various suggested revisions and with the final version as seen by the public. I hope to illuminate the differing viewpoints of the individuals involved in the development of the movie. The process depicted contains clues on issues important for historians and sociologists, as well as those in the mass media. Every genre of exposition – the scientific journal article, the historical monograph, the newspaper article, the novel, the popular motion picture, etc. – imposes a structure and a dynamic on their subject matters. In ways sometimes subtle, sometimes gross, different messages are conveyed not always matching the intentions and needs of the creators of the exposition, their audiences, or the actual participants in the events described.

Origins of the Film

Shortly after Hiroshima, contacts between scientists in the Manhattan District

229

Terry Shinn and Richard Whitley (eds.), Expository Science: Forms and Functions of Popularisation. Sociology of the Sciences, Volume IX, 1985, 229–245.
© 1985 *by D. Reidel Publishing Company.*

and MGM spawned the suggestion for a movie on the building of the A-Bomb (2). These scientists were part of the so-called atomic scientists' movement which eventually resulted in the establishment of the Federation of Atomic Scientists and the well-known *Bulletin of the Atomic Scientists*. Doing a commercial movie was one, atypical incident in the efforts of individuals in the movement and other scientists to educate the lay public about the nature of the new weapon and its implications for both domestic and international policy. Besides the use of the periodical press and public lecturing, many individuals had personal contacts with influential persons. Talks on radio also occurred, the only other use of the newer forms of mass media. Unlike the MGM film, these talks were essentially like conventional public lectures.

Only in this instance was there an attempt at something markedly different from familiar expository forms. Even here, the awe of the new power caused MGM to approach the project with exceptional care. Sam Marx, who later produced the film, visited Oak Ridge in 1945 and then spoke to President Truman in Washington. Truman was friendly but non-committal. To avoid his possible hostility, an MGM official assured Truman of the company's high intentions. People "sit in theatres and listen" for entertainment "but in a film of this nature we are certainly going far deeper than ordinary entertainment." MGM foresaw "a great service to civilization if the right kind of film could be made." (3)

MGM hired a successful screenwriter, Robert Considine, to prepare the initial story with the advice of the men from the atomic scientists' movement. They were active in the early stages of formulation of the script because of their hope the film would further their viewpoint, as well as yield money for their meager treasury and even funds for scholarships (4). By early 1946 these younger and generally little-known individuals had given up those hopes as the evolving script in their eyes glorified the military and "put foolish words" in the mouths of scientists. They did not wholly understand what was happening and expressed confidence that the leading scientists would never permit themselves to be so depicted (5). What they did not know was that General Leslie R. Groves on the last day of 1945 had signed an agreement with MGM giving permission to depict him in return for $10,000 and the right to review the script. Only the military participants personally received cash for their permission to be depicted in the film. All of the scientists gave their releases to MGM gratis. Perhaps they assume the film was a professional obligation not calling for cash (6).

The Original Script

Considine's original story was elaborated and converted into screenplay by Frank Wead. To get the consent of the prominent individuals in the plot (no longer a legal requirement), Wead's script, completed in March 1946, was submitted to many of the participants in the development of the A-Bomb (7). As in the early discussions with those in the atomic scientists' movement, dramatic continuity was provided by two fictional males; Matt Cochran, a young physicist, and Jeff Nixon, a young Army Engineer Colonel on Groves' staff (later depicted on the screen by Robert Walker). Matt was given a young bride, Jeff a girl friend serving as the General's secretary (8).

The script opens with a newsreel showing the burial of *The Beginning or the End* under a grove of redwood trees so that, no matter what, five hundred years later the truth about the A-Bomb will be known. J. Robert Oppenheimer (eventually played by Hume Cronyn) next introduces the story which starts with Lise Meitner working in Berlin who flees to Bohr in Copenhagen when Nazis take over the laboratory. Word of the new work on uranium fission comes to America, and Albert Einstein writes a letter to President Roosevelt with the assistance of Matt Cochran (later depicted by Tom Drake). The bomb project is launched, leading to a reenactment of Enrico Fermi's first controlled chain reaction at Stagg Field at the Metallurgical Laboratory of the University of Chicago. Introducing the scene, the script advises: "Tremendous history is about to be made by unhistoric looking people." Soon the Italian navigator appears: "Dr. Fermi, scientifically detached from the world, enters. . . ." In a harsh review of the film, *Life* criticized the dramatic qualities of the "biggest event since the birth of Christ." (9) But Matt has qualms about continuing in the development of such a terrible weapon. Convinced to stay, he has to leave his bride behind. Vannevar Bush regretted these passages which he saw as "an American trait . . . to tie a serious matter and a romance together." (10)

Skipping the other important work of the OSRD period, the script enters into the domain of the Manhattan Engineering District where Groves (played by Brian Donlevy) exhorts industry to join up. In the released film, the

DuPont representative then grandly waives all patent rights, an easy position for DuPont to take fictionally (if not really) as those very conservative gentlemen Vannevar Bush and Leslie Groves had no intention whatsoever that any such patents would go into private hands because of the nature of the technology. We next get a panorama of great factory structures, endless rail shipments, and cryptic production lines.

The script switches to Los Alamos where rather little is shown, given the requirements of secruity. There is a dramatic account of the first A-Bomb explosion at Alamogordo, quite impressively recreated in the studio. Jeff and Matt, who have appeared throughout, now go to Tinian to prepare the first two bombs for their use against Japan. In an impossible accident, Matt suffers a fatal radiation injury while setting up the Bomb one evening all by himself. Hiroshima is devastated in a spectacular film sequence reaffirming Hollywood's skill at special effects. (Apparently little, if any, of the footage derived from the actual hombing.) Matt dies, and the screenplay (and the picture) ends with his now pregnant widow, Jeff, and Jeff's girl friend talking inspirationally how the new world coming will justify Matt's sacrifice. This bare outline does not do justice to the nuances of the screenplay, some of which are treated later.

Metro-Goldwyn-Mayer's Dilemma

MGM realized that their A-Bomb film was an unusual, difficult project but the full extent and nature of the problems only became known in three stages: (1) up to the preparation of the Wead screenplay in March 1946; (2) the reactions to the screenplay from April into the autumn; (3) from October 1946 (when a first complete film was shown to interested parties and sneak previewed) to January 1947. MGM received strenuous complaints in the last stage forcing extensive cutting and reshooting. By February 1947 the final print was available for release. The reactions of the scientists in stage (1) did not prepare the company for what occurred later.

As General Groves was bluntly told, MGM was not an endowed institution like Harvard but a commercial organization (11). To make a picture salable, it was necessary to fictionalize for dramatic purposes. An MGM memo sent to Albert Einstein conceptualized the point: "It must be realized that dramatic truth is just as compelling a requirement on us as veritable truth is on a scientist." (12) "Veritable truth" consisted of a great mass of details. To achieve dramatic truth required selection and compression – Matt Cochran to stand for all the young physicists and Jeff Nixon for all the engineer officers under Groves. "Vertiable truth," presumably a complex knowable reality, is a difficult concept for philosophers, historians, sociologists, and others who have to deal with the intractability of imperfect bodies of evidence. As disclosed by their letters and memoranda, the MGM officials were sophisticated and intelligent enough to realize the problems. "Dramatic truth" was a kind of abstract of "veritable truth" capable of commercial dissemination to a mass audience.

The depiction of Fermi's great Stagg Field experiment provided two examples of the conversion of veritable truth to dramatic truth. Matt Cochran's hesitation about continuing stood for all the qualms of those who had strong feelings about dropping the Bomb on enemy targets, like the scientists who later endorsed the Franck Report in the Metallurgical Laboratory. Deliberately, all such individuals appeared in the film in one fictional Stagg Field scene as men who withdrew because of scruples after the experiment succeeded. Correspondence and the script make clear that these were intended to be Quakers. The film does not explicitly identify them as such nor did any such incident occur in "veritable truth." By hinting at Quaker pacifism, the film glides silently by strongly felt issues, blurring why more than traditional pacifism was involved (13).

Another problem was the desire on the part of both MGM and the scientists and engineers to show the internationalism of the effort. Besides the early European scenes, the screenplay has Bohr later playing a visible, consequential role in the A-Bomb project. But depicting the participation of the Canadians and the British posed problems for "dramatic truth." It increased the casting and complicated the plot. Groves was conscious of the importance of Canada as a past and as a future supplier of uranium. He was less adamant than the scientists about crediting British participants in the bomb project like Rudolph E. Peierls, James Chadwick, and William G. Penney. MGM, consequently, had its way in symbolizing the Commonwealth's role by having a delegation of observers at the Stagg Field experiment, a complete fiction. Besides, MGM argued, they were not against a British presence as they expected "British shillings" to provide an appreciable portion of the profits. They were even willing to contemplate making a special Commonwealth version, presumably with a greater specific role for Commonwealth scientists (14).

Selecting from the mass of details did more than simplify a complex sequence of events. "Dramatic truth" acted as a pressure to mold the screenplay and film into a familiar narrative form with stock characters and stock situations as far as possible. Hollywood had little experience with the realities of scientific research, let alone the unique circumstances of the A-Bomb project. What they had done in the past were stories of heroic physicians and inventors, triumphs of individual wills. Here they faced a great collective enterprise. Giving Leslie R. Groves as the hard-driving organizer of a great industrial enterprise was an easier challenge than displaying Bush's managerial skills in directing research and development or Oppenheimer's role on the mesa in New Mexico. Hollywood had difficulties in depicting situations of lesser moral ambiguity and tragedy than presented by the A-Bomb. Success stories where virtue triumphed were more comfortable and familiar. Even without the agreement with Groves, there is little, indeed, to suggest an inclination on MGM's part to present the anti-military viewpoint of the atomic scientists' movement so soon after the conclusion of a popular, victorious conflict. Not that it was impossible for Hollywood to produce a great, meaningful film on the A-Bomb project. Given the prevailing situation in the industry, the probability was low of achieving the necessary critical and artistic insight into the story of the Manhattan Project. Perhaps more important was the need to couple such insight with the skill to succeed within the constraints of the commercial genre or somehow to transcend those limitations.

Reactions of Key Participants

J. Robert Oppenheimer and his wife told Sam Marx in no uncertain terms of their hostile reaction to the screenplay in April 1946. Marx had no problem adjusting to the criticisms of factual details and depiction of personalities. Oppenheimer's private views were, in fact, quite mild: "[the] script is not bad generally but that 'real' characters are stilted lifeless and without purpose or insight." (15) Reassuring Oppenheimer, Marx wrote that "the character of J. Robert Oppenheimer must be an extremely pleasant one with a love of mankind, humility and a pretty fair knack of cooking." The film would make plain that Oppenheimer, not Groves, was in command at the Alamogordo test. Fresh from a reading of the Smyth Report and a viewing of newsreels Hume Cronyn added: "I gather that simplicity, warmth and a complete lack of affectation are essential to your character." Oppenheimer signed a release shortly afterwards in May 1946 (16). When queried incredulously by a scientist in the atomic scientists' movement, Oppenheimer defended his signing by asserting the main points were satisfactory: "namely scientists were ordinary decent guys, that they worried like hell about the bomb, that it presents a major issue of good and evil to the people of the world." Although the screenplay was not "beautiful, wise, or deep . . . it did not lie in my power to make it so." (17) A fictional Oppenheimer consequently appeared in movie houses, an earnest scoutmaster who accidentally had a Ph.D. in theoretical physics from Göttingen.

If Oppenheimer withdrew from further meaningful involvement after May 1946, Groves and Bush continued to interact with MGM into the late fall of 1946, particularly after seeing the first film version. Groves was quite explicit about his intentions. After checking for possible security violations, he was determined that the film would not reflect any discredit on anyone engaged in the Manhattan Project (18). In fact, of all the participants whose reactions are presently known, Groves was the most assiduous in objecting to inaccuracy of details, tone, and interpretation, much to the annoyance of MGM.

As to discredit, he was most alert to depiction of the Army in general, the Corps of Engineers in particular, and especially himself. As late as November he complained that the film falsely implied that the Army (and its chosen instrument Leslie R. Groves) was handed a complete project requiring only routine subsequent steps. Groves insisted he had signed big contracts even before Fermi's chain reaction. Robert Walker as his aid outraged Groves. The fictional Jeff Nixon, zestfully portrayed by Walker, chased women, was disrespectful to his superiors, and was too long haired for a combat zone like Tinian. A real Corps of Engineers Colonel did not behave that way, and a real Corps of Engineers general officer would not tolerate such a person on his staff (19). As to his own film image, the pudgy, slightly rumpled Groves had no objection to the handsome, dapper Donlevy (20).

Groves did not get Walker's depiction of Jeff Nixon to conform and only reluctantly conceded other points. He ended up essentially conforming to MGM's plans. Perhaps he took comfort from one of his aids' report on the final film version. Although regretfully overlooking the possible economic impact of atomic energy, security was maintained with no danger of arousing popular revulsion. Public impact would be minimal because the film would flop (21).

Despite strong reservations about the screenplay and the first film version, Vannevar Bush was careful to limit his responses to MGM to the depictions of OSRD and himself as its Director. Particularly outrageous to him was the original screenplay's crediting Lyman J. Briggs as having the crucial discussion with President Roosevelt on launching the A-Bomb project. Briggs, the Director of the National Bureau of Standards, headed the early Uranium Committee which was absorbed by OSRD before it launched the full-scale effort which became known as the S-1 project.

Once that was corrected, Bush also strongly objected to the suggested dialog between himself and the dead President. Obviously a historic moment, Bush took the matter very seriously. But so did MGM in its own way. They wanted to depict the dead, still popular President, even to showing his well-known black Scotch terrier Fala. MGM also saw the scene as introducing an essential element of dramatic tension.

Bush did not relish the dialog about the uncertainty of the costs where he almost reluctantly concedes the project may even require as much as two billion dollars. Admitting that costs did go upwards, Bush did not welcome the implication of administrative uncertainty. But Bush compromised. More annoying was the text having him say that it was uncertain whether the A-Bomb could fit into a plane. Nor did he like the text saying that serious doubts existed if the A-Bomb could be finished for use before the end of the conflict. On the contrary, Bush insisted he knew the weapon could fit into a plane and be ready in time. As the responsible administrator of the wartime scientific mobilization, he only advised President Roosevelt to launch the project after receiving advice from some of the best scientists and engineers in the world. The released film retained in softened form the doubts about size and timing but added Bush citing the advice of the National Academy of Sciences. It was important to MGM to enhance the tension of a deadly race with Nazi Germany (22).

On viewing the first film version of the scene with President Roosevelt, Bush became concerned about its ending as depicted by the actors. After a discussion of the possibility of a full-scale project, Roosevelt thanks Bush, saying he will consider the matter. The veritable Bush objected to how the dramatic Bush reacted as he left, displaying dissatisfaction at not getting an immediate decision by facial expression and body language. MGM thought the scene a success; the sneak preview audience applauded. Bush's spokesman made clear what was objected to. The scene implied that American science through its spokesman [i.e., Bush] "is arrogant enough to feel it should either make the decision itself or force the Commander in Chief into making it then and there." (23) The released film has a rather prosaic parting of the two men followed by the President placing a call to Winston Churchill. By December 1946, Bush could write Bernard M. Baruch that "history was not unreasonably distorted" by the film (24).

Albert Einstein agreed to his depiction by a quite different path. Having been early told by the atomic scientists' movement the film reflected the military view, he twice declined permission to MGM. But the film company persisted, offering to change objectionable details. They very much wanted Einstein's appearance. Einstein apparently let Leo Szilard handle further negotiations. Szilard telegraphed him on July 27, 1946 to sign up, which Einstein did that very same day (25). When Groves viewed the first film version, he correctly complained that an early scene purporting to show an experiment at Columbia University with Fermi, Eugene Wigner, and Leo Szilard simply slowed the action. The scene's presence, MGM explained, was insisted on by Einstein (26).

Not all scientists agreed to their depiction. James B. Conant, the President of Harvard, and a key administrator in the A-Bomb project, only agreed to being shown at the Trinity test but not to have any words placed in his mouth. From the standpoint of MGM, the most serious refusal was from Niels Bohr. The early scenes in the screenplay featured him in Europe. As part of the tensions of the race to beat the Nazis to the A-Bomb, much was made about smuggling Bohr out of Copenhagen and then bringing him to the United States. Bohr's essentiality for the A-Bomb project was more than strongly implied, and he was falsely placed at the Alamogordo bomb test.

In May and July, MGM used John Wheeler of Princeton as their go-between, assuming that Bohr would eventually agree to his depiction, perhaps with a few changes. In October Bohr turned down MGM, citing the many inaccuracies of the plot. Because Lise Meitner had also refused permission, the company assumed she had influenced Bohr. They offered Bohr a private showing of the first version. Not only did Bohr decline, but his lawyers sent warning letters to MGM. By December, at least, MGM was cutting the original film and reshooting scenes, a process continuing into January (27).

The A-Bomb Decision

Dropping the bomb on Japan provided a problem for dramatic truth, especially after the build-up of tension over the menace of a Nazi nuclear weapon. In the original script Niels Bohr shocks Oppenheimer and others when he brings the news that the Germans are sending atomic experts and materials to Japan by submarines. Another, later scene has General Groves telling President Roosevelt and Secretary of War Stimson that the Japanese will meet an invasion of their homeland with atomic weapons as an argument for dropping the bomb. Bohr's intransigence and Groves' firm denial of his use of that argument eliminated those passages.

The original screenplay has a fictional German physicist named Schmidt in Lise Meitner's laboratory. Later, the scenario has a submarine leaving Hitler's doomed Reich carrying Schmidt and sundry atomic secrets, eventually to surface in Tokyo Bay. There Schmidt disembarks amid rejoicing that the two countries could continue developing the decisive weapon for victory. The Japanese rush Schmidt off to a modern laboratory they have established for him in the city of Hiroshima. Schmidt did not survive to the final film version (28).

An unexpected, vociferous source of objection to the film, in particular the depiction of the decision to drop the A-Bomb, was the prominent political commentator Walter Lippmann. A viewing of the first version outraged him. He could not understand how so many eminent scientists agreed to their incorporation into such a banal "American success story." Particularly appalling to Lippmann was what he viewed as a libelous depiction of Roosevelt and Stimson in the scene with Groves. Not only were the men denigrated in his opinion, but so too was the seriousness of the elaborate, careful process preceding the decision. Even worse, to Lippmann, was the one scene with Harry Truman, whose visage did not appear. (Because of that, Truman's permission was not necessary.) As an actor spoke, the camera shot over his shoulder to a listener as the dramatic Truman's voice expressed concern over U.S. losses and unconcern over Japanese deaths: "But I think more of our American boys than I do of all our enemies. . . ." Lippmann's letters of protest forced MGM to reshoot the scene with President Truman simply expressing the belief that dropping the bomb could save Allied deaths in an invasion of Japan (29). The vertiable Truman refused to intervene to avoid the charge of engaging in censorship but in a private letter complained that the brief scene was objectionable in implying he had simply made a snap decision (30).

Just why Truman's action was important was not specifically elaborated, although the scenes of devastation at Hiroshima at least hinted that this was not simply a bomb bigger than a conventional weapon. Wead's screenplay had the newsreel announcer say at the beginning: "A message to future generations! Come what may, our civilization will have left an enduring record [i.e., the MGM film] behind it. Ours will be no lost race." That, and the very title, certainly suggested catastrophic possibilities. The implications were not absent from the minds of Sam Marx and his colleagues. For example, when James Franck, T. R. Hogness and Harold C. Urey on September 9, 1946 protested the use of Lise Meitner in the film even under a fictitous name, Marx agreed but added a reference to John Hersey's piece on Hiroshima in the *New Yorker* "[which] is making many readers feel that the creators of the atomic bomb are the world's greatest war criminals, it should be a relief to many scientists that a motion picture of this magnitude is on its way, hailing their achievement as the most magnificent triumph of modern times." (31)

The filmed scenes at the Metallurgical Laboratory made much of monitoring for radiation hazards, preparing the audience for Matt Cochran's fate. In the script and in the released film are dialog at Alamogordo between Oppenheimer and General Thomas F. Farrell, Groves' deputy, about the possibility of the fission "going around the world," that is, converting the planet to a fireball. Oppenheimer rates the possibility as less than one in a million. Farrell tells Groves that those odds are too small, implying at least imprudence on the part of the scientists. After the bomb goes off, when questioned again about whether he had not really worried about that catastrophic possibility, Oppenheimer replies: "In my head, no; in my heart, yes." That concern was in the air after the A-Bombs dropped on Hiroshima and Nagasaki, but not among those in the project who had earlier determined it was not possible with a nuclear weapon of that size and nature (32).

Focussing on a non-existent peril diverted attention from real perils. The original screenplay treated radiation and burn hazards at the Alamogordo test by announcing that injury to the skin "is best overcome by covering or use of lotion freely." Groves firmly criticized that and the wearing of dark glasses as untrue. In the film only the dramatic Oppenheimer wears goggles with dark lenses to peer at the blast.

Lost somehow to the final film version is a bit of dialog in the original screenplay between Oppenheimer and Bush. As they watch the mushroom cloud at Alamogordo, Oppenheimer says: "The cloud is dissipating nicely." Bush replies: "That's one fear we can forget." (33) The exchange rings true for that particular point in history when many responsible individuals in the Manhattan Project and OSRD regarded long-term radiation hazards with what we can now describe as a mixture of ignorance and wishful thinking. But well before the end of 1946, the tests at Bikini ("Operation Crossroads") had disclosed disturbing possibilities. In *The Beginning or the End* the film audiences saw a turtle walking across the ground at Alamogordo right after the test, no doubt a dramatic truth symbolizing that life survives nuclear explosions.

Did It Matter?

In a notably jaundiced review of *The Beginning or the End, Time* magazine wrote: "The picture seldom rises above cheery imbecility." The film was a commercial, historical, and artistic flop. At least seventy-five films of that year grossed more at the box office (34). Although the *Time* reviewer went on to lecture Hollywood: "regard [the] audience as capable of facing facts, even problems which may prove unsolvable [and] stop treating cinemagoers as if they were spoiled or not-quite bright children," his conclusion was relatively cheery. There was no harm done unless *The Beginning or the End* stopped the making of the better picture (35). Of course, no one knows the reactions of the millions who did see the film.

The lack of success of the film probably reinforced the attitudes of the historic actors, shared by the *Time* reviewer. Despite words about bringing truth to the audience, in the last analysis it did not matter or did not matter very much. The Army Corps of Engineers had reáched the same position before the release of the movie. In knowingly signing up with MGM, Arthur Compton, Enrico Fermi, J. Robert Oppenheimer, Vannevar Bush, Albert Einstein, and others all agreed to not unreasonable distortions of history (as

Bush put it), to deviations from veritable to dramatic truth. What were unreasonable were a small number of gross deviations from fact and violations of perceptions of self and of standards of propriety. Beyond that was little apparent concern for the viewing public.

Perhaps the veritable participants agreed out of a sense of play, of vicariously becoming part of Hollywood's great make-believe world, figuratively rubbing shoulders with individuals accorded almost mythic status not only in the United States but many other countries. Many individuals in the Manhattan Project played themselves recreating past events in the March of Time documentary *Atomic Power* released in August 1946 (that is, during MGM's filming). It showed, for example, Conant and Bush stretched out on the ground awaiting the bomb blast at Alamogordo. The two men were filmed on a sand strewn garage floor in Boston (36).

Joining the sense of play, perhaps, was a sense that the real "history" was elsewhere. If "history" was elsewhere – not at MGM in Culver City, California, nor on a Boston garage floor – where was it? Perhaps in their memories, perhaps in the scientific and technical literature? Perhaps "history" was over, gone, with no tangible existence? Perhaps they sensed that "history" was dispersed in their unpublished personal papers and in the archives of institutions. I doubt it. Certainly, many did not like what resulted when historians and others began poking around memories and archives (37). Although they would fight for freedom of information for the advancement of science, some were quite willing to disregard the strictures of *Time* magazine and consider limiting what the public should be told of the possible horrors of modern warfare. James B. Conant, for example, later wrote a report for the Defense Department along these lines (38). In all sorts of contexts, it did not matter that veritable truth was compromised. It is hard to avoid the conclusion that compromises with veritable truth are more likely the further from familiar forms of professional communication. And a Hollywood saga was far from the style of the *Physical Review*.

When the first film version was finished, it represented Wead's screenplay as amended slightly because of the complaints of various participants. At a sneak preview, MGM was delighted with the overwhelmingly favorable response (39). They may have had a hit on their hands before Bohr and the others forced cuts and reshooting of scenes. Given MGM's record of popular successes, perhaps the original, unrevised script would have yielded a successful film, artistically and commercially. Who can estimate the effect on tens of millions of viewers if Schmidt had disembarked in Tokyo Bay and left for his laboratory in Hiroshima?

Popularizations have consequences even if not always precisely definable. Because it does matter, we can regret MGM won the cooperation and assent of so many key individuals. The subject was unsuitable for the kind of treatment MGM had in mind. Because it does matter, we can express relief that MGM had to get their assent and consequently had to compromise its original dramatic vision. Think of how Hollywood has warped the perceptions of so many inside the United States and in other countries about the settlement of the American West. Hollywood did not need the written assent of the long dead, original settlers and of the American Indians.

Although I have located no direct consequence of this film on the public presentation of science and scientists – at least not in a wide range of later correspondence of nuclear physicists, other scientists and records of scientific organizations – one can speculate about two indirect effects. First, there was a noticeable increase in interest after 1947 in reaching the lay public but in forms where professional control was paramount. The reformed *Scientific American*, television documentaries, and countless books by scientists resulted. But now scientists, engineers, and physicians have attracted the attention of the world of belle-lettres with results not always pleasing to fastidious scientists and historians of science. Brecht and Koestler are now joined by far lesser talents implicitly following MGM's precedent.

A second possible consequence hinges on the very difficult matter of the general public's perception of scientific integrity. The aura of secrecy around the Bomb soon engendered uneasiness about whether the whole truth was being disclosed. As more and more came out about such matters as the problem of fallout, there was an erosion of confidence, not only in governmental agencies but also in scientists as sources of objective truth. The film, if remembered at all, became another instance of evasion by those popularly charged with being bearers of truth. If that is a valid speculation, it might have furthered the trend to a greater professional role in reaching the general public to avoid repetition of such instances.

This incident suggests a troubling moral to a historian. His guild has a decided preference for anchoring generalizations firmly to detailed particulars of contexts. Is it a professional virtue or an act of self-righteousness? Does our abstracting from veritable truth to historical truth inflict any injury on the past, different from but just as real as that resulting from an application of dramatic truth? If so, how can we minimize this injury?

Notes

1. The Oppenheimer and the Bush Papers are in the Manuscript Division of the Library of Congress. The files on the movie are both in boxes 171 of the respective collections. Box 11 of the General Correspondence of Groves in Record Group 200 of the U.S. National Archives contains the record of his dealings with MGM. For Albert Einstein, see 57–147 to 57–173 of the Einstein Papers in the Mudd Library, Princeton University. I have viewed the film in the holdings of the Library of Congress. Through the courtesy of MGM/UA Entertainment Co. I have examined in their records file 1377 on the production of the film and file 7005 on obtaining permissions to be depicted from the participants.

   After completion of this paper, I learned of Michael J. Yavenditti's 'Atomic Scientists and Hollywood: The Beginning or the End?', *Film and History* 8 (1978), 73–88, with a quite different but not incompatible interpretation because of its focus on the atomic scientists' movement and the issues it raised of the public roles of researchers.
2. E. R. Tompkins to E. Fermi, January 16, 1946, Oppenheimer Papers. See also, Alice K. Smith, *A Peril and a Hope* . . . 1971 ed., pp. 293–294.
3. Carter J. Barron to H. S. Truman, November 21, 1945. President's Secretary's File 112, H. S. Truman Library, Independence, Missouri.
4. As late as March 1946 when he withdrew, Hal Wallis of Paramount Pictures hoped to make the movie and was dangling the possibility of scholarship money before the scientists. J. H. Teeter memorandum, March 7, 1946 and Teeter to Oppenheimer, March 26, 1946, both in Oppenheimer Papers.
5. W. R. Shank memorandum to W. Higginbotham, February 20, 1946, R. Noyes to Oppenheimer, February 26, 1946; Oppenheimer Papers. According to a telegram in 7005 (R. Consodine to S. Marx, May 16, 1946) on a conference with Einstein in which H. D. Smyth spoke up for the Federation, MGM sent the organization a check which was returned with a request for a larger sum.
6. Groves Agreement with MGM, December 31, 1945. Groves Papers. This does not appear in Groves' autobiography. Other documents in Box 11 disclose that the political columnist Drew Pearson had scented the deal by the late 1946, but did not publish a word of it. This is based on a review of file 7005. For his efforts on behalf of MGM, John Wheeler of Princeton had the company contribute $500 to his university. E. R. Tompkins of the Clinton Laboratory (now Oak Ridge) who actually first suggested the film received $100.
7. The script used is in the Bush Papers in two identical copies. Besides the original version dated March 22, 1946, there are a number of revisions of specific scenes dated May 10, 1946 inserted at the appropriate points in the original text. All subsequent comments refer to this document.

8. In none of the documents examined are there discussions of these two fictional female characters during the development of the script.
9. Pages 28 and 30 of the screenplay. The *Life* review appeared in the March 17, 1947 issue, pp. 75–81.
10. V. Bush to B. M. Baruch, December 20, 1946. Bush Papers.
11. Groves to W. Consodine, March 12, 1946 and attached documents. Groves Papers.
12. James K. McGuinness memorandum to L. B. Mayer, July 16, 1946. Enclosure to 57–154 in Einstein Papers.
13. Based on a comparison of the screenplay with comments in various letters in the Groves Papers, particularly the materials cited in note 11.
14. W. Consodine to Groves, March 7, 1946, Groves Papers.
15. Telegram to David Hawkins, April 29, 1946, Oppenheimer Papers. Hawkins authored the official history of Los Alamos. He and H. T. Wensel of the National Bureau of Standards who worked on S-1 for the OSRD central office were in Hollywood during the filming as technical advisors, in effect replacing the individuals from the atomic scientists' movement.
16. Marx to Oppenheimer, April 24, 1946 and Cronyn to Oppenheimer, April 30, 1946, Oppenheimer Papers. Oppenheimer signed his waiver on May 8, 1946, subject to receiving assurance in writing about desired changes. The waiver form, in the same location, reads, in part: "I understand that although you will attempt to show the historical facts with accuracy, you will, however, have to dramatize your motion picture story, and I have no objection thereto, and you may rely on my personal irrevocable consent to proceed."
17. Oppenheimer to J. J. Nickson, May 29, [1946] replying to Nickson's letter of May 17, 1946, Oppenheimer Papers.
18. Groves to Bush, June 3, 1946, Bush Papers.
19. Notes of November 15, 1948 conference with Carter Barron and Groves to Barron, November 19, 1946, Groves Papers.
20. *Ibid*. Groves was sensitive to being portrayed as treating industrialists rudely.
21. Albin E. Johnson to Groves [January–February, 1947], Groves Papers.
22. Bush to F. G. Fassett, Jr., July 15, 1946 and Marx to Fassett, July 19, 1946, Bush Papers. Fassett worked for Bush at the Carnegie Institution of Washington and helped him with his writings and with public relations.
23. Fassett to Marx, October 26, 1946; Marx to Fassett, November 14, 1946; Fassett memorandum to Bush, November 13, 1946, Bush Papers. The quotation is from the October 26 letter.
24. Bush to Baruch, December 20, 1946, Bush Papers.
25. The declinations occurred on May 26 and June 24, 1946. The July events are in exchanges between Marx and Einstein, 57–156 to 57–161. The Szilard telegram and Einstein's permission are in 57–163 and 57–164.
26. Barron to Groves, December 4, 1946, Groves Papers.
27. The Bohr account is based on copies of correspondence in the Einstein Papers (Bohr to Wheeler, May 16 and July 25, 1946; Bohr to Consodine, October 9, 1946) and in the Oppenheimer Papers (Marx to Oppenheimer, October 21 and December 4, 1946); file 7005 has much on the unsuccessful MGM efforts.
28. From an April 24, 1946 memo of an MGM conference in file 1377 there was agreement that the account of Schmidt's trip was fictional, although Consodine insisted

such a submarine was sent but turned back. Meitner insisted there were no Nazis in her laboratory. Schmidt, it appears, was inserted in the script so that the audience would not confuse Bohr and Hahn and that Hahn would not be labeled as a Nazi. For Groves' objections to other aspects of this part of the screenplay, see Groves to Barron, April 15, 1946, Groves Papers.

29. Lippmann to F. Aydellotte, October 28, 1946, Oppenheimer Papers. Traces of Lippmann's vehement reaction occur elsewhere. See Bush to J. B. Conant, November 27 and December 6, 1946; and R. P. Patterson to Bush, December 2, 1946, Bush Papers. The original dialog with Roosevelt, Stimson, and Groves is on 163 of the Wead screenplay; changes dated April 30, 1946 have the Truman words Lippmann objected to on 83–83A.

30. In Bush to Baruch, December 20, 1946, re censorship. Truman to Roman Bohnen, December 12, 1946. President's Secretary's File 112, H. S. Truman Library, Independence, Missouri. From file 1377, we know that Truman did see an early version of the script, as did his secretary Charles G. Ross, the source of Bush's information. (Ross to Barron, April 19, 1946.) Ross saw the revised script but that neither Truman nor his family saw the first film version. (Strickling to Barron, December 6, 1946 and Ross to J. K. McGuinness November 4, 1946.) The sources are unclear as to whether Truman saw the revised script.

31. The opening words indicated the date 2446 for the expected opening of the buried cache of the reels containing the film. The "twenty-fifth century," was selected, I suspect, for that future date was evocatively familiar, as in the popular pre-World War II comic strip, "Buck Rogers in the Twenty-fifth Century." File 7005 has the letter of the three scientists and Marx's draft of his reply [September 17, 1946].

32. The point here is that uncertainty existed about the nature and extent of the explosion at the test site. The men involved had calculations of what might occur but could not vouch that the explosion would exactly match the calculated effects. Later work indicated that the estimated power of the explosion at Hiroshima, 20K of TNT, was too high.

33. Page 99 of the screenplay.

34. *Variety*, January 7, 1948. Of 369 releases only seventy-five grossed two million dollars or more.

35. The *Time* review is in the issue of February 24, 1947.

36. Raymond Fielding, *The March of Time, 1935–1951*, New York, 1978, pp. 291–293. Bush figured prominently in the *March of Time* film. His papers contain part of the script with a number of jaundiced comments. Bush refused cooperation until the script was satisfactory. *Atomic Power* was far shorter than the MGM film and brought the story up to the current debates of early 1946 on atomic policy.

37. For example, see Oppenheimer to G. Seaborg, May 3, 1962, Oppenheimer Papers, for comments on Hewlett and Anderson's *The New World – 1939/1946* (1962), the first volume of the Atomic Energy Commission's official history.

38. Secretary of Defense Louis Johnson to Truman, August 22, 1950, White House Official File 192, H. S. Truman Library, Independence, Missouri.

39. Marx to Oppenheimer, October 16, 1946, Oppenheimer Papers. Up to the world premier before a gala audience in Washington, at least some MGM officials were certain they had a big hit on their hands. (Barron telegram to E. J. Mannix, January 7, 1947, in file 1377.)

PART III

THE SOCIAL APPROPRIATION OF SCIENCE

INDUSTRIAL SCIENCE AS A "SHOW"

A Case-Study of Georges Claude

CHRISTINE BLONDEL

Musée National des Sciences, des Techniques et des Industries, Paris

This paper deals with a scientist, industrialist, scientific popularizer and French politician of the twentieth century: George Claude (1870–1960). We shall try to see to what extent the scientific discourse of an industrial physicist, involved in applied research, differs from that of a scientist engaged in fundamental research. More specifically, we shall examine Claude's methods of popularization and his use of science for political purposes. It will be demonstrated that like his research work, Claude's popularization as an industrialist and a politician was centerd on the problems of power rather than around those of the *transfer of knowledge*. We will see how his claim that science has a right to political power was related to other forms of power which he exploited, those powers of technology over nature and industry within the economy.

In 1886 Claude entered the École Municipale de Physique et de Chimie Industrielles de la Ville de Paris (1). This had been founded four years previously to answer demands from laboratories in the public and private sectors for chemists sufficiently well qualified to undertake not only the setting up of experiments, but also management duties. At that time, the beginning of the IIIrd Republic, the aim was to encourage within the French chemical industry the type of research to which the French attributed the success of industry in Germany. The school was original in that it closely linked physics with chemistry and considered both laboratory and workshop to be of utmost importance.

However, Claude's perception of science was not formed by the School alone, he was also profoundly influenced by the work of Jules Verne.

Without hesitation I recognize Jules Verne as one of my masters. He was the first who

Terry Shinn and Richard Whitley (eds.), Expository Science: Forms and Functions of Popularisation. Sociology of the Sciences, Volume IX, 1985, 249–258.
© 1985 *by D. Reidel Publishing Company.*

knew how to show me science as *amusing* and *entertaining* while so many scientists only perceived and showed it as boring and unyielding. He was the first who knew how to make me understand the variety and *incredible power of its potential*; it is certainly as a result of reading his delightful science fiction that I developed my taste for research (2).

These two elements, *entertainment* and *power*, were, as we shall see, the foundations of Claude's popularization and, ultimately, his appropriation of science for purely social purposes.

These twin forces, then, formal schooling and science fiction, formed the corner stones of Claude's two series of industrial projects. The first of these revolved around technological developments and industrial profitability. By mastering the methods of handling gases at extremes of temperature and pressure, he was able to develop a whole series of new industrial processes. After each discovery he founded a company, on average about one a year. The most important of these companies was *L'Air liquide*. He was equally ambitious in the domain of military technology: his research included industrial liquefaction of chloride, liquid oxygen bombs and trench guns. The second series of projects, developed in the 1920's and 1930's, was in part a reaction against the baneful consequences of the applications of science. He concentrated his attention on looking for new sources of energy, including thermal energy from the sea. At the same time he indulged in some strange attempts to extract gold from the sea, to construct a pipe between the Red Sea and the Mediterranean, and to locate aircraft which had fallen into the sea. "Fantastic" ventures which were worthy, as Claude like to point out, of Jules Verne himself.

The Exposition of Science, Technology and Inventions

George Claude's writings cover a very wide range. His purely scientific texts consist mainly of articles published in the *Comptes Rendus* of the Académie des Sciences (3). Unlike much of his exposition, these are traditional in their presentation. There is always reference to the theoretical work which underlay his research and there is an implicit recognition of the dominance of theory over experiment and basic research over applied research. At the same time he made applications for patents which specified the technical procedures involved. Thus the viability of an industrial process was, above all, economic. These academic publications supported the ambitions of industrial researchers, like Henry Le Chatelier, to gain recognition from the Académie for what was then called "Industrial Science". Acknowledgement was gained in 1918 with the creation at the Académie of the "Section des sciences appliquées à l'Industrie". Claude was himself elected to this section in 1924.

Unlike many scientists, he did not wait for official recognition to begin popularizing science and technology. At the age of 24 when he was still only an engineer, he started a review called *L'Étincelle Électrique*. The aim of this review was "To make the study of electricity as pleasant as possible . . . . To bring an attractive science within the range of the comprehension of ordinary people . . ." (4). It included the expected articles on the applications of electricity, the registration of patents and the activities of learned or industrial societies. His attraction to ideas taken from science fiction is also evident, ideas like using discharge tubes for lighting or harnessing the power of tide and waves to make electricity. At this time he was already vigorously expressing the anti-parliamentary feelings, so important to his subsequent popularizing activities (5). His attempts to popularize the many virtues of electricity were made more accessible in the book *L'Électricité à la portée de tout le monde* (6). It treats the themes of "fairly electricity" with its implications in daily life and the atom with its mysteries and associations with basic knowledge. The physics presented here dealt with subjects already popular in science fiction. In fact the success of the book was enormous. More than 60,000 copies were sold, nearly double the number of Jean Perrin's famous book, *Les atomes* (7). Perrin's work was also aimed at a large public, although his technique of popularization was quite different. Claude addressed himself to "all those who . . . deal with the practical aspects of electricity (What they want) is not to learn about its *nature*, nor to know *why*, it is quite simply to learn about the *effects* it produces . . ." (8) (see also Cloître and Shinn). The strategy of Georges Claude's popularization in this book is clear; mathematics and theory are excluded not only because they frighten the reader and turn him against science, but also because they are basically of no use to him. The success of this particular method of popularization re-enforced much of his own scientific strategy which was based on the same contempt for theory.

The second book which he wrote for a large audience, *L'Air liquide, sa production, ses propriétés* (1903), sees the development of a new strain of thought. In the preface to the book Arsène d'Arsonval, his friend and patron, professor at the Collège de France and member of the Académie, underlines that "this book shows how *applied* science can correct some ill-conceived laws of so-called *pure* science" (9). Here he referred to predictions made in the 19th century about the properties of gases which were later proved to be wrong. Claude himself took part in these corrections. Once again he underlined several contradictions between the predictions of the theoreticians and the results of actual experiments. As an example, he cited the recent discovery of a violent chemical reaction at a very low temperature, while physicists postulated the "death of matter" in these conditions: "So, another beautiful theory is compromised, or at least we have to say, once again, that it is an exception which proves the rule" (10). Emphasising this type of disparity within the context of popularization Claude moved further and further away from pure theory. He often stresses in this book the difficulty which industry has in moving from theory to practice. To Claude this difficulty made applied science independent of pure science and created a sphere of autonomy with regard to it.

Much later, but still in the same vein, in 1923, under the ironic title 'Some Ideas . . . SGDG on Invention and Scientific Research', he lectured to the science students at the Sorbonne. This title refers to patents submitted SGDG, that is "Sans Garantie Du Gouvernement" (without government garantee). He recommended that anyone who wanted to make discoveries of practical use should be sure of all the possibilities offered by science, but also not to rely ". . . on that cautious documentation which informs you . . . but dampens your enthusiasm. Ignorant of everything . . . (one does not feel) incapacitated at every moment by ideas or facts which are often wrong or debatable" (11). The experimenter who is in continuous contact with reality, touches a reality much richer than that of the theorist who must always purify the real in order to extract phenomena he can account for. Here Claude is closer to physiologists than to physics theorists. Each experiment was considered an integral whole. A purely theoretical approach despite all its equations gives only a partial view of reality.

This pre-eminence given to experiment is, however, quite different from a traditional empiricist discourse; Claude's aim was not to base knowledge on the results of a set of experiments. It is the sequence of events during those experiments, not a corpus of all the experiments on a given subject, which gives a scientist power over nature. This type of scientific discourse and popularization does not depend much on past experience and history.

While the pure scientist often refers to the history of his discipline whose values he acknowledges, even if he questions them, to show how he fits into a succession to contributions, the inventor insists on the chance aspects of his research.

Popularization in Practice

We will now analyse Claude's strategies of popularization and attempt to see how they reflected his views on science and research. As we have seen, he acknowledged Jules Verne as having shown science to be *pleasant*, that is likely to entertain, and *powerful*.

Although his scientific Notes for the Académie des Sciences already included several photographs (of factories and apparatus) it was in *L'Air liquide* that he most used pictorial representation. He was quick to have himself photographed doing experiments on this strange liquid, whose properties can be made to appear spectacular. Liquid air makes all bodies, metallic or organic, as strong and as fragile as glass. As it boils it spreads out and becomes surrounded by clouds of condensed atmospheric steam. It was a splendid subject to demonstrate "Les Merveilles de la Science" to borrow the title of Louis Figuier's book (12).

He was not, however, satisfied with publicizing his photograph alone. Claude wanted to go before the public in person. The first appearance before an audience of the neon tube, which he developed in 1910, occurred in a place not usually associated with serious minded science, the Luna-Park of Paris. Here Claude set up a stand called "Scientia". In addition to his experiments on liquid air, he made phantasmagoric lights in the national colours of red and blue, by alternately lighting orange-red neon tubes and bluish mercury gas tubes. Furthermore he arranged all his lectures around these displays which became part of his repertoire. For Claude, experiments, apart from proving scientific facts, were also for illusion, excitement and *pleasure*.

Using modern inventions, he dramatized not only the potential of modern technology, but also the power of his personality. In 1936 he had a commercial film made of his attempts to use the thermal energy of the sea (13). He built a plant, initially on the coast of Cuba in 1928 and then on a boat which he brought into the bay of Rio. It was designed to produce electricity by using the difference in temperature between the surface of the sea and that at several hundred meters of tropical water. The film showed not only the tremendous task of assembling a 2,000 meter long pipe to draw cold water from the ocean and the construction of rails to bring it to the coast, but also and principally, Georges Claude himself. The film started with Claude demonstrating the experiment which shows that if water is boiled in a balloon flask at $20\,^{\circ}$C at a very low pressure and then condensed into another balloon at $4\,^{\circ}$C, it gives a flow of steam capable of driving a small turbine. Science is shown as both the authority and the starting point of the industrial researcher. But the film then deals with the individual as entrepreneur, and shows his problems with staff, his failure, his short success and his ultimate abandonment of the project.

Dramatization and the emphasis on "I" and "Me" are fundamental characteristics of Claude's popularization. An inventor like Claude did not present science and technology in a way related to the internal logic of the scientific field concerned. Unlike the pure scientist, he did not introduce himself as a man who "reveals" the secrets of nature by lifting "a corner of the great veil" (14). As we said above, for the industrial researcher, it is not his field of studies, but his actual procedure that is important. Claude demonstrated the structure of his research, thus relating his disappointments and errors and affirming the importance of, above all, chance. If a "do-it-yourself" quality is revealed, Claude's insistence on his failures allowed him to emphasize the correlation between an inventor's determination and his "moral energy".

This type of industrial popularization allows the inventor to call himself a creator of vocations: "success is within everybody's reach . . ." (15). In fact if one chooses the right subject and persists, fortune may come in the end! He not only masters nature, but proves his moral value by doing so. This moral value, added to his realistic managerial qualities, ought to allow him to organize other human activities, in particular public affairs. We see here a convergence between industrial popularization and moral and political considerations.

Industrial Exposition and Politics

Finally we will examine the relationship between science and politics in Claude's career. His most important political activities took place during the second world war, when he was a prominent collaborator, but his 1928 campaign is more important from the point of view of his attempt to popularize science in the political field. Already, during the 1914 election campaign, he had pilloried France's weakness in industry and armaments when compared with Germany. But after the war, his nationalism grew to become an anti-political and anti-bureaucratic attitude. Not only the refusal of various military and civil commissions to accept his military inventions during the war, but also the choice by the French Government of the Haber patent for the synthesis of ammonia, rather than his own patents, were, for him sufficient proof of the total incompetence of the Government in the fields of science and industry.

How did these incompetent men come to power? By *words* and "because they can yell at public meetings". This is what Georges Claude wanted to change. Firstly members of the "élite", that is those who can prove their ability, especially their professional ability, must no longer refuse to enter the political arena because they are afraid to grapple with words in public. Secondly they must lay *proof* of their value before the electorate. So, standing against a radical candidate and backed by l'Action Française (extreme right), Claude did not reply to any of the political problems currently being debated. He wanted to establish himself at a different level, a level which could be called "scientifico-industrial".

At Georges Claude's meetings, the spoken promises which were used to sway the electorate were replaced by experiments and actions. Peasants were invited to attend a real scientific spectacle. He put science on show: "As I want to present myself in terms of science and industry . . . I can manipulate my material as no other candidate ever has . . ." (16). He put on the stage the contents of a five ton lorry: air-containers, blackboards, oxygen and acetylene cylinders, transformers and neon-tubes, vacuum pumps, welding torches etc. At the end of the meetings he even gave the farmers of Seine et Marne small bags of nitrogenous fertilizer which was the byproduct of an ammonia plant which he had in the district.

Along with all this Claude related the way in which he had made his discoveries. He explained both the principle of oxy-acetylene welding and the economic importance of ammonia-synthesis. The power of science was presented through the description of a personal quest, there was no overall view of the current state of the sciences, of the possibilities that they offered, or the techniques which might be useful in industry.

This tenacious attachment to his own history was justified by borrowing the "scientific ethic" that one should not speak of what one does not know. Like all scientists entering the political field, he explained the economic importance of science and technology and introduced himself as a future supporter of science in parliament. But unlike the leftist scientists already in or close to power, like Paul Painlevé, Jean Perrin or Paul Langevin, Claude considered that only the practical applications of science were important. He never advanced the argument that an increase in knowledge merited an increase in resources to laboratories.

He emphasised that practical uses, which are what really count in science, can suddenly emerge out of organised research; and it was, above all, necessary to have governments who could recognize and appreciate this. Then, and here Claude goes much further, science must assume power itself. Science is no longer a small area in a whole world of thought, to which power gives greater or lesser credit, it is a very model of rationality which has proved itself and should reach the whole of society. The scientific method had already proved successful in enterprises, for organizing work. This method ought to become an alternative to traditional political practice, one should apply to nations the methods that have already proved successful in factories. This attempt by Claude to oppose science to politics was quickly registered by the press covering the 1928 campaign: "Science opens fire on politics" (17).

His election defeat, even though it was only by 250 votes, reinforced his conviction that there was no room for his sort of "élite" in the system. The excessive value he laid on show and individual experiment achieved its culmination in a strange event which nearly ended Claude's life. In 1942 he was a star of the collaboration, holding numerous conferences and publishing in major newspapers. In front of the audience of one of his conferences he actually attempted to commit suicide. After recalling the memory of Christ and Joan of Arc and explaining that only a *personal* and indisputable sacrifice could convince the public of the genuineness of his collaboration, he swallowed a tube of strychnine (18). His attempt failed because he had eaten a large meal before the conference, but it showed vividly his faith in the power of dramatization and of individual experiment.

In concluding, we would like to underline the links between the scientific, popularizing and political activities in the particular career of Georges Claude. We cannot answer the question "why" we find this type of activity with this type of researcher, but there were other researchers in industrial science like Henry La Chatelier whose scientific and expository practices show similar tendencies. In the case of Georges Claude, we can discern elements that are common to all his activities. He accorded absolute preeminence to experiment over theory and to practical applications over basic research. The continual references to individual experience are at once like a scientific and like a moral training of that individual.

These common traits were joined in a particular conception of science. The ultimate aim of science was not knowledge, because knowledge of the universe still remains inaccessible to man, but the domination of nature. This alone is possible. Here lies the real power of science. Science had already spread its power to industry, Claude wanted to extend it to the rest of society. We should not be surprised that Claude was checked in his dream of enlarging the area in which scientific rationality can act and as a consequence enlarge his own social and political domain. What is astonishing is that despite all the setbacks, the dream persisted, and he continued to have the illusion that society could be treated like nature.

Acknowledgements

I would like to thank Terry Shinn of GEMAS who helped me to devise this paper, Bernadette Bensaude-Vincent who made some excellent criticisms, Mesdames Monnerie, Sonia Lehrer and Olga Yovanovitch from the École Supérieure de Physique et Chimie Industrielles for their help with research into the sources, Monsieur Racinet from the company l'Air Liquide, and Louisa Dunlop for her help in translating and editing. This work was carried out in the Musée National des Sciences, Techniques et Industries as part of the extension of the centenary celebrations of the founding of the École Supérieure de Physique et Chimie Industrielles de la Ville de Paris.

Notes

1. To my knowledge there is no historical study of Georges Claude. The following may be consulted: Georges Claude, *Ma vie et mes inventions*, Paris, 1957.

    On the École Supérieure de Physique et de Chimie Industrielles, see: Charles Lauth, *Rapport général sur l'histoire et le fonctionnement de l'École Municipale de Physique et de Chimie Industrielles*, Paris, 1900; Terry Shinn, 'Des sciences industrielles aux sciences fondamentales, la mutation de l'École Supérieure de Physique et de Chimie (1882–1970)', *Revue française de sociologie,* **XXII** (1981), 167–182.

2. Georges Claude in the preface to A. Jacobson and A. Antoni, *Des anticipations de Jules Verne aux réalisations d'aujourd'hui,* Liège, 1937, p. VIII.

3. These communications are listed in Georges Claude, *Notice sur les travaux scientifiques de M. Georges Claude,* Paris, 1913 and *Notice sur les travaux scientifiques et industriels de M. Georges Claude (1913–1924),* Corbeil, 1924.

4. *L'étincelle électrique,* 1894, cover page of all the issues.

5. *L'étincelle électrique,* 8 December 1895, no. 7, p. 81.

6. *L'électricité à la portée de tout le monde,* Paris, 1901.

7. Jean Perrin, *Les atomes,* Paris, 1913.

8. *L'électricité à la portée de tout le monde,* 10th edn., Paris, 1908, p. 6.

9. Arsène d'Arsonval in the preface to Georges Claude, *Air liquide, oxygène, azote, gaz rares,* Paris, 1909, p. 2 (underlined in the text).

10. Georges Claude, *L'air liquide, sa production, ses propriétés, ses applications,* Paris, 1903, p. 105.

11. *Bulletin scientifique des étudiants de Paris,* Paris, 1923, p. 12, partly reproduced in Georges Claude, *Ma vie et mes inventions,* Paris, 1957, p. 59.

12. Louis Figuier, *Les merveilles de la science, ou description populaire des inventions modernes,* 4 vols., Paris, 1867–1891.

13. Film 'L'énergie thermique des mers' produced by J. de Cavaignac (Société Les Cîmes). The rights belong to the 'Films du Centaure', Paris.

14. A. Einstein to P. Langevin about L. de Broglie's thesis in 'Paul Langevin et Albert Einstein d'après une correspondance et des documents inédits', Luce Langevin in *La Pensée,* no. 161 (février 1972), p. 22.

15. *Bulletin scientifique des étudiants de Paris,* 1923, p. 5.

16. Georges Claude, *Souvenirs et enseignements d'une expérience électorale,* Paris, 1931, p. 93.

17. *Le Matin,* 12 avril 1928, 'La science ouvre le feu sur la politique. La campagne chimique de M. Georges Claude', p. 1.

18. Robert Aron, *Histoire de l'épuration,* vol. 1, 1967, pp. 301–311.

POPULAR POLITICAL ECONOMY FOR
THE BRITISH WORKING CLASS
READER IN THE NINETEENTH CENTURY

MAX GOLDSTROM

The Queen's University of Belfast

Political economy was popularised for two distinct purposes. The first is exemplified by the work of that body of writers that chose to simplify the subject's "laws" for the student and the educated layman, in the interest of advancing the "science". The second objective, with which this paper is chiefly concerned, was the control of working class behaviour through dissemination of certain selected aspects of the subject. Writers in this area sought to expound political economy as a series of unchangeable laws, disobedience of which brooked disaster for the working man. But the working man persisted in behaving in ways that flouted these supposedly immutable concepts, and over time much of the teaching was exposed as fallacious. With the theories overturned, the process of feedback forced first the theorists, then the popularisers, to modify their positions. By 1880 the second objective had been abandoned — while the first flourishes to this day.

I

Political economy dates back to the 1770s (1) but the attempts by the disciples of Adam Smith, Malthus and Ricardo to spread their ideas to a wider audience did not begin until after the ending of the Napoleonic Wars. From that time a small number of writers, amongst whom Mrs Jane Marcet and Miss Harriet Martineau were the most prominent, published tracts designed to explain the intricacies of political economy to a lay audience. The work of writers like these is well known (2). This paper is concerned with the rise and decline of a general movement to popularize political economy among the lower orders. The rationale of this more general movement was to diffuse the

259

Terry Shinn and Richard Whitley (eds.), Expository Science: Forms and Functions of Popularisation. Sociology of the Sciences, Volume IX, 1985, 259–273.
© *1985 by D. Reidel Publishing Company.*

subject as widely as possible because its evangelists were convinced that if the lower orders could be made to grasp the basic concepts of political economy they would be receptive to middle class values. In current terminology this paper examines the use of political economy to exercise social control (3).

To see the rise of the subject and its eventual decline in a proper perspective we must go back to the 18th century. The origins of the subject can be traced to the 1780–1790 period, a time when churchmen and intellectuals detected, or thought they had detected, a threat to the stability of English society. They did not appreciate the scale of the change that was underway, nor did they guess that it would lead to the major upheaval that we now call the consequences of the industrial revolution. They did not even know the population was rising. But they nevertheless sensed that traditional, stable relationships between the social classes were deteriorating.

These fears were compounded by the anxieties felt by the propertied classes as they learned of the excesses of the French Revolution, anxieties that increased as small, vociferous groups urged the extension of revolutionary measures to England. Particularly alarming was the popularity of Thomas Paine's *Rights of Man*, published in 1791. (This allegedly sold 1.5 million copies by the end of the century) (4). Employers looked uneasily at their servants, and wondered how they could shield such simple and gullible minds from evil influences.

The problem was how to influence the lower orders. There were those who favoured enforcement of the status quo through existing legal channels; a counter-argument came from the school of thought that was not opposed to quelling disturbance by resort to legal sanctions, but reasoned that social control techniques would reach out into the minds of the lower orders. Persuasion, as opposed to repressions, was less expensive a policy than policemen and prisons.

The founders of what was to become political economy for the masses were not economists; they were simply anxious to demonstrate to the lower orders that God's "invisible hand" was at work, and that they could not expect to improve their lot. At that time there was just one effective channel of communication with the lower orders, namely the churches. The wealthiest and most influential church organisation in the late 18th century was the anglican Society for the Promotion of Christian Knowledge. The SPCK had direct access to the pulpits, the Sunday schools and the small but increasing number of day schools. Any defender of traditional values was drawn naturally to the SPCK, and an examination of the minutes of the Society show the extent to which individuals were pressing the Society to publish their books (5). One lady, Mrs Sarah Trimmer, persuaded the Society to publish her moralising tales, and to distribute them widely to the servant classes.

Mrs Sarah Trimmer (1741–1810) had a very wide circulation, with tales of country folk who were guided by the scriptures, the parson, and the squire, and who accepted without question that it was "the duty of poor people to labour for their food and raiment" (6). Others followed in her footsteps after 1795 by launching the Cheap Repository Tracts. These Tracts were, by the standards of the time, very appealing to the reader; the ballads and moral tales were nicely illustrated with woodcuts, and the prices were low. Financed by the evangelical Clapham Sect, they were designed to compete with the traditional reading matter of the lower orders, i.e., the dying confessions of murderers, romantic tales of highwaymen and a wide assortment of other such low and lewd material.

A typical example of the Cheap Repository Tracts is a song written by Mrs Hannah More (7), a leading figure in this organisation. She called it *Turn the Carpet, or the Two Weavers*. Dick, a weaver, complains that life is unjust – he has little to eat, he has a large family and a sick wife, while the rich man has all he wants. A fellow weaver explains that God's designs cannot be understood by simple people, just as a stranger, knowing nothing about weaving, could not predict how a half-woven carpet would look when it was completed because it was woven 'inside out'.

> What now seem random strokes, will there
> All order and design appear;
> Then shall we praise what here we spurn'd,
> For then the *Carpet shall be turn'd*. (8)

It is remarkable that although Mrs More cites "God's plan" and "God's laws" as the explanation for the seeming injustice that Dick and his like endure, her sentiments foreshadowed so closely the teachings of the popular political economists forty years later. Pamphlets of this kind were sold or thrust at people by the million, and organisations like Cheap Repository Tracts proliferated.

The effort and expense that were invested in this campaign to stiffen

Christian values and instil 'acceptance' in the souls of the lower orders was huge. But was anyone persuaded? Historians are generally agreed that the attempt was a failure, and that Cobbett was right — "it would hardly be decent to describe" the ways in which the literature was used. The lower orders rarely deviated in the nineteenth century from a deeply rooted taste for robust and earthy reading matter (9).

The more perceptive of the campaigners acknowledged the passive resistance to their message. They hoped that a way forward might be through the schools, and that concentration of energies in the direction of the teachers and pupils of the day and Sunday schools would have a more lasting effect. Children were so obviously more suggestible. Mrs Trimmer more than anyone else realised this; she stole a march on her rivals, so to speak, with her *Charity Spelling Book* (10). This book was designed to teach children their letters, syllables, and words, and proceeded to suitable reading matter such as: "Those who are rich, will not help the poor if they will not try to be good." (11) It was placed on the SPCK list and distributed to all anglican schools at a heavily subsidised price. In 1811, when the National Society for Promoting the Education of the Poor in the Principles of the Established Church was set up, Dr Andrew Bell, the architect of the Society's Monitorial System, used the *Charity Spelling Book* as the basis for his National Society school books (12). Thus Mrs Trimmer was in the position of being read by millions of children for thirty years or more after her death. Her closest contender was William Allen, the Quaker educationist, who had his own textbook, *Scripture Lessons*, for the nonconformist schoolchild (13). Allen explained the object of *Scripture Lessons:*

We have made them [the Scripture Lessons] to bear upon those duties in a very striking and prominent way without any comment whatever; but merely in the words of the Scripture; such as the duties of subjects to government in the words of Scripture; the duties of servants to masters in the words of Scripture . . . . (14)

However, the evidence we have is that children in the 1830s were as resistant to these ideas as their elders, a generation earlier, and promptly forgot what they had learned on leaving school. Well before the mid-point of the century almost everyone in the world of education, from civil servant and churchman to college tutor, was in agreement that their values were failing to reach the working man and his family. Education for the future was to be built upon a foundation of useful knowledge. In this new approach the "science" of political economy was to play an important role.

II

The exponents of popular political economy, writing after the Napoleonic Wars, endeavoured to explain the subject to the well-educated layman. They did not set out to produce literature to contain the labouring poor, as they were alleged to have done (15). The best known works of these exponents are James Mill's *Elements of Political Economy* (1821), J. R. McCulloch's *Principles of Political Economy* (1825) and the first publication of Mrs Jane Marcet, *Conversations on Political Economy* (1816). The latter is said to have had a wide readership amongst middle class women who felt the need to be informed in what was a fashionable subject in the post-Napoleonic period (16). The 'conversations' of the title were between a teacher and her pupil:

Mrs B. In our last conversation I think we came to the conclusion, that capital is almost as beneficial to the poor as to the rich; for though the property of the one, it is by its nature destined for the maintenance of the other.

Caroline It comes to the labourer in the form of wages; but as we must allow the capitalist a profit on his work, I should like very much to know what proportion that profit bears to the wages of the labourer?

Mrs B. It varies extremely, but the wages of the labourer can never be permanently less than will afford him the means of living, otherwise he could not labour (17).

The critics who were so scathing about popular political economy made no distinction, however, between the serious contributions (like that quoted above) and the tracts that were to appear from the 1830s, directed specifically at a working class readership. These tracts represent the full expression of middle class fear of revolution and breakdown in society. When the 1831 Census was published it appeared that Malthus had been proved right. The population of England and Wales had increased from 8.9 million in 1801 to 13.9 million in 1831, an increase of over 50%. Crime, particularly juvenile crime, was rampant in towns, and in the countryside rick-burning was not unusual. Strikes, hunger, reform agitation, formation of trade unions, the appearance of the working class press and the beginnings of the Chartist movement were collectively frightening phenomena; a hostile, sullen, alien population seemed to be outbreeding the middle classes. Many propertied people were resigned to coming chaos. Particularly hurtful to the older reformers was that so many literate working class people, indebted for their literacy to the church schools, were indifferent to studying the bible and the moralising tracts. For the rare individual who attempted "sound" reading matter there were multitudes who bought Sunday papers and material such as the *Newgate Calendar*. The radicals argued that the working classes were reading seditious and salacious works because religious material published for their edification was so clumsy and dreary. In 1825 a group of radicals led by Jeremy Bentham and a publisher, Charles Knight, established the Society for the Diffusion of Useful Knowledge. In 1832 they published a weekly paper, *Penny Magazine*, in which there were well-written articles on such topics as science, geology, geography, history and political economy. The open contempt of this particular group for religious moralising, and in some individual cases for religion, led it into conflict with the SPCK, which duly produced a rival publication, *Saturday Magazine* (18).

The academic discipline of political economy was called upon throughout the nineteenth century to shape government policy. But with the advent of the tract writers in the 1830s the subject was harnessed quite openly as a force that might help to influence working class behaviour. In 1832 Harriet Martineau began publishing a series of stories, *Illustrations of Political Economy*, to assist the poor in "managing their own welfare". *The Manchester Strike*, (1832) demonstrating the futility of strikes, was representative. It was very well reviewed:

If the masters knew their own interest, this little work would be circulated by tens of thousands among their labourers; and the philanthropist, who feels for the deplorable state of society in Manchester, could not spend a year better than in devoting himself to the circulation of its ideas and pictures (19).

In 1833 Mrs Marcet entered the field with a rival publication (20). The publications of both ladies sold in substantial numbers by publishing standards of the time — Miss Martineau's first story sold several thousand copies. Considering that she was trying to reach an audience of millions her influence on the working classes should not be regarded as significant; moreover, most readers would have been middle class — the young Princess Victoria was among their numbers (21). Despite their biographers' claims neither

Mrs Marcet nor Miss Martineau achieved anything like 'household name' status.

The one person to succeed in reaching the working classes and to have their name linked with political economy in every school and college in the land was Richard Whateley. He was Drummond Professor of Political Economy at Oxford from 1829 to 1831, but even though he was at this point still at an early stage of his career, he craved a wide audience. In 1832 he published his lecture notes as *Introductory Lectures on Political Economy*, intending the work for the lay adult reader. His golden opportunity came with his appointment, in 1831, as Archbishop of Dublin. Using his ecclesiastical contacts he persuaded the SPCK in 1833 to publish a simplified version of his *Introductory Lectures* in *Saturday Magazine* (22). In the same year he published his *Easy Lessons on Money Matters for the use of Young People*. This, because it, too, was put on the SPCK list, was offered at a subsidised price to schools and colleges, and consequently sold in vast numbers for the next fifty years. Not only did *Easy Lessons* outsell all its competitors in Britain, but was translated into several languages (23).

Whateley's missionary zeal marks the beginnings of what must be one of the most bizarre episodes in British educational history. In Ireland, in 1831, the British government embarked on a major new educational system for the country, introducing a rigidly controlled syllabus. Richard Whateley was appointed as one of the Commissioners and took a leading part in drawing up the syllabus and preparing a set of textbooks. It was an opportune time for him to ensure that lavish extracts of *Easy Lessons* were reproduced in the Irish textbooks. These textbooks were cheap, secular in tone and superior in every way to their British rivals. They sold to English schools by the million through the 1840s and 1850s, and established a pattern that was to be imitated by British textbook compilers for thirty years or more (24).

The nonconformist British and Foreign School Society set about publishing its own series of school textbooks towards the end of the 1830s, and the anglican National Society about five years later, both societies drawing heavily for the content and format on the Irish series. Other organisations followed suit. All the textbook series contained a substantial quota of political economy, which might appear as a formal subject in its own right, or in the guise of fable, fairy tale or poem. The more advanced textbooks of each series allotted about 10% of their space to the subject. They all had extracts from

Whateley's *Easy Lessons*; Mrs Marcet's fairy tales were less in evidence, and Adam Smith appeared here and there. Miss Martineau's works are conspicuous by their absence — probably because, as a Unitarian, she had no influence with the anglican or nonconformist establishment (25).

All the compilers were concerned that political economy should be understood by very young children, and since Mrs Marcet and Whateley in their original form were too difficult, simplification was called for.

Division of labour was explained to the five-year-old in words of one syllable:

What a small thing a pin is; and yet it takes ten men, if not more, to make it. One man draws the wire; the next makes it straight; the third cuts it; the fourth points it; the fifth grinds it for the head; the sixth makes the head; the next puts it on; the eighth makes the pins white; and the ninth and tenth stick them in rows. What a heap of pins they will thus make in a day! More, I am sure, than you or I could count (26).

The concept of leisure preference was adapted for ten-year-olds:

When you give labour for wages, it is because you have a higher estimation of the wages, than of the profitless ease and freedom of remaining unemployed. . . . (27)

Twelve-year-olds were taught the interdependence of the classes through a fable:

"Once on a time," says the fable, "all the other members of the body began to murmur against the stomach, for employing the labours of all the rest, and consuming all they had helped to provide, without doing anything in return. So they all agreed to strike work, and refused to wait upon this idle stomach any longer. The feet refused to carry it about; the hands resolved to put no food into the mouth for it; the nose refused to smell for it, and the eyes to look out in its service; and the ears declared they would not even listen to the dinner-bell; and so of all the rest. But after the stomach had been left empty for some time, all the members began to suffer. The legs and arms grew feeble; the eyes became dim, and all the body languid and exhausted.

" 'Oh, foolish members,' said the stomach, 'you now perceive that what you used to supply to me, was in reality supplied to yourselves. I did not consume for myself the food that was put into me, but digested it, and prepared it for being changed into blood, which was sent through various channels as a supply for each of you. If you are occupied in feeding me, it is by me in turn, that the blood-vessels which nourish you are fed.' " (28)

The English educational societies recognised that teachers would need training in the subject if they were to teach it effectively, and all training colleges, whatever their denominational affiliation, used Whateley's *Easy Lessons* as a set text. Furthermore, the government inspectorate set questions on the content of school textbooks, to ensure that intending teachers had mastered the material themselves (29). By the mid-nineteenth century most schools had textbooks that contained political economy. Whilst the subject was not compulsory, it was held in high esteem by committees, boards and inspectors. Since schools were dependent on the inspectorate for their grants, and since a prime requirement for a grant was suitable textbooks, the schools by definition purveyed political economy. The 1861 Newcastle Commission Report regretted political economy was not on the formal syllabus, and urged that this be remedied. "The want of such knowledge leads him (the labouring man) constantly into error and violence destructive to himself and to his family, oppressive to his fellow workmen, ruinous to his employers and mischievous to society." (30) In 1863 the government made political economy a compulsory subject at teacher training college level. In 1871 the government added the subject to the formal school curriculum by making it eligible for payment under the Revised Code "results scheme". Thereafter schools could obtain a small sum of money for every pupil who passed an annual examination in this subject (31).

When it is asserted that the entire operation to implant political economy in the hearts and minds of young people was a failure, there is only indirect evidence. The most positive evidence supporting the assertion is our knowledge of literacy levels at the time. Most children could read when they left school, but haltingly. If their understanding of history and geography was hazy (32), it is highly unlikely that their grasp of political economy would be any better. In terms of attitude to the subject it is impossible to establish how children felt at the time, though we are on firmer ground when we look at the involvement of college tutors and pupils.

Prior to political economy being made compulsory in the colleges, not only was there very little involvement but a marked disinclination to tackle it at all. In 1858 some 330 pupil teachers presented themselves for examination before the inspectorate to do their demonstration lessons – two chose political economy (33). After 1863 the subject was made compulsory for males but nothing was done to render it more attractive to the young pupil teachers, so there was considerable passive resistance. In 1875 the Committee of Council on Education made a concession – it need only be studied in the second, final year. Ten years later the subject in its compulsory form was quietly dropped (34).

Its decline in the schools was a protracted affair. The newly-trained teachers had no choice about teaching the subject, since it was in every reader, but few troubled to purchase a work on political economy for their school, however subsidised the price. The incentive scheme referred to failed because so few children could master the subject sufficiently to pass the examinations. Numbers entered in the 1870s were minimal. The textbook compilers bowed eventually to prevailing feeling and editions appearing in the 1880s were free of the subject. The struggle to incorporate it in the school curriculum had lasted fifty years (35).

The moralising tract had given way in the 1830s to secular political economy, in the interests, as its proponents believed, of improved social control. Now, in the 1880s, with the demise of political economy, a new subject, social economy was introduced. It embraced topics like the savings banks, friendly societies, sickness and old age insurance, and the dangers of money-lenders and pawnbrokers. Its firmly moralising tone kept it in the tradition of Trimmer and Whateley, but social economy was different in one important respect; its message was that whilst children should accept that the realities of life were harsh, with self help they might better their lot. The subject provoked no controversy, and won approval in educational circles (36). There seemed no particular reason, however, for its being accorded any preferential treatment in terms of funding and timetabling; the social tensions of the 1780s and 1830s were long gone, few thought now to look to the school classroom to mould the young mind so overtly. As a subject in its own right it was taught in a number of schools and colleges through the 1880s and 1890s and thereafter became absorbed into domestic economy.

III

Though so much attention was given to teaching political economy to children, for a full half century, that does not mean that enthusiasm for popularising the subject at adult level diminished. Miss Martineau's financial success in the 1830s encouraged a number of writers to enter the field (37). The works for adults that appeared thereafter fall into two broad categories, those that simplified the writings of the academic political economists, and those intended purely for the working classes. None of them, though, enjoyed wide sales. They all, as they evolved, were influenced by the neo-classical economists and by the changing economic climate of the times. Fawcett's *Tales of Political Economy* (1874) is described in Polkinghorn's analysis as 'bright and optimistic' in tone, and quite free of the dismal theories of Malthus (38). Even this kind of political economy fades away in the last quarter of the nineteenth century — the social and economic tensions that had brought it to the fore had virtually disappeared. It was revived only from time to time in newspaper articles or in a speech by an employer or a politician during a strike or a general election.

Popular political economy for the serious reader continued to be published. Well on in the century economists, notably Alfred Marshall (39), wrote elementary textbooks on the subject and there was a small market for them. The "science" was also explained in periodical literature such as *The Economist*, other weekly, monthly and quarterly journals and, from time to time, the quality newspapers.

What impact, then, did the popularisation of a difficult subject like this have on the hearts and minds of the millions of people who encountered it? If political economy was largely unread, largely uncomprehended, or was understood only to be despised, perhaps even turned against its authors, should we consider it an entirely failed enterprise? Historians wading through the dreary writings of the Marcets and the Whateleys, evaluating the reaction of the working class reader, will find little evidence to support any other views.

Yet the objectives of the popularisers were largely realised at the end of the nineteenth century. Those anxieties that had obsessed the middle classes had disappeared. Not only had the anticipated revolution failed to materialize, but British society had achieved a level of stability that would have exceeded the hopes of the most ardent propagandists for political economy. A considerable body of working men accepted and sought to emulate middle class values. Furthermore, many working class leaders were familiar with the concepts and language of political economy. Some historians go so far as to maintain that a number of trade unionists accepted much of the teachings of the classical economists as the harsh realities of life (40). Certainly it is true that they were persuaded on occasion to accept wage reductions when employers succeeded in convincing them that labour had obtained a dangerously large share of the wage fund (41).

It is possible to present a correlation between the extent of the teachings of popularisers on the one hand and the diminution of social tension and the rise of a viable social and economic structure on the other, but this would be arguing at undergraduate level. Nonetheless, it would be a mistake to shrug off the popularisers' endeavours. The working class leaders and trade unionists referred to may have been small in number but they occupied positions of influence. Their familiarity with political economy, derived perhaps from classroom days, meant that there was a common language for the representative of the working man and his employer. The terminology of the subject gave to both sides a vocabulary through which to debate. But there could never be agreement on fundamental issues. Trade union leaders at no stage accepted that political economy was a series of "incontrovertible laws". They were bound to reject outright the point that the popularisers pressed most frequently — the pernicious effect on society of trade unions. Nor did they accept the iron law of wages as anything more than a theory. They proved to be well able to use political economy to buttress their side of an argument (42).

The implication has so far been that any familiarity on the part of the working man with political economy came through reading the authors referred to in this paper. But a number read widely, beginning with the original writings of the classical economists and moving on to more left-wing writers — John Stuart Mill, Ruskin, even Engels and Marx (43). Some working class leaders, though, would have gained their grasp of the subject in a less academic manner, for the printed word is not the only vehicle for transmitting ideas. Lectures at Mechanics' Institutes, Working Men's Clubs, discussions at trade union meetings, in the workshop or the public house, gatherings (large and small) in the Birmingham Bull Ring or Hyde Park Corner were all means of acquiring a smattering of political economy. The written form is not the only manner in which ideas can be transmitted.

More generally, it would be a mistake to consider the transmission of ideas to the lower orders as being a purely one-way process. What we have here is an example of "feedback" — a concept more familiar to the scientist than to the social historian — at work in the interaction between theorists, popularisers and the working man. When the working man saw his self interest threatened he reacted in a way that obliged the economists to modify their dictats. Told that trade unions had a detrimental effect on society, he nevertheless joined. Told that wages could not in the long run exceed subsistence level, he nevertheless pressed until he had obtained wages that *were* in excess of subsistence level. And when trade unions grew strong enough to become a permanent feature of public life, and the iron law of wages was revealed for the nonsense it was, the classical economists were forced back to the drawing board.

Notes and References

1. Maxine Berg, *The Machinery Question and the Making of Political Economy 1815–1848*, Cambridge: Cambridge University Press, 1980, ch. 3.
2. H. Scott Gordon, 'The Ideology of Laissez-Faire', in A. W. Coats (ed.) *The Classical Economists and Economic Policy*, London: Methuen, 1971, pp. 144–179; R. K. Webb, *The British Working Class Reader, 1790–1848*, London: George Allen and Unwin, 1955.
3. F. M. L. Thompson, 'Social Control in Britain', *Economic History Review* 2nd series, **XXXIV** (1981), 189–208. See also A. P. Donajgrodzki (ed.) *Social Control in Britain*, Totowa, New Jersey: Croom Helm, 1977. Phillip McCann (ed.), *Popular Education and Socialization in the Nineteenth Century*, London: Methuen & Co., 1977.
4. Richard D. Altick, *The English Common Reader, a Social History of the Mass Reading Public 1800–1900*, Chicago: University of Chicago Press, 1957, pp. 69–71.
5. I am indebted to the Society for Promoting Christian Knowledge for allowing me to use their Minute Books. W. K. L. Clarke, *A History of the S.P.C.K.*, London: S.P.C.K., 1959.
6. Sarah Trimmer, *The Servant's Friend, an Exemplary Tale ...* , London: S.P.C.K., 1824 ed., p. 7; [Sarah Trimmer] *Some Account of the Life and Writings of Mrs Trimmer ...* , London: F. & C. Rivington, 1814, 2 vols.
7. Mary Alden Hopkins, *Hannah More and her Circle*, New York: Longmans, Green & Co., 1947.
8. Hannah More, *Cheap Repository Tracts*, London: Cheap Repository, 1796, Vol. II, pp. 1–7.
9. Richard D. Altick, *The English Common Reader, op. cit.*, R. K. Webb, *The British Working Class Reader, op. cit.*
10. J. M. Goldstrom, *The Social Content of Education 1808–1870, a Study of the Working Class School Reader in England and Ireland 1808–1870*, Dublin: Irish University Press, 1972, pp. 11–34.
11. Mrs Sarah Trimmer, *The Charity Spelling Book*, London: F. & C. Rivington, 1818, Part I, p. 11.
12. Henry James Burgess, *Enterprise in Education: The Story of the Work of the Established Church in the Education of the People prior to 1870*, London: National Society, S.P. C. K., 1958, pp. 27–35.

13. William Allen, *The Life of William Allen* . . . , London: Charles Gilpin, 1846, 2 vols.
14. *Report from the Select Committee on the State of Education*, H. C. 1834, IX, (572), p. 72.
15. H. Scott Gordon, 'The Ideology of Laissez Faire', in W. A. Coats (ed.) *The Classical Economists, op. cit*., p. 191.
16. H. Scott Gordon, *op. cit*., p. 190; Bette Polkinghorn, 'Political Economy Disguised as Fanciful Fables', *Eastern Economic Journal* **VIII** (1982), 145–156.
17. Jane Marcet, *Conversations in Political Economy*, London: Longman, 1824 ed., pp. 121–122.
18. R. K. Webb, *The British Working Class Reader, op. cit.*
19. *The Spectator* cited on back cover of Harriet Martineau, *Weal and Woe in Garveloch, A Tale*, second edition, London: Fox, 1832.
20. Jane Marcet, *John Hopkins's Notions on Political Economy*, London: Longman, 1833, pp. 27–30.
21. Vera Wheatley, *The Life and Work of Harriet Martineau*, London: Secker & Warburg, 1957; R. K. Webb, *Harriet Martineau: a Radical Victorian*, London: Heinemann, 1960.
22. J. M. Goldstrom, 'Richard Whateley and Political Economy in Schoolbooks, 1833–80', *Irish Historical Studies* **XV** (1966), 131–146.
23. *Ibid*., p. 145.
24. Goldstrom, *The Social Content of Education, op. cit*., Ch. II.
25. Commissioners of National Education in Ireland, *First Book of Lessons for the Use of Schools*, Dublin 1833. Also *'Second'*, *'Third'*, *'Fourth'*, and *'Fifth'* books; Henry Dunn and John Crossley, *The Daily Lesson Books for the Use of Schools and Families*, Books I–IV, London: Hamilton, Adams & Co., 1840–42.
26. Commissioners of National Education in Ireland, *Second Book of Lessons* . . . , Dublin, 1846, p. 16.
27. Henry Dunn and John Crossley, *Daily Lesson Book No. 3* . . . , London: Hamilton, Adams & Co., 1840, p. 37.
28. [Richard Whateley], *Easy Lessons on Money Matters* . . . , London: Parker, 1833, pp. 49–51. This passage was reproduced in most advanced school books between 1833 and the late nineteenth century.
29. *Minutes of the Committee of Council on Education, 1853–4*, H. C. 1854, LI, [1787], p. 239.
30. *Report of the Commissioners Appointed to Inquire into the State of Popular Education*, H. C. 1861, XXI, [2794–I], p. 127.
31. *Report of the Committee of Council on Education, 1863*, H. C. XLVII [3171], p. 203.
32. See especially Matthew Arnold, *Reports on Elementary Schools, 1852–82*: London, Macmillan & Co., 1910.
33. *Report of the Committee of Council on Education, 1859*, H. C. XXI, [2510 Sess. 1], p. 298.
34. *Report of the Committee of Council on Education, 1875*, H. C. 1876, XXIII, [C 1513], p. 461; *Report of the Committee of Council on Education 1885*, H. C. 1886, XXIV [C 4849], p. 347.
35. Goldstrom, *Richard Whateley and Political Economy in School Books, op. cit*., p. 145.

36. W. M. Williams, 'On the Teaching of Social Economy', *Transactions of the National Association for the Promotion of Social Science*, London, 1857, pp. 509–17; W. L. Blackley, *The Social Economy Reading Book* . . . , London: National Society, 1880. See also the Inspectors' reports in the annual volumes of the Committee of Council on Education.

37. See, e.g., E. K. Blyth, *The Life of William Ellis*, London: Kegan, Paul & Co., 1889; W. A. C. Stewart and W. P. McCann, *Educational Innovators*, London: Macmillan, 1967; Simon Denith, 'Political Economy, Fiction, and the Language of Practical Ideology in Nineteenth-Century England', *Social History* **VIII** (1983), 183–99; Robin Gilmour, 'The Gradgrind School of Political Economy', *Victorian Studies* **XI** (1967), 207–224.

38. Polkinghorn, 'Political Economy Disguised as Fanciful Fables', *op. cit.*, p. 149.

39. Alfred and Mary P. Marshall, *The Economics of Industry*, London: Macmillan & Co., 1879.

40. See, for example, R. V. Clements, 'British Trade Unions and Popular Political Economy 1850–1875', *Economic History Review* **XIV** (1961), 93–104.

41. H. A. Turner, *Trade Union Growth, Structure and Policy, A Comparative Study of the Cotton Unions*, London: George Allen & Unwin, 1962, esp. pp. 108–226.

42. See for example the spirited defence by trade union leaders before the Royal Commission of 1867–1869. I am indebted to my colleague K. D. Brown for allowing me to read his unpublished paper 'British Trade Unions before the Royal Commission of 1867–1869'.

43. 'Character Sketches. 1 – The Labour Party and the Books that Helped to make it', *Review of Reviews*, London, 1906, pp. 568–582.

PART IV

A PRACTITIONER'S VIEW OF POPULARISATION

IMPACTS OF PRESENT-DAY POPULARIZATION

VICTOR K. McELHENY

MIT, Cambridge, Mass.

As a popularizer of science, I wish to enter a plea for greater attention from sociologists, philosophers and historians of science to present-day communications by scientists of the facts and ideas involved in their work to persons beyond their immediate circle.

I urge these studies because of the conviction, largely impressionistic, that popular communication of science and technology arises from a strong demand from the public for such information. I believe that this demand is directly linked to the growth of the scientific and engineering enterprises and of their impact on social decision-making.

If we accept that technical issues, including those of medical care, environmental pollution, alternative sources of energy, and nuclear weapons, are an important fraction of all public controversies, then popular scientific communication is closely linked to the governance of our societies, and thus is worthy of intensified investigation by humanistic and social-science scholars.

At present, popular communication of technical matters proceeds largely on faith. It is assumed that people want this information, and are willing to pay their agents — in this case journalists — for obtaining an increasing amount of such information. It also is assumed, at least by the journalists if not by the scientific professionals whom they contact, that translation of scientific information into popular terms will make decisions on public policy more rational than they would be otherwise, and thus reduce by some undetermined percentage the risk of disastrous decisions, such as those resulting in wars.

Notions such as these deserve more rigorous examination than they have received. I believe this could be achieved, with consciousness of difficulties and limitations of various methods, in several ways:

(1) Polling of national samples about their exposure to and attitudes about

Terry Shinn and Richard Whitley (eds.), Expository Science: Forms and Functions of Popularisation. Sociology of the Sciences, Volume IX, 1985, 277–282.

scientific information in popular media, as was done in the studies, 'The Public Impact of Science in the Mass Media' (Robert C. Davis, Survey Research Center, The University of Michigan, 1958), and 'The Attitudes of the U.S. Public Toward Science and Technology' (Jon D. Miller, Kenneth Prewitt and Robert Pearson, National Opinion Research Center, University of Chicago, 1980).

(2) Searching archives of past national public opinion polls in the United States, such as those stored at the Roper Center of the University of Connecticut at Storrs (E. J. Dionne, Jr., *The New York Times*, 21 April 1980, p. B2), and other countries, for answers to particular questions bearing on public attitudes toward technology, with special attention to secular trends emerging from repeated asking of identical or similar questions.

(3) Greater examination of such resources as data from past Field polls in the American state of California to trace the evolution of public opinion during referendum campaigns bearing on technology, such as those seeking restrictions on nuclear power, where evidence may be obtained about the persuasiveness of particular attempts to influence public opinion and about the volatility of opinion on technological issues placed before electorates.

(4) Use of sales figures of such products as cigarettes, particular pahrmaceutical drugs, or foods, as probes of changing public attitudes toward particular aspects of technology and the influences of those changed attitudes on consumer behavior.

(5) Consideration of studying audiences for a particular popular communication, such as a television series on a scientific or technical subject — examples would be 'The Ascent of Man', 'Connections', 'Cosmos', or the British 'Nature' series on animal behavior that was shown in December 1983 and January 1984 on American non-commercial television — before and after the communication is broadcast or published, to measure possible changes in attitudes and levels of information as a result of exposure to the communication.

(6) Studying particular patterns of interaction between journalists and scientists, such as the interviews arranged for by the recently established Media Resource Service of the Scientists' Institute for Public Information in New York City; or observing a group of journalists covering a particular event, such as the 1975 Asilomar conference on possible risks from recombinant DNA research, and following their later reporting of that event or related topics.

(7) Making a comparative content analysis over a limited period in periodicals of one type but differing in emphasis or geography, such as two months' coverage of technology, medicine and science in *The New York Times, The Wall Street Journal* and *The Boston Globe*; or in *The Times* of London, *Le Monde* of Paris and *Frankfurter Allgemeine Zeitung*.

(8) Preparing a complete list and written summary of the content of all shows in the 'Horizon' series of the British Broadcasting Corporation, which has been produced for more than 20 years, to begin observing long-term trends, both in topics chosen for popularization and in levels and methods of presentation.

The examples presented above all have to do with the explanation of technical topics to a broad public audience of people assumed to have only an elementary preparation in the sciences or engineering.

It is important, particularly for a science journalist like myself who is concerned directly with the types of communication listed above, to emphasize that such communications are only one part of a wide spectrum of communications between researchers and persons outside their immediate circle. These are the communications embraced by the conference title of 'Expository Science'.

There is a multiplicity of types of communication beyond a researcher's immediate circle. A list of 20 occurs to me:

1. Briefing a researcher about to join a research group.

2. Conversation with or seminars for colleagues in an academic department of division of an industrial or government research laboratory.

3. Professional papers written for and reviewed by scientists trained in the same discipline, as for journals like the *Physical Review*.

4. Professional papers aimed at researchers across a range of fields, as appear in *Science* or *Nature*.

5. Review articles in similar journals, summarizing a line of research or even a whole field, and often containing elements of speculation or advice about future directions of research.

6. Codification of research for novices, as in the writing of textbooks or chapters or textbooks.

7. Popular lectures about scientific or technological subjects for naive audiences, such as primary or secondary school classes, or civic discussion groups.

8. Expositions of technical matters to boards of directors of companies,

research institutions or alumni of educational institutions, with the aim of influencing decisions about investment or donation of money.

9. Consultation with staff of industrial companies, such as production or sales managers.

10. Consultation with government agencies on such matters as environmental regulation, design of weapons systems, or the allocation of research funds.

11. Appearance at formal regulatory hearings, such as inquests into the deaths of persons, consideration of the safety of nuclear reactors, or the investigation of engineering disasters such as airplane crashes.

12. Appearance at legislative hearings, where the passage of new statutes or the administration of existing ones is considered.

13. Participation in committees of scientific societies or of scientific academies making reports on the future directions of fields such as astronomy or physics, or summarizing knowledge on a controversial question, such as alternative energy sources or acidity in rainfall.

14. Participation in press conferences concerning a scientific discovery, a technological application, or the implications of such a development for political decision-making.

15. Participation in interviews with print or broadcast journalists.

16. Composition of or review of a news release concerning discoveries, applications or their implications.

17. Letters to editors of professional journals.

18. Letters or so-called 'op ed' articles for popular periodicals.

19. Popular articles for magazines or newspapers, such as those for *Scientific American*.

20. Service as an expositor for television programs, as with Philip Morrison, Carl Sagan, Richard Leakey, Don Johansen, or Sergei Kapitsa.

Such a typology of scientific communications beyond the researcher's own laboratory emphasizes for the scientific journalist an important fact. The type of communication to the general public that involves the journalist as translator is only a late stage in a multi-step process of making technical information available to wider and wider circles with the community of scientists and engineers.

Anyone wishing to study expository science as it exists today must also keep in mind the multiplicity of means of exposition to broad publics, all of which take part in translation to a general public that seems, by most of the measures available to us, eager for such information — either for themselves or their children.

It seems possible to list at least seven media of popular or near-popular exposition of technical subjects:

1. News reporting in the pages of scientific journals, such as *Science* and *Nature*, which both competes with and prepares the way for coverage in media reaching broader audiences.

2. Popular publications by professional scientific organizations, such as *Physics Today* (issued by the American Institute of Physics), *Chemical and Engineering News* (issued by the American Chemical Society), *Science 85* (issued by the American Association for the Advancement of Science), and *Psychology Today* (once commercial but now issued by the American Psychological Association).

3. Popular publications from other organizations, such as the weekly *Science News* (published by Science Service), and *Discover* (published by Time, Inc.).

4. Journals of opinion and criticism, such as *The New Yorker* or *The New York Review of Books*, *The National Review*, *The Nation*, *Commentary*, and *The New Republic*, to give only American examples.

5. Science, technology and medicine coverage in general news pages and special sections or columns of periodicals like *The New York Times*, the *Wall Street Journal*, *The Economist*, *Le Monde* or *Die Zeit*.

6. Radio reporting, such as is heard frequently on National Public Radio in the United States, or on non-commercial services in Canada, Great Britain and other nations.

7. Television coverage, as in feature programs and news broadcasts.

The existence of a large number of different types of scientific exposition and of means of reaching broad publics should guarantee that investigators of scientific communication today would find an ample number of case-studies of issues that (a) have been confronted recently, (b) have reached stages of completion defining the limits of an investigation, (c) are of urgent social importance and immediacy of impact, (d) involve many levels of explanation to laypersons, and (e) involve a large body of published material available for investigators.

The kinds of issues I am thinking of are: (a) major programs for the exploration of space, such as Apollo or the Shuttle; (b) ethical dilemmas arising from the use of advanced techniques such as organ transplants or genetic counselling; (c) possible risks from research using recombinant DNA techniques; (d) changing perceptions of commercial applications of such techniques; (e) changing perceptions of the desirability of harnessing nuclear energy for generating electric power; and (f) popular concepts of the practical implications of electronic technology for communications and computing.

The major reason for urging greater attention to contemporary communication of scientific facts and ideas to broad circles is simple: the scientific and technical enterprise is very much larger now than it was even quite recently, and both that enterprise and its impact are increasing very rapidly.

Conditions, both material and intellectual, affecting both the learned communities and the general public, are changing with remarkable speed. We are talking about rapid and profound changes both for the audiences for scientific information and for the people generating that information.

INDEX